LABOR AND POLITICS
IN ENGLAND
1850-1867

LABOR AND POLITICS
IN ENGLAND
1850-1867

By

FRANCES ELMA GILLESPIE

1966

OCTAGON BOOKS, INC.

New York

Reprinted 1966
by special arrangement with Duke University Press

OCTAGON BOOKS, INC.
175 FIFTH AVENUE
NEW YORK, N.Y. 10010

LIBRARY OF CONGRESS CATALOG CARD NUMBER: 66-28368

6-30-67

Printed in U.S.A. by
NOBLE OFFSET PRINTERS, INC.
NEW YORK 3, N. Y.

PREFACE

Students of English social movements in the nineteenth century have in general expressed the opinion that English workingmen, during the two decades after 1850, made little positive contribution to the politics of the period. Such significance as these years possessed in this connection has been considered to be of a negative kind only. The one striking exception has been the recognition of the importance of trade-union political activities in the late sixties, chiefly for purely trade-union objects. A certain lack of conviction as to the adequacy of the few general observations usually made to cover this chapter in the history of the political labor movement in England is the source out of which this study grew. It appeared worth while to re-examine the evidence with a view to giving the chapter, if possible, a more substantial character. It seemed possible that a re-evaluation of its importance, even in English political history as a whole, might be rendered necessary if all the available data should be assembled. This study presents such data as I have succeeded in collecting and such conclusions as the evidence seemed to me to warrant.

To the members of the History faculty at the University of Chicago who gave me assistance in prosecuting this investigation I wish to express my sincere gratitude. Among these I desire to mention especially Dr. Conyers Read, until recently a member of that faculty, who first suggested that I undertake this study and whose encouragement and assistance, given generously throughout the course of my research, were invaluable. In England I met with great courtesy from all from whom I sought aid. To the authorities and attendants at the British Museum, the Goldsmiths'

Library of the University of London, the British Library of Political Science, the library of the Bishopsgate Institute, and the Manchester Free Reference Library, I express my thanks. To Mr. R. H. Tawney I am very grateful for suggestions and valuable letters of introduction.

FRANCES ELMA GILLESPIE.

Chicago, 1926.

TABLE OF CONTENTS

LABOR AND POLITICS
IN ENGLAND
1850-1867

CHAPTER I

THE SIGNIFICANCE OF THE PERIOD

This study takes as its point of departure the end of the Chartist agitation. One distinct phase of the English labor movement had wrought itself out through thought and action and disillusionment, and those whose necessities had fashioned it found themselves without a workable theory or policy, but with problems only less pressing for solution than in the years just behind them. The next two decades were to be for English workingmen a critical period of transition and adjustment. This is the period of the present investigation, the aim of which is not to present an analysis of all the important endeavors of the working classes, but to weave from many irregular and sometimes tenuous threads the pattern of their political history.

It will be immediately objected, perhaps, that these decades were characterized preëminently by an absence of political interest and activity on the part of English workingmen. To test the validity of that general assumption is one object of this investigation. That there was any clearcut, easily labeled political labor movement in this period, comparable in distinctness of organization and aim with the Chartism that preceded it or the Labor Party that was eventually to follow it, cannot for one moment be maintained. But that, on the other hand, this was a period barren of working-class political interest and achievement would seem to be an opinion equally untenable.

The failure by 1850 of the organized class movement, which aimed at independent political action, and the subsequent direction of the activity of workingmen toward a more or less deliberate merging of working-class interests in general liberal interests, operate to obscure the fairly distinct and conscious share the working classes had in the adjustment of political relationships that took place in the next two decades. The Chartist movement had made the upper and middle classes aware of the wage-earning classes with a distinctness that left no debate as to the latent power residing in the laboring masses. It is possible that the chief result of the whole Chartist effort was just this fact. The governing classes were compelled to recognize for the first time that in the workers there was a new political element to be reckoned with in all future calculations of policy. Continued disregard of working-class opinion was henceforth impossible—impossible not only because of working-class insistence, but also because of this consciousness on the part of those above them of the power that could be called into existence through the wise or unwise handling of working-class problems. The broad lines of political development from 1850 on were in no small part drawn with reference to this new factor.

Not all middle and upper-class politicians were conscious of this altered situation and shaped their policies accordingly. Nor is it to be assumed that those who did have eyes to see would have given ready attention to the wishes of the working classes, if the latter had not often prodded their rulers to a realization of their power and their problems. The working classes did not always do this with deliberate purpose. Their action upon the political consciousness of the alert members of the ruling classes was indirect as well as direct. The influence of workingmen in the politics of the period should, therefore, be studied in both these aspects: that which they exerted consciously, and that which their increasing weight, through organization, wealth, and intelligence, was able to exert because of the mere fact of its existence. The second factor told heavily as a supplement to the first. Deliberate action on the part of workingmen became less and less a matter to be ignored, as their mass importance grew.

This potential power in the hands of wage-earners was regarded differently by the different groups among other classes. These diverse views tended to bring about different alignments in the country and in parliament and, working with other directive forces, had a large share in that evolution of parties and policies which is the outstanding feature of English domestic politics during the period under consideration.

The issue, as it presented itself in its widest form, was one of the issues of Chartism-democracy; or, as it took practical shape, the political recognition of the working classes. The Chartists had brought the possibility of democracy down from the realm of speculation and high constitutional debate into the hot arena of mass agitation. To most upper- and middle-class leaders after 1850 it was a grave question whether the issue could ever again be elevated to the rarer atmosphere of calm and judicious consideration, where it could be sterilized to innocuousness. To them democracy meant danger to the institutions of the country. Their policy had to be, therefore, to keep the issue deadened, if possible, and to combat it cautiously but persistently, if it should be revived.

Certain groups of the middle class, however, saw in a mitigated democracy a force which could be used to effect the one object to them most desirable; namely, the further liberalization of the government and of policy. They believed that if working-class power could be evoked within measure—the stream turned on until sufficient flood should gather to float their great measures over the bar of a conservative opposition—such limited democracy would promote the reformation of England along most desirable lines.

The first reforms contemplated were the completion of free trade and an alteration in the basis of taxation. These groups, under the leadership of John Bright, pursuing a policy in harmony with their purposes, became the most active force in reshaping issues and parties in parliament and in the country.

Such, in broadest statement, was the shape the question of working-class participation in politics took in the minds of the upper social classes. But, like most broad statements, it must at once be modified, and the modifications are of equal importance with the generalizations. Within all of these larger groups thus taking a certain attitude toward the question of democracy, subdivisions were constantly being created by the operation of other currents and interests. Singleness of view was repeatedly broken into complexity because of the action of forces inseparable from the main consideration.

Of these corollary considerations, beyond question the most disturbing were the economic implications of democracy. A study of the expressions of the opinion of the time—through the press, in parliament, by means of pamphlets, and in public addresses—offers the temptation to assert that the economic issue was the solid substance that upper and middle class politicians saw under the garb of democracy. That which gave the significance of living reality to the whole issue was the power to effect economic change, which it was believed political power would confer.

The reason for this conception of the problem is easy to understand. The reform of 1832 had implied the political recognition of economic power and it had resulted in further economic and social changes, such as the new Poor Law and the repeal of the Corn Laws. The Chartists had demanded political democracy for the ultimate purpose of providing a better distribution of wealth in the interest of the masses. Thus, on the two occasions when an advance in a democratic direction had been before the country, the chief aim had been to effect alterations in social and economic conditions. The two concepts, therefore, became inextricably joined in the minds of the great majority of the governing classes. Most of those who desired to use the political power of workingmen and most of those who feared it desired and feared it alike on economic grounds. One important exception must be made. The nonconformists saw in democracy a powerful ally in their struggle to disestablish and disendow the established Church. In proportion, therefore, as the nonconformist body was not identical with the other extreme liberal groups, they added to the number and influence of those who kept the question of democracy in the forefront of English politics.

The purpose of these few paragraphs is to indicate the reaction of the more powerful social groups in England to the new factor in political life born of the Industrial Revolution. But what of the great populations in factory towns and mining districts whose interests were as vitally concerned as those of their superiors? To what extent were they active agents in shaping the policies of which they to so large an extent were the very center?

This question is difficult to answer. It can be answered adequately only after a careful examination of the evidence, which is often sparse and unsatisfactory. Those were the days when labor was yet too obscure to find its way easily into respectable print, and, when admitted, it was often only to have its aims and acts denounced or distorted. It was yet too weak to have many spokesmen of its own in the press, in parliament, or in the public at large. Yet a careful searching of the extreme liberal press, of the pamphlet literature, which reached considerable proportions at times when the working classes were especially under discussion, as in 1859 and 1866, and of the few organs of working-class expression, such as their trade-union documents and the few weekly newspapers that they put out or supported, together with an examination of discussions in parliament and reports of commissions—this accumulation of evidence seems to warrant certain conclusions that can be accepted as safe. Some of these conclusions have already been embodied in Mr. and Mrs. Webb's *History of Trade Unionism*. Others have been touched upon more or less sketchily in Beer's *History of British Socialism* and in certain biographies of men such as Bright and Gladstone. But no extended effort to reconstruct the political thought and action of the whole body of English workingmen in this transitional quarter of a century has yet been made, the reason being, doubtless, that the period seemed to promise so slight a yield in the political field, as compared with the economic, as scarcely to warrant the effort.

And yet beween 1850 and 1870 political developments were taking place which meant for the first time the incorporation of the working classes in the body politic. It would be most unlikely that they played a negligible part in effecting changes so vital to themselves, or that the changes could have taken place without their participation. If they were being incorporated in the body of voters, it meant that they had to enter into political relations with other classes and groups; adjustments of policy had to be made according to interests, and certainly it would be dangerous to assume that the millions of men who were fashioning such effective instruments in the economic field as trade-unions and coöperative societies were wholly passive in the hands of upper-class manipulators when it came to politics.

The argument has been generally accepted that this very absorption of the working classes in their attempts to work out their redemption along economic lines did in fact render them passive in political matters; that they ceased after 1850 to trust in political methods. This argument, however, requires certain modifications. It could apply in its entirety only to that minority of the working classes who during this period were being directly benefited by the various working-class organizations. These doubtless were the most progressive elements, but they cannot be taken to stand for the whole of their class. The fact is, that just at this time they were beginning to take on the characteristics of an aristocracy of labor, apart from the rank and file.[1] Furthermore, even organized labor intermittently recognized the bearing of politics upon economic status. Finally, this argument assumes that the working classes had no motive in seeking political power except for the advancement of their economic interests. In a preceding paragraph the statement was made that in the minds of the majority of the upper classes the economic implications of democracy were of paramount concern. That statement designedly excluded the working classes, with the purpose of later making distinctions somewhat fine, but fundamental.

Chartism bequeathed to the next generation of workingmen two potent ideas which bear on this question. One was that until the workers gained political power their social status could not be greatly improved. They would always be at the mercy of the capitalists who, through their control of the government, would manipulate taxation, the public debt, the currency, the poor laws, and the regulations as to property and profits solely for their own benefit. If workingmen could carry their democratic program, it would give them control of parliament and

[1] Sidney and Beatrice Webb, *History of Trade Unionism*, London, 1920, pp. 217, 218.

power to reverse the process. A second legacy of Chartism was a belief in the rightness of democracy.[1] To its more enlightened followers, Chartism was not just a "knife and fork question." It was justice. It was a recognition of the dignity of humanity. It would remove from labor the brand of an inferior caste. It would permit workingmen to stand with feet firmly planted on the solid ground of citizenship and look the world in the face with the assurance of self-respect.

The heirs of these two Chartist conceptions retained or modified them according to changed conditions. The need of an economic revolution became gradually less evident after 1850, and the possibility of it was by that date known to most to be hopeless. Conditions of labor were still harsh, but the more progressive workingmen, despairing of direct Chartist methods, turned to those that could be undertaken without political power, chiefly trade-unions and coöperation. These methods won their way and, together with other forces making for general prosperity, began to effect a gradual amelioration of conditions for the favored minority, and to a smaller extent for the masses.

It became at once evident, however, that the adoption of these non-political methods did not obviate the need of political power. This need merely assumed an altered shape. Political power was now required to safeguard the new methods themselves. Restrictive laws on organizations and special legislation against labor had to be combated. And so workingmen found the general Chartist principle of political power as a lever for economic advancement still indispensable; only now it was to be political power acting indi-

[1] For evidence of the prevalence of the belief in natural right *cf.* M. Beer, *History of British Socialism,* I. 288 ff; J. West, *History of the Chartist Movement,* pp. 81 ff; M. Hovell, *History of the Chartist Movement,* p. 30; William Lovett, *Life and Struggles of Wm. Lovett in His Pursuit of Bread, Knowledge and Freedom,* etc., London, 1876, p. 127.

rectly through the promotion of voluntary effort rather than through direct, social legislation. The middle and upper classes sensed the reality behind the indirection. What difference if competitive economics was to be set aside by the direct legislation of the Chartist, or thwarted by the non-political interference of the trade-unionist?

Working-class leaders, therefore, like their Chartist predecessors, realized the necessity of a democratic reform of parliament as an auxiliary to the economic advancement of their class. The Chartists had believed in the independent political action of labor. The newer generation of labor leaders did not; but they could not allow the possibility of such a policy wholly to lapse. The mere discussion of that possibility acted as a coercive influence upon those inclined to be unresponsive to, or afraid of, labor's demands.

These considerations afford one reason for continued working-class political interest during the years under discussion. This general fact has to a certain extent been recognized by students of the history of English labor. The steadiness and persistence with which such motives spurred labor on to political activity in this period, supposed to be so non-political, have, however, never been adequately described. This aspect of the working-class demand for the franchise was apparent to the more discerning of the upper and middle classes and served to weaken the support the cause of franchise reform was receiving from certain sections of these classes on other grounds. Only when these facts are duly perceived can we understand this period of transition and of readjustment in the political relationships of classes.

Another aspect of the lingering Chartist influence consists in the persistence of unorthodox economic ideas long after 1850. Working-class leaders were coming to rely upon methods of self-help rather than upon state action, it is true. In order to gain an opportunity to apply these new methods, they had to make it clear that they were not attacking the existing system. They were forced to defend their actions on the ground of individualistic, competitive economics.[1] But this economic theory was adopted by trade-unionists slowly and largely from motives of expediency, at least up to the decade of the seventies. They never ceased to be inconsistent and haphazard in their application of *laissez faire* to labor problems.[2] For instance, factory legislation was uninterruptedly advocated by trade-unionists. As for the non-unionized masses of labor, research reveals scattered but significant evidence of the steady persistence of heterodox economic views among them. This fact is of considerable importance politically, as modifying the general attitude of class to class. It was difficult for the average middle-class politicians to differentiate the various sections of the working-class world and estimate the importance of their opinions accordingly.

In such ways as these did the Chartist conception of political power as a means to economic ends, however disguised or diluted, continue to be a political factor. How important a factor it was has never been adequately appraised.

The influence of the second inheritance from Chartism —a belief in the suffrage as a right—has been to a large extent ignored. A careful study of the literature of the period leaves no doubt that the belief that the rights of citizenship should go with its duties was ineradicably lodged in the minds of the great masses of working men, trade-unionists and non-trade-unionists alike. The vote was not property nor a trust in the hands of a few for the many.

[1] Webb, *op. cit.*, pp. 201, 239.

[2] See Webb, *op. cit.*, pp. 368-70, for a discussion of this change of theory. Two strong groups of unions never adopted middle-class economics; namely, the cotton operatives and the coal miners.

It was a right due to every full-grown man in England. Without it the laborer, even though a member of a powerful trade society or holder of shares in a coöperative store, bore the stigma of social and civic inferiority. He was something less than an Englishman. Undeviatingly, therefore, the great body of the working classes held in their hearts to the spirit of the six points of the Charter. They cherished it all the more as they advanced in self-respect. Almost without exception, every expression of working-class opinion on the franchise between 1850 and 1867 was in favor of manhood suffrage, and during this period no other slogan could win a rousing response from the unenfranchised masses. The influence of this allegiance to democracy was conspicuous.

It will be objected, perhaps, that there was no agitation during this period. No agitation took place comparable with that of 1832 or 1842, certainly. Such agitation is usually due to the pressure of grievances not to be borne, in the shape of naked physical suffering or of actual oppression on a wide scale. Such grievances were decreasing after 1850. It is no valid argument, therefore, to maintain that the absence of agitation proves the absence of political interest and conviction. On the contrary, given the absence of those causes without which no mass agitation had ever taken place in England, the volume of evidence that exists as to the part taken in politics by men who had not even the right to direct participation therein argues a notable amount of interest and thought. Nor were there wanting the definite formulation and promotion of policies according to carefully reasoned plans. Methods and policies had to be different after 1850, because conditions changed, and theories gradually changed with them. But method and policy both existed and were acted upon with a fair degree of steadiness. In place of agitation, there was steady pressure. Above all, the pressure was exerted not by labor alone, but in conjunction with strong groups from the middle classes. For labor's new policy came to be not independent action, but coöperation with those of the other classes who would coöperate. This fact is vital, not only in the political history of labor, but also in that of England as a whole. It meant the transformation of Whiggism into Liberalism, or better into Liberal-Laborism, and the further development of Conservatism in the direction of Tory democracy. Participating in this evolutionary process, guiding or being guided by it, were Disraeli, the adjustor of the landed classes to democracy; the Manchester School under Bright; the nonconformists under Edward Baines and Samuel Morley; certain prominent independent radicals of such varying types as John Stuart Mill and Joseph Cowen, the miners' champion of Tyneside; and, conspicuously in its later phase, Gladstone, who drew to himself the diverse liberal currents and became the embodiment of the new Liberalism. Not least among the forces reshaping parties and policies were the leaders and masses in the ranks of labor. Their general policy was, to state it again, coöperation with the middle classes. But, again to repeat for the sake of emphasis, in so far as the economic aspect of the issue, whether in the guise of trade-unionism or not, lifted its head, just so far did the policy of coöperation find itself in difficult straits.

All of these currents and cross-currents in English politics in this third quarter of the nineteenth century became inevitably complicated with others remotely related, such as foreign policy and the Irish question. The sum of all creates the intricate fabric of English politics during a period when the impact of the new and growing industrialism was forcing a continual readjustment in conformity with its needs.

The preceding pages have attempted to present in summary the developments in English politics which it is the task of the remainder of this discussion to endeavor to make as clear as possible in detail. The necessity must be held in mind of considering the problems that present themselves from two points of view—from that of the upper and middle classes, as well as from that of the working classes themselves. The object will be to place labor in its relation to the politics of the period as a whole.

CHAPTER II

A NEW POLICY: CONDITIONS ATTENDING
ITS INAUGURATION

When workingmen stopped to take stock of their situation as the second half of the nineteenth century opened, they were confronted on every hand with difficulty and uncertainty. In the decades just passed they had been driven by direst necessity to attempt to devise means of protection against the social and economic forces that had threatened to submerge them. An appeal to the government for legislative action had tardily resulted in incipient factory legislation because supported by a section of upper-class opinion.[1] Trade-unions had been organized, but up to 1850 were more of the nature of a series of experiments in organization and method than effective weapons of defence.[2] Excursions into Owenism and syndicalism proved fruitless of benefit. Finally, the desperate workingmen of the thirties and forties, convinced that all measures short of a social revolution were ineffective in the face of the enormity of existing evils, became alienated completely from all other classes in the state and set about organizing the great class movement known as Chartism.

Their social and political isolation and their consciousness of the lack of a will on the part of the governing classes to seek for an adequate solution of their problems had developed in English workingmen a sense of class

[1] See G. von Schulze-Gaevernitz, *Social Peace, a Study of the Trade Union Movement in England*, London, 1893 (tr. Wicksteed and Ed. Wallas), pp. 67-75, for interesting comments upon the Conservative attitude. For the influence of the Coleridgean school, see Beer, *History of British Socialism*, I. 273-4; II. 177. For factory legislation, see B. L. Hutchins and A. Harrison, *A History of Factory Legislation*, London, 1911, pp. 1-95.

[2] Webb, *op. cit.*, ch. iii, and pp. 137-154, 170-174.

solidarity. The pioneers of Ricardian socialism preached to them the gospel of the right to the whole produce of labor. This added to their class consciousness the cementing force of an intellectual sanction and the objective of a social revolution. The fact that these workers were Englishmen with strong traditions of constitutional action determined the method whereby they strove to effect the sweeping changes desired. That method was by attempting to secure control of parliament through the enactment of complete democracy. Chartism was, therefore, a class movement for economic and social ends by political means.[1]

The movement was without a possibility of success. The masses who supported it were not capable of reasoned and organized action. Suffering impelled them to demonstrate and demand, but without a sufficient understanding of the fundamental elements in their problem. The leaders were torn between two opposing policies and were sometimes, conspicuously in the case of Feargus O'Connor, little above their followers in wisdom and understanding. And finally, the forces of property and power arrayed against the movement insured its hopelessness from the start, unless it should develop into a violent revolution. This workingmen were not ready for.

Chartism, however, as a political labor organization whose object was to promote social and economic amelioration, made a strong appeal to the English working classes. Its ideals sank deep into their hearts. It continued to be looked back upon as right in its spirit, if wrong in its methods, long after it had ceased as an organized move-

[1] The best discussions of Chartism are E. Dolléans, *Le Chartisme*, 2 vols., Paris, 1912; M. Hovell, *The Chartist Movement*, Manchester, 1918; J. West, *History of the Chartist Movement*, London, 1920; P. W. Slosson, *The Decline of the Chartist Movement*, New York, 1916; and Beer, *op. cit.*, I. 280-347; II. 3-105; also F. F. Rosenblatt, *The Social and Economic Aspect of the Chartist Movement*, N. Y. 1916; and R. G. Gammage, *The Chartist Movement*, edition of 1894.

ment. By 1850 its strength had been dissipated. Numerous Chartist sects, however, continued and played a larger part in the political world than has usually been conceded. One cause of the disintegration of Chartism was the gradual improvement of economic conditions after 1850.[1] The improvement was only comparative, however.[2] At no time in the decade after 1850 could the masses be said to have attained to a decent standard of living, and fluctuations of trade brought periodic distress. These facts go far to explain the persistence of the unorthodox economic beliefs characteristic of Chartism long after the middle of the century, as will appear later in the course of this study.

By 1850 the thinking portion of the working classes began to realize that the solution of their problems would have to be by different methods from those which they had supported in the years just passed. A new phase of the labor movement was at hand. On its economic side, it meant the steady perfecting of the machinery of collective bargaining and of coöperative distribution. On its political side, it

[1] Other causes were the baneful influence of O'Connor and his land scheme; failure of the revolution in France and of the national worshops (cf. Foxwell's "Introduction" to Menger's *The Right to the Whole Produce of Labor,* p. cl.) ; failure of the Owenite colony at Queenswood; and the emigration of many of the leading spirits of the movement.

[2] Slosson, *op. cit.,* p. 129, shows that wages between 1840 and 1848 had advanced, but rose but slowly after that for several years. In the cotton industry only in 1852 did wages, which had fallen steadily since 1841 except for a recovery in 1845-6, reach the average level of the bad years 1837-41 (p. 137). In 1853 they had risen slightly above that level, but by that year the prices of foodstuffs had reached a higher point than at any time since 1841 except in 1846-7. Then came the Crimean War, which pushed prices up still more and produced considerable dislocation of industry. The influence of the gold discoveries upon prices and real wages is indicated by a table in Porter, *Progress of the Nation,* p. 56, summarized as follows: between 1830 and 1852 money wages were fairly stationary, but prices were falling, hence real wages were rising slowly; 1852 to 1870, wages were "rising fast," prices were "rising," hence real wages were "rising considerably." For a table of prices showing the effect of the Crimean War, see L. Levi, *Annals of British Legislation,* I. 29.

meant the abandonment of the policy of independent class action in favor of the only practicable alternative; viz., an alliance with those elements of the middle classes with whom for any reason alliance was possible. The total abandonment of all political activity by workingmen was never a fact. They believed in democracy as a recognition of their rights and were willing to assert that belief. Furthermore, they were repeatedly made aware of the power of government to interfere with the effectiveness of their methods of self-help. In addition, they sought constantly to extend the scope of factory legislation. All of these reasons imposed upon the more intelligent among them the necessity of a continued participation in politics. To the first phase of this new period in the history of English labor politics, it is now possible to turn.

The work of building up a public opinion among the middle and working classes in favor of their political reunion began about 1842. The schism between them had developed in the years of the first reform agitation, and the chief reason for it had been the inherent opposition between political liberalism and social democracy. Francis Place, who understood both classes with their aims and creeds as few other men of the time did, sensed both the need and the difficulty of the coöperation of the two classes. He had been watching with alarm the formation of the group of social revolutionary thinkers among the working classes in London, who were later to be the creators of Chartism.[1] In 1831 they had organized the National Union of Working Classes (the Rotundists), which opposed vigorously the middle-class reform bill and finally adopted a social-revolutionary program to be effected by class action. So widespread did the influence of such teachings

---

[1] For an account of the whole movement drawn from the Place MSS see G. Wallas, *Life of Francis Place*, pp. 265-322. See also West, *History of the Chartist Movement*, pp. 49-70.

become, that Place and other advanced Radicals saw almost equal danger in seeking the support of workingmen
for the reform bill and in not seeking it. Without a great
popular agitation it would be impossible to push the bill to
safety, yet such an agitation involved the danger of a social-
revolutionary struggle which would unite the Whigs and
Tories against all reform. Such a conflict of interests, of
theory, of method, and of aim, rendered the situation in-
calculably difficult. To use the working classes, yet not
to give them any oportunity to enforce their separate demands, was the procedure successfully followed, but it
created angry opposition and a sense of betrayal among
workingmen, which Place had most dreaded. He had
feared that "the working people would see in the proceedings the old desire to use them for a purpose and then to
abandon them. The gap between the working and middle
classes would be widened, and the rancour that exists would
be increased, and all chance of reconciliation put off for
years."[1]

Before the year was out the people were "awake to the
treason of their allies,"[2] as Place had prohesied would
happen when "the Reformed House of Commons . . .
shall, as it must, prove how inadequate will be the Reform
Bill to satisfy the expections of the people." In 1834 came
the new Poor Law.[3] By 1835 Place saw that the Radicals,
even Hume, were not willing to press for democratic reforms in the House.[4] Fierce hatred of employers was
rapidly developing around the prosecutions of trade-unionists, as in the cases of the Dorchester laborers and the

---

[1] Wallas, *Life of Place,* p. 281.

[2] W. J. Linton (a Chartist) on the "History of Chartism" in the
English Republic, Vol. 1851-1855, pp. 78 ff.

[3] Schulze-Gaevernitz, *Social Peace,* p. 42, calls this "the signal for
the dissolution of the union between the proletariat and the bourgeoisie."

[4] Wallas, *Life of Place,* pp. 334, 351.

Glasgow cotton spinners.[1] There was, also, united opposition to industrial measures by most of the upper-class groups.[2] By 1836 the alienation of workingmen from their political allies was complete, and the great working-class movement had begun.

By 1840, however, the difficulties in the way of the success of independent working-class action began to be apparent to the more enlightened of its adherents. The middle-class Radicals at the same time began to consider the possibility of a reconciliation. Hume interrogated Place in 1840 on the chances of workingmen following if he would take the lead in demanding in parliament as many points of the Charter as they could get. Place advised patience. In the meanwhile, he was, as Wallas expresses it, trying to coach the middle-class Radicals in the difficult art of acting with the suspicious and intractable working· men of that day. The situation had become complicated by the question of repealing the Corn Laws, which was opened by the League at the moment the Charter was being formulated. Chartists believed this to be a device to thwart their movement and that the middle classes were not sincere in their professions of zeal for the welfare of the working class in the repeal agitation, since they refused assistance in gaining the Charter, which would render possible at once the repeal of all obnoxious laws. But by 1840 or 1841 the League was beginning to win over the upper-grade artisans and operatives.[3] Lovett (in prison) cor-

[1] Webb, *op. cit.*, pp. 144 ff. and pp. 170 ff.

[2] J. H. Rose, *Rise of Democracy*, p. 61. Hutchins and Harrison, *A History of Factory Legislation*, pp. 1-95, *passim*, for the attitude of the various classes toward factory legislation. E. Hodder, *Life and Work of the Seventh Earl of Shaftesbury*, London, 1888, II. 30, 82.

[3] For relations between Chartists and the Anti-Corn Law League see Dolléans, *Le Chartisme*, II. 16-90; Hovell, *op. cit.*, pp. 193ff.; Lovett, *Life and Struggles*, p. 173; R. Garnett, *Life of W. J. Fox*, pp. 255-9; T. Frost, *Forty Years' Recollections, Literary and Political*, London, 1880, pp. 26, 27; H. Solly, *These Eighty Years*, London, 1893, I. 569.

responded with Place, each trying to win the other to the
support of his movement.   There was among the middle
classes a distinct and growing tendency to make overtures
to Chartists, for the former began to realize the great extent of the Chartist agitation and also the forbidding attitude of the government toward any further electoral reform[1] and toward the repeal of the Corn Laws.[2]   Certain Chartist leaders were willing to meet them half way,
notably Lovett, Bronterre O'Brien, and George Jacob
Holyoake. Lovett in 1841 tried to form a new association
to be open to "all creeds, classes and opinions," which
should work toward promoting education and creating a
public opinion in favor of the Charter.[3]   It received
nominal support from several Radical leaders—Place,
Hume, John Stuart Mill, Lord Brougham, Milner Gibson,
James Stansfeld, and T. S. Duncombe; in fact, "virtually
all the intellectual Liberals."[4]   At about the same time,
Place founded the "Metropolitan Parliamentary Reform
Association" for the purpose of promoting reconciliation.
Its objects were to be the same as those of the Charter,
though the word Charter was not to be used.   All the
Radical members of parliament joined it, but it lasted only
a year.[5]

Of all the tentative efforts at reunion of the two classes
put forward at this time, however, the most significant and
the most instructive was that called the Complete Suffrage

Hovell (p. 215) says every variety and combination of views on the
subject existed among Chartists. Dolléans thinks Chartists were almost
universally hostile (II. 23). He states that the free traders used every
means to give the public the impression that the majority of workingmen were favorable to the League, but this was not true. Those favorable to the League were in a great minority (II. 29-90).

[1] Russell's declaration of finality was made in 1837.
[2] Beer, *op. cit.*, II. pp. 113-114.
[3] Lovett, *Life*, p. 248; Hovell, *op cit.*, pp. 208, 209; West, *op. cit.*,
pp. 159, 160, 174.
[4] West, *op. cit.*, p. 160.
[5] West, *op. cit.*, p. 179.

Movement. It was a deliberate overture made by the free-traders and Radicals to the Chartists, but the inspiration of it was as much nonconformist as free-trade or Radical. This is a significant fact. It shows for the first time since 1832 the three great groups advancing toward the alliance that was later to command very largely the course of political events and result in the new Liberal party of Gladstone. These groups were the Manchester School, the non-conformists,[1] and labor. All of them might be induced to meet on the common ground of the old Radical democratic platform. It was their diverse economic interests that made such a *rapprochement* difficult. The nonconformist group now undertook to be the mediators, standing, as they did, in close sympathy with both of the other groups and believing in democracy on the Manchester and Radical grounds of its necessity for good government and on the religious ground that "every man should be treated as if he had within him the germs of a noble character."[2]

The immediate inspiration of the new movement was a series of articles in the *Nonconformist*[3] by Edward

[1] Many nonconformist bodies were distinctly opposed to politics at this date, but radical groups among them were developing a political interest and program. The most conservative were the Wesleyan Methodists; the most democratic and advanced were Baptists and Unitarians. For an interesting discussion of this, see H. U. Faulkner, *Chartism and the Churches*, N. Y., 1916, pp. 84-120.

[2] Thus Rose, *The Rise of Democracy*, p. 126, describes Sturge and other prominent nonconformists of the time. Also see S. Hobhouse, *Joseph Sturge, His Life and Work*, London, 1919, p. 66, for a speech made by Sturge in 1840 setting forth a typical nonconformist program of reforms; namely, separation of Church and state, free trade, wide extension of the franchise, the ballot, abolition of the property qualification, abolition of capital punishment and of slavery. Sturge, says Hobhouse, soon came to believe in all the points of the Charter. E. Barker, *English Political Thought from Herbert Spencer to the Present Day*, p. 120, says one root of the belief in natural rights has been Dissent, with its emphasis on the independence of conscience. The doctrine of natural rights has always been a chief basis of the demand for universal suffrage.

[3] Founded in 1841 by the radical wing of the Congregationalists who were urging the disestablishment question upon the official leaders,

Miall, its editor, in 1841 on the subject of "The reconciliation between the Middle and Labouring Classes." Joseph
Sturge had the articles published as a pamphlet. It reached
a fortieth edition in the course of several years.[1]
Joseph Sturge became advocate and organizer of the new
movement. He was a Friend, a Corn Law Leaguer, and
an alderman of Birmingham. He negotiated with Cobden
concerning the project, and Cobden expressed both his approval of Sturge's leadership and his sense of the difficulties ahead by writing him: "You have so much of established reputation to fall back upon, that your standing
with the middle classes would not be endangered by a
course which might peril the character and endanger the
usefulness of most others."[2] Sturge believed democracy
to be the only means of relief from the evils of the time.
He also believed that Chartism had come then (in 1841)
to a parting of the ways, when its intelligent section, now
advocating persuasion and education against a policy of
physical force, ought to be supported in its efforts.

Sturge, therefore, early in 1842, at the close of an Anti-
Corn Law League meeting in Manchester, gathered a large
conference, with Place in the chair, at which he proposed the
initiation of a movement to secure for the people "the
fair, full, and free exercise of the elective franchise."   The
free-traders felt urgent need of the support of the factory
operatives,[3] and knew that some of the anti-O'Connorite
Chartists were coming to believe in free trade. The hostility
between the two industrial classes seemed temporarily to
be much assuaged.   The *Spectator,* for instance, had come

who opposed any political action (Faulkner, *op. cit.,* p. 98).   It became
a spokesman for extreme liberalism in all its phases.

[1] Statement made by R. Kell in nominating Miall for Bradford in
1869, reported in the *Morning Star,* October 2, 1869. Also see Hobhouse,
op. cit., p. 72, and West, *op. cit.,* p. 173.

[2] Hobhouse, *op. cit.,* p. 72.

[3] Rose, *op. cit.,* p. 121.

out for the six points of the Charter.[1] The project received without difficulty a large free-trade and Radical support, including that of Cobden, Bright, W. J. Fox (Unitarian preacher and orator for the Anti-Corn Law League), Sharman Crawford, M.P., the Reverend Thomas Spencer, George Thompson, M.P., and others.[2] The proposed movement was welcomed by an influential Chartist section, especially by Lovett and O'Brien. At a conference of both classes in Birmingham it was the endeavor of the middle classes to present the Chartist program, without in any way acknowledging the Chartist organization. The National Complete Suffrage Union was formed, the matter of drawing up its program being deferred to a later time. The movement spread to a great many industrial towns.

But the project was foredoomed to failure because the time for it was not yet ripe. The mass of the workingmen were still too revolutionary, and times were desperately hard. A few months after the formation of the Union came an attempt at a general strike in Lancashire, followed by wholesale arrests, when feelings on both sides became exasperated anew. The majority of operatives and miners were not ready for *laissez faire,* but still adhered to a belief in state interference, and so long as they held that view the gulf between them and the capitalist class was unbridgeable. The more violent party of Chartists denounced the move as treachery and an attempt to weaken the class war.[3] The inevitable break came even among the

[1] Statement made in West, *op. cit.,* p. 174.

[2] The large religious element in its support is shown by the fact that it had about two hundred ministers among its adherents, and by the general tenor of its petition to parliament in April, 1842, which based its appeal for universal suffrage upon natural right, British constitutional precedent with regard to taxation and representation, and upon "holy religion." This petition is quoted entire in Faulkner, *op. cit.,* App. I. p. 121.

[3] O'Connor and the *Northern Star.* See Beer, *op. cit.,* II. 125. Doléans, *op. cit.,* Vol. II. 102 ff., gives a speech of G. J. Harney at Sheffield which sums up the Chartist arguments against the movement.

adherents of the movement at the end of the first year over
the question of adopting the official program of the Union.
The middle-class members of the committee ignored Lovett
and the other working-class members and tried to avoid
adopting the term "Charter," which Lovett considered a
vital point. This break was not over the matter of mere
words, as Beer points out, but was because the Charter
had come to signify a whole program of social reform. To
give that up would be to exchange social democracy for
political.[1]

Upon this rock the Complete Suffrage Movement split.
"Apparently, then, class jealousy was more powerful than
all attempts at conciliation, and the secret or openly expressed desires of the working-men levellers were too
strong to admit any thorough coöperation with middle-class
democrats like Joseph Sturge, who sought parliamentary
reform only for the redress of the more glaring grievances
of the age."[2] To such an alliance upon such terms
workingmen were eventually to come. The Complete
Suffrage Movement prefigured it and revealed the fundamental nature of the obstacles to its realization. The
evolution of an opinion among the working classes upon
social issues that would be more in harmony with that of
middle-class Radicals, and, on the part of the Radicals, an
increased sense of their dependence upon democratic sup-

[1] Beer, op. cit., II. 128, 129.
[2] Rose, op. cit., p. 125. Further details of this most interesting
movement are in West, op. cit., pp. 173-199; Dolléans, op. cit., II. 90 ff.;
Hovell, op. cit., pp. 242-265; Lovett, Life, pp. 262-289. He states that
at the Birmingham conference one object was to get workingmen to
promise to use the vote for free trade (p. 279). The debate in parliament
on the second Chartist petition, in 1842, is significant. Several free-
traders spoke in support of the motion to permit the petitioners to appear
at the bar of the House. On this occasion Lord John Russell and
Macaulay both opposed, on the ground that universal suffrage would
mean the destruction of the institutions of the country, which were based
on property. For an account of this see Beer, op. cit., II. 135-7.

port—these were the two prerequisites.   To a study of such developments let us now turn.

The Corn Law movement absorbed the attention of the Radicals from the failure of the Complete Suffrage Movement to the free-trade victory of 1846.   The unity of the working-class agitation had been shattered to fragments, only temporarily reaching a state of coherence again in 1848.   Chartism, as a body of ideas, however, was still vigorously propagated by a multitude of associations with most diverse panaceas for the ills of the times.   By 1847 the Manchester leaders were free to take up again the question of democracy.   Their interest in it lay in the fact that they needed it to complete their victory over the landed interests, against which the war had not by any means ended.   Ricardo taught them that the interests of industry and land were diametrically opposed, since rents and profits varied inevitably in inverse ratio.[1]   Protection must be totally abolished and trade set free from every restriction; profits from industry must be increased and those from land decreased by a substitution of taxation upon real property for taxation of industry; and the whole burden of taxation must be lightened by a policy of rigorous economy at home and peace abroad.   To put into effect these policies, which would complete the emancipation of capitalistic industry and open up to it vistas of almost unlimited expansion, more power in parliament was needed by the industrial classes.   A wide extension of the franchise and a redistribution of seats in favor of the towns and the industrial counties became, therefore, an essential feature of their political objective.   To the slogans peace and retrenchment was added, therefore, a third—reform.

[1] Cf. Beer, *op. cit.*, I. 149, 153. Foxwell, in the "Introduction" to Menger, *The Right to the Whole Produce of Labour*, p. xli, says that Ricardo's teachings made political economy the tool of a political party.

Such was the cry of the Manchester School. It was also the cry of the nonconformists. Many of the latter advocated peace from principle, and an increasing number saw the need of electoral reform in order to effect an object to them most important, the establishment of the religious equality. If the working classes could be induced also to accept this program, without any sinister interpretations, then a power could be created in England before which no opposition could stand. The nature of the Manchester policy and its relation both to the democracy and to its opponents, the territorial party, was expressed with much discernment by a working-class journal in the early fifties. The Manchester party, it declared, represented commerce in its inevitable war with feudalism, and this gave them popular support because of the long-cherished antipathy of the people to the dominance of the territorial aristocracy. They advocated enfranchisement of the people because they knew that political strength came from them and because "their family traditions are those of the people." But, on the other hand, theirs was decidedly a class movement, and democracy knows no class. Hence they feared the people. So also did their enemies, the aristocracy. Both would try to call in the aid of the people in their war with each other. All sorts of bait would be offered them. The traders disliked social changes more than political, the aristocracy, political more than social; this indicated the manner in which tenders would be made to the people.[1]

By "reform" the Radicals meant more than mere electoral reform. This was to be preliminary to a long program of changes, which should completely liberalize English institutions in harmony with Radical and Dissenting views, such as colonial reform, prison reform, fiscal reform, drink reform, army reform, religious reform, edu-

[1] The *Political Examiner,* two articles, April 5 and May 11, 1853.

cational reform, and reform of the press laws.[1] Practically all of these measures would appeal to working-class sympathy, and some of them had been, or soon were to be made, distinctly working-class issues, as for example education and reform of the press laws. On the broad basis of liberalism, therefore, it was certainly not vain to hope for the political assimilation of the two great industrial groups with each other. The fact that they were both industrial ought irresistibly to compel united action against their common opponents, the landlords; and it would so compel it if the working classes could be made to understand political economy and know that their interests were not diverse from, but were intimately bound up with, those of the employing class and that both must obey the irrefragable laws of economics for their common salvation. The most serious obstacles to this desired consummation were likely to be two: working-class belief in the antagonism of their class interests to those of capital and the appeal of Conservatism to certain working-class elements and interests, such as had produced Tory-Chartism and was even now producing Tory-democracy.

In 1848 efforts at reunion were revived in earnest. As Morley, in his life of Cobden, points out, the moment seemed opportune for the Radicals to form a strong party.[2] The old parties were confused and disintegrated over the repeal of the Corn Laws. Further, the strength of labor as an organized movement had been hopelessly broken, it appeared. Bright, in consideration of all these elements in the situation, began early in this year to urge the formation of a new party along the lines of the Anti-Corn Law League, which should gather up the energy of the innum-

[1] For a catalogue of such measures advocated by a typical Radical and nonconformist, see Garnett, *Life of Fox,* pp. 325-6, 353. Also see the introduction, p. viii.

[2] J. Morley, *Life of Richard Cobden,* Boston, 1890, p. 334.

erable little movements and associations that were spring-
ing up in all parts of the country.[1] To Villiers he wrote:
"We can have a party out of doors more formidable than
we had in the League and can work the Constitution so as
to reform it through itself."[2] He wished to call it the
"Commons' League." Financial and parliamentary reform
were to be its two objects; the tactics to consist in strengthening the party by attending to the registration of voters,
increasing the number of county voters in towns by the
promotion of the purchase of forty-shilling freeholds, and
general organization and propaganda. But Cobden was not
sympathetic. He declared that he was not so sanguine as
he used to be as to the good effect of a wide extension of
the franchise.[3] He believed they should concentrate upon
financial reform and seek to extend the franchise only by
the freehold scheme.

In the meantime, others were moving toward the same
general end. Joseph Hume, at the time of the spectacular
failure of the Chartist demonstration in April, had invited
the working classes through O'Connor to coöperate with
him in an attempt to gain a substantial measure of reform.[4]
O'Connor stated that he had become convinced of the
expediency of abating some of the demands of the Charter
for the sake of gaining the measures Hume advocated, on
the condition of the sincerity of Hume and his followers,
and that he (O'Connor) had so advised his supporters.
Hume's program came to be called the "Little Charter,"
its demands being household suffrage, the ballot, triennial
parliaments, and a more equal distribution of seats according
to population. When Hume brought it up in the House

[1] G. M. Trevelyan, *Life of John Bright*, p. 183.
[2] *Ibid.*, p. 184.
[3] Morley, *op. cit.*, p. 335.
[4] From remarks by O'Connor in the House of Commons in connection with the postponement of Hume's bill. *Hansard*, IIC. 1307-8.
This was in May.

in 1848, it received the support in debate of Cobden, R. Bernal Osborne, and C. P. Villiers, and, in the division, of eighty-four members to three hundred and fifty-one in opposition. The supporters included most of those Radicals who were to take the lead for fifteen years in promoting the movement now begun—Manchesterites like Bright, Cobden, and Gibson; the nonconformists, Fox, Berkeley, and Trelawney;[1] independent Radicals like Sir De Lacy Evans, a metropolitan member, and Thomas Wakley; and the friends of the Chartists, Sharman Crawford, Sir Joshua Walmsley, and Colonel Perronet Thompson. In the opposition were the solid phalanxes of Whigs and Conservatives.[2]

Still other groups were trying to promote a new political alignment. Sturge again offered to Chartists to adopt universal suffrage as the basis of a party.[3] Edward Miall's tract, which had inspired the Complete Suffrage Movement, was reprinted and was discussed favorably in Chartist journals.[4] The principle of universal suffrage was, throughout 1848, advocated in several journals—Douglas Jerrold's *Weekly Newspaper,* the *Leeds Times,* the *Nonconformist,* and another important journal of Dissent, the *British Banner.*[5]

Thus from several middle-class quarters came tentative offers of coalition. The working classes on their side found themselves torn with doubt and dissension on the question of the attitude to be assumed toward the proposed policy. There were two related elements in their problem: could and should class activity be abandoned, and,

---

[1] Berkeley soon became the maker of an annual motion for the ballot, and Trelawney of one for the abolition of church rates.

[2] For the debate and vote, see *Hansard,* C. 156 to 226.

[3] The *English Republic,* February 5, 1852.

[4] The *Republican* (ed. by the Chartist, G. G. Harding), 1848.

[5] Enumerated in *The People* (ed. by the Chartist, J. Barker, at Wortley), May 27, 1848, in an article on "Chartism and Unitarians."

secondly, could their social objectives be modified and should they be divorced from politics? Upon the answers to these questions hinged both their acceptance of middle-class overtures and the very continuance of such overtures. In 1848-50 there could be no unanimous answer. Utter confusion of aim existed. Factions innumerable were proposing schemes as varied as they were numerous. A survey of the most important of these reveals the disunion that prevailed.

Some groups of workingmen were beginning to place their whole faith in the coöperative movement. Their conception of coöperation was not yet free, however, from a belief in it as an agency for the redemption of the wage-earning classes. Christian Socialism, from 1848, became a potent influence to this end.[1] The humanitarian and religious feelings of such men as Frederick Denison Maurice, Charles Kingsley, and J. M. Ludlow had nothing but scathing condemnation for the existing competitive system, with its apparently inevitable consequence of dividing class from class and increasing the wealth of the rich and the poverty of the poor. This group of earnest friends of labor had met in the week following the Chartist failure of April 10 and organized a movement to direct working-class energies into coöperative enterprise, which would develop a Christian society instead of the cut-throat régime of individualism.[2] They began in May to issue their short-lived Politics for the People. Its chief burden was that government cannot touch the deepest social ills and that Chart-

[1] See C. W. Stubbs, Charles Kingsley and the Christian Social Movement, N. Y., 1899; H. De B. Gibbons, English Social Reformers, London, 1892; Charles Kingsley, Yeast, and Alton Locke, London, 1850; Politics for the People; The Christian Socialist; and The Journal of Association, three Christian Socialist journals that followed each other in rapid succession, 1848-1852; and C. E. Raven, Christian Socialism, London, 1920.

[2] Stubbs, op. cit., pp. 103, 104.

ism was thus based upon a false foundation.[1] The Charter, according to Kingsley, was "a poor, bald, constitution-mongering cry as I ever heard. That French cry of the 'Organization of Labour' is worth a thousand of it, and yet that does not go to the bottom of the matter by many a mile."[2] A moral and religious revolution that would socialize industry alone would bring permanent social peace. Conferences with Chartists and trade-unionists were held constantly during 1848-50, and competition was denounced as "a hateful, devilish theory which must be fought with to the death."[3] Attempts were made to organize coöperative production among the most oppressed trades, as the tailors, and in 1850 the Society for the Promotion of Working-Men's Associations was formed, tracts were issued, and the influence of the movement became fairly widespread.

Its political influence was to depreciate all political activity and interest. Many leaders were not democrats. Maurice was not, nor Kingsley; Ludlow, Thomas Hughes, and Lloyd Jones were, whole-heartedly.[4] Politically, it was also an influence working against harmony between the middle and working classes because of antagonistic economic interests and theories. Kingsley, says Beer, be-

[1] Thus Kingsley wrote to Chartists, in *Politics for the People*, May 13, 1848: "I think you have fallen into . . . the mistake of fancying that *legislative* reform is *social* reform, or that men's hearts can be changed by Act of Parliament." Quoted also in Stubbs, *op. cit.*, p. 117.

[2] Stubbs, *op. cit.*, p. 117.

[3] *Ibid.*, p. 129. Also C. E. Raven, *Christian Socialism*, London, 1920, p. 138.

[4] See C. F. G. Masterman, *F. D. Maurice*, London, 1907, p. 61. He said Maurice's ideal was the Tory one "of kings reigning by the grace of God." Also, F. Maurice, *Life of F. D. Maurice*, N. Y., 1884, II. 29. As to Kingsley, see Masterman, *op. cit.*, p. 66; H. De B. Gibbins, *op. cit.*, p. 160; Holyoake, *Bygones Worth Remembering*, London, 1905, I. 90. Kingsley believed the upper classes to be the natural leaders of the people. Hughes and L. Jones were to be later among the most important leaders of the working classes in their economic and political struggles, Hughes as member of parliament and Jones, an ex-Chartist and tailor, as an influential journalist. On Ludlow, see Raven, *op. cit.*, p. 62.

lieved the great battle of the day was that of the Church, the gentleman, and the workman, against the shop-keepers and the Manchester School.[1] In fact, Christian Socialism was more closely akin to non-political, voluntary Owenism and to Tory-democracy than to Liberalism.[2]

But Christian Socialism could not afford a platform upon which the whole of the working classes could stand, because large sections of them were not ready to repudiate politics. When Lloyd Jones, a Chartist, was sent to Lancashire to spread Christian Socialist doctrine, he failed completely for this reason and brought upon the movement the denunciation of the foremost Chartist of the time, O'Connor's successor in leadership, Ernest Jones, who henceforth kept up a crusade against it, insisting that political power would gain its objective, which without political power was impossible of realization.[3] George Jacob Holyoake, a great influence among workingmen for many years before and after this period, consistently opposed the subordination of political to social reform, and hence opposed this early movement.[4] Some Chartists welcomed it.[5] As to working-class and Chartist journals, some opposed, as for example, the *National Instructor*, which condemned the movement as futile.[6] Others supported it, as George Julian Harney's *Democratic Review*,[7] the *Leicestershire*

[1] Beer, *op. cit.*, II. 183.
[2] Beer, *op. cit.*, I. 122, shows that both Christian Socialism and Tory-democracy were a product of Coleridgean philosophy, whose adherents became "the spiritual leaders of the new conservatism, imbuing it with a sense of social righteousness and love of the people. They are the fathers of Tory Democracy and Christian Social reform."
[3] Beer, *op. cit.*, II. 186; R. G. Gammage, *History of the Chartist Movement*, pp. 382, 3; F. Maurice, *Life of F. D. Maurice*, II. 157.
[4] G. J. Holyoake, *Bygones Worth Remembering*, I. 96.
[5] Walter Cooper became a lecturer for it. See *Democratic Review*, February, 1850. The *Christian Socialist*, January 18, 1851, records a conference at Manchester at which a number of Chartist leaders were present.
[6] Quoted in Slosson, *Decline of the Chartist Movement*, p. 176.
[7] February, 1850.

Movement,[1] and, more significantly the *Operative*, the organ of the newly formed Amalgamated Society of Engineers and their organizer, William Newton.[2] Throughout 1851-2 the *Operative* was arguing in favor of the coöperative as opposed to the competitive industrial principle: it furnishes conclusive evidence of the influence of the idea of salvation through coöperative workshops upon the engineers in these years.[3] In fact, say the Webbs, various unions vied with each other in setting up self-governing workshops.[4] The *Operative* recounts that the Glassworkers at their national conference in May, 1852, discussed coöperation and decided to draft plans for undertaking it.[5] So rapid was the increase of coöperative societies of all types that, whereas in 1850 there were only fifty in existence, two years later there were two hundred and fifty, with a membership of a hundred and fifty thousand.[6]

Nevertheless, the movement had failed by 1854. Its influence had, however, been great. Its leaders were the

[1] March 23 and March 30, 1850. The latter number stated that the framework knitters were much interested. The movement was regarded as a means to secure for labor what it should receive as the sole producer of wealth.

[2] "The First Report of the Society for the Promotion of Working Men's Associations. To which is Appended a Report of the Co-operative Conference in London . . . 26th and 27th of July, 1852," in the Goldsmiths' Library, London, lists William Newton as a delegate to the conference. "Transactions of the Co-operative League, 1852" (in the Goldsmiths' Library) contains a MS list of members of the League, among whom were several Chartists or men who were to be influential with the working classes later—William Cunningham, later M.P., John Locke, also later M.P., Robert Cooper, Chartist, Robert Owen, Louis Blanc, George Dawson of Birmingham, a middle-class friend of workingmen, James Hole, and John Holmes, both workingmen of Leeds of importance later, and William Newton.

[3] See a series of articles in February, 1851, also December 13, 1851, January 31, 1852, February 27, 1852. An article in the issue of February 22, 1851, attacked the journal for its policy, saying that it "teems with invectives" against competition.

[4] *Op. cit.*, p. 226. They say the movement ceased to have practical importance among unions after 1852.

[5] May 22, 1852.

[6] Slosson, *op. cit.*, p. 190.

friends of trade-unions in the days when they had few
friends; they secured a law to legalize coöperative enterprise[1] and worked for improvements in education and sani-
tation.[2]   Politically, its influence was to offer an obstacle
to the assimilation of working and middle-class theories
and policies.   So inimical were certain Christian Socialist
leaders to a Liberal alliance that Ludlow advised in the
Journal of Association on the eve of the election of 1852
that workingmen vote for a Tory who set his face against
extension of the franchise, but who also opposed a reduction of wages, rather than for an extreme Radical reformer
who "buys labour in the cheapest market."[3]   In the conferences held with workingmen the debate often turned on
political action and its advisability.   In one such discussion
Lloyd Jones insisted that the free traders meant freedom
only for themselves, and E. Vansitart Neele deprecated all
political action as useless.   On the other hand, F. J. Furni-
val, Washington Wilkes, and W. E. Forster urged coöpera-
tors to make use of their electoral power to further all reforms, especially in the franchise.[4]

Such confusion of views characterized the English
working classes at the middle of the nineteenth century, in
whatever relationship they may be examined.   Let us turn
now to trade-unions.   What was their attitude toward
economic policy and toward politics?

[1] 15 and 16 Vict. c. 31.
[2] They founded the Working Men's College in London in 1854.
Stubbs, *op. cit.*, pp. 168-9, gives an account of Kingsley's work for sanitary reform.
[3] Volume for 1852, p. 170.
[4] *Ibid.*, pp. 157, 159, 171.   Forster, who later as a member of Gladstone's cabinet had charge of the Education Bill of 1870, was in 1850
writing in the *Leader* on coöperation and arguing for the right to labor
and to the use of the lands of the country. (Quoted in Wm. Pare's
Claims of Labour and Capital, London, 1854, Part II, p. 27.)   See also
Journal of Association, 1852, pp. 86 ff., for a conference on the question
of state intervention.

Since 1842 they had been increasing in strength and had in several cases taken the form of national organizations of single trades.[1] Their policy came increasingly to be to apply themselves to resisting industrial and legal oppression through the building up of strong, permanent societies able to oppose employers upon more equal terms and with peaceful weapons instead of the strike wherever possible. The year 1850 is memorable in the history of trade-unionism as witnessing the origin of the amalgamated union formed by the combination of several competing societies. It elaborated a new method of combining the ordinary purposes of collective bargaining with the insurance features of the many friendly societies with which workingmen had become familiar.[2] Such increased membership and funds necessitated an improved management. Consequently regular salaried officials came to be employed, in whose hands the guidance of trade-union affairs came more and more to be lodged. The first of these amalgamated unions was the Amalgamated Society of Engineers. Its organizer was William Newton.

So much for the externals of trade-unionism about 1850. An investigation into its spirit and attitude toward the great social and political problems then engaging working-class attention makes it clear that, while eventually trade-unions were to abandon all ideas of social revolution, even all sense of the solidarity of labor, and become, as the Webbs say, associations only for the protection of the vested interests of the members, an aristocracy of labor removed from the masses and accepting middle-class economics and philosophy[3]—while this was the general course of trade-union development after 1850, by that year and for several years afterward such development had not gone far enough

[1] Webb, op. cit., chapter iv.
[2] Webb, op. cit., pp. 204-14.
[3] Webb, op. cit., p. 297.

to warrant any such description.   And it was with the actual situation that politicians of those years had to deal. • They could only draw inferences from what was apparent and shape their tactics accordingly; and there were more symptoms of dangerous beliefs among trade-unionists then than of the reverse.

Notably, there were the proceedings of the "Metropolitan Trades' Delegates" from 1848 to at least 1855. Here certainly were promulgated doctrines as much at variance with middle-class conceptions as were those of Chartists or Socialists. The initial meetings of these delegates seem to have been in the late summer of 1848. The *Labour League* (organ of the Association of United Trades) reports in the issue of August 12 of that year that a series of meetings had recently been held at the Bell Inn, Old Bailey, to consider the extent and causes of the present evils of the working classes. The delegates published a report on unemployment and its attendant evils.[1] A petition to parliament in behalf of the reforms they suggested was ignored. Whereupon, they decided to form a society of the London and provincial trades to organize public opinion to force these reforms upon an unwilling parliament. In the spring of 1849 they issued their Address to the Trades of Great Britain and Ireland, which was published in the *Power of the Pence* and later as a pamphlet, a copy of which is in the Goldsmiths' Library.[2] It stated that they had been delegated by the

[1] This report is summarized in the *Labour League*. The *Britannia*, March 15, 1851, referring to the petition to parliament at this time, says it placed the number of unemployed in London at one half of the total number of working men (200,000), and the partially employed at one third.

[2] A note on the back by the librarian or the collector reads: "A very interesting manifesto for a National Trades Union . . . On the whole, a more reasonable program than we should find today, or generally at that time." This report was discussed in Harney's *Democratic Review* by A. A. Walton, one of the most persistent advocates of direct labor representation at the time of the passage of the Act of 1867 and after, and Labor candidate for Stoke-on-Trent in 1874.

trades of London to frame a constitution for a "National Organization of Trades for the Industrial, Social, and Political Emancipation of Labour." They therefore submitted a program that embraced nationalization of the land as the only solution for unemployment; manhood suffrage; a state supported system of secular education; expansion of the currency; home colonies for the unemployed; securing of the benefits of machinery to the whole community; restriction on foreign imports that competed with home industry; local boards of trade of an equal number of employers and workmen to act under the supervision of a minister of labor as impartial arbitrators in industrial disputes; the imposition of a graduated property tax in lieu of all other taxes. This remarkable program of social reconstruction ends with an appeal to the trades to "unite in one firm and indissoluble bond" to bring about its adoption. The address was signed by James O'Leary, chairman, and A. E. Delaforce, temporary secretary.

About a year later the Trades' Delegates issued a second address, dated April 11 and signed by John Segrave, president, and Delaforce as secretary.[1] The organization had evidently by that time taken on a regular form. It had been charged with the duty of attempting to ascertain the "natural and social" causes that affected labor. The body of this address, setting forth the conclusions of the members, is an argument against orthodox political economy and unrestricted free trade. The aim of the new system, they say, is cheapness, but cheapness comes from reducing wages or from cheap machine production, which means unemployment. "It has become a matter of the very highest importance that every working man . . . should be made acquainted with the delusion that prevails regarding Adam Smith's writings" and those of the other economists, McCulloch, Malthus, and

[1] Published in the *Champion*, Vol. 2, No. 1, and in the *Britannia*, April 20, 1850.

Mill, which are admittedly "popular, plausible, and loose hypotheses." Then follows a severe arraignment of the new middle-class government based upon self-interest, "the accumulative principle of social action instead of the distributive." But their power can be overthrown if the trades will support this organization in a "temperate, firm, and constitutional manner." This address was issued as a pamphlet. The first edition was soon exhausted, and a second was published.[1]

That the object of attack by this body was the Manchester School is evident. At the meeting that adopted the above address, Richard Oastler, the Tory factory reformer, was a speaker.[2] The protectionist party were much interested in these proceedings. This is evinced by the fact that one of the Tory papers published the address in full, commenting that "the representatives of labour in this vast city deliberately and unanimously proclaim to the world their conviction that the so-called Free Trade legislation of recent years is not only injurious in practice, but that it is radically false in principle."[3] It stated that the manifesto was said to express the sentiments of nearly twenty thousand individuals. In a later number, this same paper stated that the Metropolitan Trades' Delegates were giving great assistance to the National Association of United Trades in organizing effective resistance to the free-traders.[4]

Still a third manifesto was issued in March, 1851.[5] It stated that unemployment in London in the trades depending upon home consumption was as great as in 1848, thus prov-

[1] A copy is in the Goldsmiths' Library, entitled, Address of the Metropolitan Trades' Delegates to their Fellow Countrymen on the Interests and Present Position of the Labouring Classes of the Empire. London, 1850.

[2] The *Champion*, April 20, 1850.

[3] The *Britannia*, April 20, 1850.

[4] *Ibid.*, May 11, 1850.

[5] Published in the *Britannia*, March 15, 1851.

ing the decreased purchasing power of the people, and that wages among those employed were much lower than in that year. Thousands were being denied "the right to labour."

In the autumn of 1852, after the election, which turned chiefly upon the free-trade issue, this body sent out a "Proclamation of the Working Classes of Great Britain" with the sub-title, "Free Trade vs. Protection."[1] Its object was stated to be to make known the true sentiments of the working classes in view of Villiers' motion in the House of Commons to approve and extend the free-trade policy. It professed to present resolutions adopted "at a large meeting of the working classes" convened to consider the subject. Those resolutions condemned the political economy that taught unlimited competition as destructive of honest dealing, morality, and the national resources, and advocated a policy of protection.

There is a possibility that active protectionist propaganda was being carried on among the London trades which contributed to such pronouncements.[2] However that may be, it was with workingmen who were issuing such manifestoes as these that Hume and Bright had to deal in entering upon their task of amalgamating the two great industrial groups into one party. Their sense of the difficulty of the undertaking must have been equalled only by their realization of its necessity.

Another organized body that preached economic heresy was the National Association of United Trades for the

[1] Published in The *Albion,* another protectionist journal, December 1, 1852.

[2] At a meeting of the Journeymen Bakers in London in 1850 to promote legislation in their behalf, George Frederick Young, president of the protectionist association called the National Association for the Protection of Industry and Capital, was present and pledged his Association to assist the bakers. Some collector wrote on the back of this pamphlet in the Goldsmiths' Library: "Protectionist movement taking up the sweated trades against the Manchester School." The pamphlet is entitled, "Meeting of the Journeymen Bakers of the Metropolis. From the *Morning Herald* of July 1, 1850."

Protection of Labour. It was formed in 1845 and lasted for over fifteen years.[1] Its policy was to be conciliation in the economic field and parliamentary agitation for measures in the interest of labor. The disasters of the bad years, 1847-8, struck it a severe blow, but in 1848 it was reorganized, started the *Labour League* as its organ, and continued its activities. In the prospectus of this new journal[2] the united action of all classes was urged for the removal of the maladies of the time, which were asserted to be social in their nature. The trades must become reconciled to a slow, persevering attempt to create a favorable public opinion. "The ever growing mass of poverty, ignorance and destitution, which results from the present system, must be dealt with effectually . . . or it will overthrow the system itself." The objects of the National Association of Organized Trades for the Protection and Employment of Labour (the body's amended title) were stated to be: (1) to protect industry from capital by means of mediation, arbitration, and financial support; (2) coöperative production to employ surplus labour and men on strike; (3) to operate upon public opinion and parliament for such measures as the prohibition of sweating, the regulation of hours, the employment of surplus labor by the government in useful public works, sanitary reform, and the appointment of a ministry of labor.

The next number of the *League* made a pronouncement as to politics: "no re-enactment of the Reform mania of 'thirty-two nor of the Free Trade deception of 'forty-six." Workingmen must work out their own political and social salvation and not be the dupes of party.[3] And again: both old parties stood equally condemned in the eyes of the producers of wealth, since neither had the desire to effect re-

[1] See Webb, *op. cit.*, pp. 186-196, for an account of this organization.
[2] The *Labour League*, August 5, 1848.
[3] August 12, 1848.

medies for social and industrial wrongs. With a certain set
of *political* reformers cheapness in government and in goods
was a cardinal principle; but to them "the sons of toil"
must not look for aid.[1]

If it was difficult for Radicals to find common ground
with the Metropolitan Trades' Delegates and the National
Association, what was the case with such individual trade
unions as the new Amalgamated Society of Engineers?
Their denunciation of competition under the strong influence
of the Christian Socialists breathed in every number of the
Operative, their journal during 1850, 1851, and 1852.[2]
This journal also expressed political opinions which must
have commanded the general support of the Engineers, or at
least of their executive council. It believed strongly in the
efficacy of political power, declaring in one article that the
people's miseries were due to the fact that they "are not
wise unto political salvation."[3] It advocated direct labor
representation as a means to "provide by law that capital
shall be just to labour," and to effect great reforms, social
as well as political.[4] William Newton, the chief contributor
to the *Operative,* stood for Tower Hamlets in the election of
1852 distinctly as a labor candidate.[5] The very success of
the recent amalgamation raised visions of greater things.
"When every trade is organized, then would be the proper
time to confederate them in such a bond as would get for
labour its fair value, and for the labourer his proper consid-

---

[1] March 17, 1849. Testimony before the Committee on the Expediency of Boards of Conciliation in 1856 showed that the Association
then had a membership of five or six thousand. See L. Levi, *Annals of
British Legislation,* London, 1857, II. Series A.

[2] *E.g.* as to Christian Socialist influence, just after the lock-out,
1852, a large delegate meeting was addressed by Neale, Hughes, Ludlow,
and Jones, and it resolved to start a coöperative enterprise. The *Operative,* May 1, 1852. Cf. Webb, *op. cit.,* p. 215, for the coöperative
attempts of the Engineers.

[3] February 15, 1851.

[4] August 9, 1851.

[5] See below, pp. 100 ff.

eration in society."[1]   Again,[2] it declared that the reform
of 1832 did nothing for the people, but that it, with the repeal of the Corn Laws, had established a complete oligarchy
of the monied class.   Another article proclaimed "the in-
alienable rights of labour" and prophesied that labour would
unite to overthrow the whole existing system of competition
and political exclusion.[3]   A striking comment upon the
Manchester peace advocacy was inspired by the incessant
iteration of a belief in the pacific influence that would flow
from the impressive display of British economic power in
the great Industrial Exhibition of 1851.   Peace, it declared,
is much to be desired, "but we doubt that competitive commercialism is really a peaceful creed." In fact, "the era of true
peace must be also an era of justice between man and man,
as well as between nation and nation, and when we gather
figs from bramble bushes we shall expect that from competitive commercialism."   The danger of war is from Russia,
yet "we have striven fruitlessly to comprehend how barri-
cades of calicoes, piled never so high, are to preach love and
brotherhood to the Cossack and the Calmuck, and we have
been forced to come to the unwelcome conclusion, that men
are crying 'Peace, peace!' where there is no peace."[4]

   The Flint Glass Makers, as well as the Engineers, were
alive to political questions and gave ready ear to economic
heresies.   They are reported as having held a 'soiree' in Birmingham in honor of George Dawson, a prominent middle-
class Radical of that town, because of his steady liberal
principles, especially his advocacy of the cause of Hungary.
The editor of the *Flint Glass Makers' Magazine* spoke on
"the people as the source of political power," and William
Newton, the engineer, on "Labour, the legitimate source of

[1] October 18, 1851.
[2] December 6, 1851.
[3] February 28, 1852.
[4] 1851, pp. 65 ff.

all wealth." Scholefield, M. P. for Birmingham, one of the
staunchest friends of democracy, was present and insisted
in his address that parliament must legislate upon social
questions.[1]

Evidence of the nature of that which has here been presented establishes the fact that trade-unionism was not yet
ready to enter into the place being prepared for it as the left
wing of the Liberal party. There was, nevertheless, considerable indication of tendencies that could be developed
in that direction, and these have been described in the pages
of Webb's *History of Trade Unionism*.[2] Those tendencies were toward the adoption of a more pacific trade policy
by the substitution of conciliation and arbitration wherever
possible for the strike and a tentative acceptance of competitive economics in some notable instances. The energy of
the unions was being more and more directed to the resistance of legal oppression, suffered through the interpretation of the law regarding masters and servants by middle-
class juries and magistrates. In the better paid trades,
say the Webbs, men were keenly desirous of learning the
facts about their industrial and social condition so as to
base their actions upon a broader understanding of forces.
Some trades were establishing libraries and classes for
instruction and putting out trade journals, one of the best
of which, the *Bookbinders' Trade Circular,* was promulgating "a theory of Trade-Unionism, from which Mc-
Culloch himself would scarcely have dissented."[3] A profound suspicion of the wisdom of strikes was being voiced
in many quarters. In fact, after 1845 "the leaders of the
better educated trades had accepted the economic axiom
that wages must inevitably depend upon the relation of Sup-

[1] Reported in the *Operative,* May 15, 1852.
[2] Pp. 182 ff.
[3] Webb, *op. cit.,* p. 197.

ply and Demand in each particular class of labour,"[1] and were consequently emphasizing the necessity of selfishly limiting the supply of labor by apprenticeship and emigration. This "new spirit, by 1850, was dominating the trade union world."[2]

This spirit was certainly the most significant influence at work so far as future developments were concerned, but to the middle-class observer of the years of 1848 to 1854 this spirit was harder to discern than the, to him, dangerous spirit of the manifestoes of the metropolitan trades, the denunciations of competitive economics rife in many quarters, and the talk still frequent of the "rights of labour" and the duties of the government to labor. It would seem, in fact, that the conversion of the Engineers to orthodoxy, for example, could hardly be said to have been an ascertainable fact to the world at large much before the issuance of an address by their executive council in 1855 to explain the objects and nature of their organization. This address expressed to employers the hope that they would cease to regard such bodies with disfavor, since they were not designed to injure employers' interests, but rather to promote them by elevating the character of workmen.[3]

It must be noted also that, whatever may have been their formal anouncement of a pacific policy, the unions during this period waged industrial wars of the first magnitude, carried on by strike and lockout. These contests stimulated class solidarity and in some cases induced to political activity on the part of labor that was impressive witness to its purpose, if not its power, to influence legislation in its own behalf. There were three of these great contests: the Wol-

---

[1] Webb, *op. cit.*, p. 201.
[2] *Ibid.*, p. 202.
[3] *Address of the Executive Council of the Amalgamated Society of Engineers to the Fellow Workmen throughout the United Kingdom and the British Colonies,* London, 1855.

verhampton Tinplate Workers' strike in 1850, the Engineers' strike and lockout in 1851, and the great strike of
the Preston cotton spinners in 1853.[1]

The case of the Tinplate Workers possesses more than
ordinary interest. It was the opening episode in the campaign carried on for a quarter of a century by organized
labor for the repeal of all restrictive or special legislation
against itself. A long legal battle developed out of the
prosecution of the strikers under the law of Masters and
Servants and the law of conspiracy as applied to offences
alleged under the Combination of Workmen Act of 1825.[2]
The trials dragged through a year, ending with convictions
and thus setting a new and adverse precedent for the interpretation of the law. The trade-union world was much
agitated. The *Operative* used the inequalities of the law
relating to Masters and Servants[3] as a text from which to
preach the need of political power. "If the people had a
suffrage—if workmen had the power of making law as well
as masters—these anomalies would soon be swept away—
one punishment applicable to all alike for one offense would
be the motto under which Parliament would legislate between employers and employed."[4] But the people have not
the vote. What then can they do? "Let the results of the
Tin-plate Workers' case be waited for and then let the Parliamentary recess be so occupied that the legislature shall not
be permitted to meet again without such a petition for a
Social Bill of Rights for the workmen as has never yet been
presented. Let some great and well-organized society, such
as the Amalgamated Engineers, take up the movement, and
invite all other trade unions to join them. Let every man

[1] There were also the strikes of the Kidderminster carpet weavers
(1853) and the "fierce and futile" strike of the Dowlais ironworkers in
the same year. (Webb, *op. cit.*, p. 224).
[2] Webb, *op. cit.*, p. 194, note 1, for this strike.
[3] For the operation of this law, see Webb, *op. cit.*, p. 240.
[4] July 19, 1851.

of the millions who has a master . . . be invited to range himself beneath the banners of his tribe, the tribe of the servitors, the most numerous on the earth." After the case was ended, the *Operative* wrote: "Much as we may dread the excitement, the turmoil, the strife of agitation, we must agitate in earnest . . . and it must be a combined, not a piecemeal agitation. It must ring through all the land wherever a toiler is to be found. If the struggle must come we must raise the war-cry of a whole class."[1] In the next issue the plan was elaborated. The working classes must unite for their own emancipation, but should agitate for one thing at a time. The first object should be the amendment of the Master and Servant law. This would arouse the solidarity which was a prime requisite for the larger movement. "As the war cry of a class, it is not to be surpassed." Our petition would be laid upon the table, but "a basis for a great organization would be attained, and, in short, a *beginning* would be made toward that emancipation of labour, which by some means must come sooner or later."[2] Plans were then outlined for an agitation similar to the agitations for Catholic Emancipation and repeal of the Corn Laws.

In the meantime, the National Association of Organized Trades was acting. The report[3] of their central committee upon their proceedings throughout the greater part of the years 1851-3 foreshadows in a remarkable way the proceeddings of the Junta for similar legislation fifteen years later. It was this body that appealed the case to a higher court,[4]

---

[1] October 11, 1851.

[2] The *Operative*, October 18, 1851.

[3] Report of the Central Committee of the United Trades on the Proceedings connected with the "Combination of Workmen Bill" in the Parliamentary Session, 1853. It was addressed to members of the Association and to the trades generally in the belief that it might be of use in the future in a similar movement. It is in the Goldsmiths' Library.

[4] Compare the account in the *Bookbinders' Trade Circular* for November, 1853, in which the statement is made that a committee of London trades collected the money for this appeal and conducted it,

and when the verdict of conviction was confirmed, they
decided to demand of parliament a declaratory act to remove
the possibility of such a construction being placed upon certain clauses of the Combination of Workmen Act as to
render prosecutions for conspiracy possible and also an
amendment of the law as to Masters and Servants. Henry
Drummond, T. S. Duncombe, president of the Association,
and Lord Goderich, a Christian Socialist and a democrat,
took charge of the measure.   The Committee instituted
"quiet but persevering" agitation among the metropolitan
and provincial trades by means of circulars and deputations.
Members of the Committee visited at least two hundred
organizations.   They also effected a "vigorous canvass" of
members of parliament.   A memorial was presented to
Derby's government, and, the report goes on to say, had it
remained in power there would have been no opposition.
They then took the matter up with Aberdeen's government,
but Palmerston, home secretary, was hostile to the bill on
the ground that the law was sufficiently liberal and would
become dangerous if enlarged.   The bill was beaten by a
vote of seventy to fifty-seven.   The Report analyzes the vote,
showing thirty-six Conservatives, thirteen Radicals, and
eight Whigs for the measure and eight Conservatives, fifteen Radicals, and forty-seven Whigs against it.   The bill
was brought up again, however, and the Committee succeeded in securing the aid of Cobden, Milner Gibson, Hume,
and several Radicals, with which assistance it passed the
House of Commons, only to be thrown out by the Lords.[1]

and that the Association did not contribute a farthing to it.   Mr. and
Mrs. Webb accept this as the true version of the matter.

[1] For the first debate on the bill in parliament see *Hansard*, 3d.
series, CXXV. 646-7, 1427-8.   For later stages of the bill, *ibid.*, CXXVI.
1117-24; CXXVII, 1017; CXXVIII. 247; CXXIX. 1322 ff.   In the
Lords, Lord Kinnaird sponsored the bill, but he finally withdrew it,
"seeing the temper of the House."

This report was discussed by the *Bookbinders' Trade Circular*,[1] which was the most middle-class in its point of view of all the trade journals. It considered that the failure of the Committee was not due to any lack of agitating ability. "We doubt whether it was ever excelled in any matter of equal magnitude." Rather it was the result of a lack of sufficient care in basing the arguments for the bill upon exact facts. The harsh criticism of the *Circular* against this body now and later[2] was due in large part, beyond doubt, to its decided antagonism to all political action. Not more legislation but greater intelligence on the part of workingmen to keep them out of the clutches of the law was the chief need, it believed.[3] The bill was opposed by such manufacturers' journals as the *Woollen, Worsted and Cotton Journal*[4] and the *Economist*.

This incident in trade-union history has been considered somewhat at length because it foreshadowed in a striking way the political tactics to be adopted by trade-unionists for the next twenty-five years; skillful parliamentary agitation for legislation, the marshalling of the trades in support, the perception on the part of some that political power in the possession of the people was a necessary prerequisite to success, and the cautious fear on the part of others of even this limited amount of agitation. Also, on the other hand, it reveals the fears of the employing class of any mea-

[1] November, 1852.

[2] February, 1857. It opposed allowing the Association to handle important affairs of workingmen, such as watching bills in parliament.

[3] January, 1854. As to the future of the National Association of United Trades, in addition to the information concerning it in Webbs' *History of Trade Unionism*, pp. 186-195, there is an item in *Reynolds's Newspaper* of November 3, 1861. G. A. Fleming, its president, and Winters and Humphreys, secretaries, with Charles Sturgeon, standing counsel, waited upon the new Lord Chancellor to congratulate him upon his appointment and to thank him for his constant readiness to assist them in industrial legislation. The Chancellor, in reply, spoke of frequent communications with the Association, which had impressed him with its intelligence and moderation.

[4] June, 1853. This also quotes from the *Economist* in like vein.

sure designed to strengthen combinations of workmen. The
deputation from the employers to Sir George Grey, the home
secretary, showed their willingness to bring pressure to bear
upon the government in order to secure coercive or legislative action against unions.[1] Furthermore, it must be
apparent that such vigorous activity as was here displayed
by the trades inevitably became a factor in the political adjustment of classes then in process of development.

Another effective piece of parliamentary agitation occurred two years later, which adds to the sum of proof that
workingmen were not politically inert. It was reported
to the Metropolitan Trades Committee in session in 1855
that a bill affecting the friendly societies had been introduced into parliament, which would endanger the status of
trade-unions. At once a sub-committee was appointed to
look after the matter. It waited upon members of parliament, watched the proceedings in Committee, had remedial
clauses inserted, and had a petition relating to the bill signed
on behalf of unions representing nearly forty thousand
members. Eighty-seven societies contributed to the fund to
carry on the agitation, and the Committee included William
Allan, chairman, and William Newton. The result was to
give trade societies what was considered to be legal recognition for the first time, by permitting them to register under
this act.

The Bookbinders had had one of their officers upon the
committee, and, at the happy conclusion of its labors, their
Circular pointed a moral for workingmen by declaring that
this case proved they had the power by moral suasion to
take part in legislation and that such methods would serve
to promote harmony between the upper and working classes.
It is not difficult to discern in this a jibe at agitators for
political reform.[2]

[1] *Bookbinders' Trade Circular,* April, 1853.
[2] Full account in *Bookbinders' Trade Circular,* December, 1855.
See also Webb, *op. cit.,* p. 243, note.

Simultaneously with the agitation with reference to the Master and Servant Act came the great Engineers' strike and lockout, a result of the formation of the Amalgamated Society.[1] The masters answered the strike of the men against piece work and overtime by a lockout covering Lancashire and London and the organization of a Central Association of Employers of Operative Engineers in December, 1851. A pamphlet issued by their Executive Committee justified the lockout as necessary "to arrest the encroachments of irresponsible dictation," for it was better that workmen suffer now "than linger under a permanent oppression."[2] Then, much underscored: "All we want is to be let alone. With less than that we shall not be satisfied. Until we accomplish that we shall not reopen our establishments." Arbitrators have offered their services, but "we alone are the competent judges of our own businesses." Collective bargaining was repudiated thus: "Artisans and their employers are respectively individuals—each legally capable of consent—each severally entitled to contract." The new Amalgamated Society foreboded "a war of classes" and was promulgating "new and dangerous principles of social and political economy."

The conflict developed into a war on trade-unionism itself through the masters' demand that the men sign a repudiation of the union before being taken back into employment. Meetings were held all over Lancashire and Yorkshire to resist; even non-society men joined in.[3] In Manchester, in the Free Trade Hall, the greatest indoor meeting ever held by the working classes up to that time took place in February, 1852. William Newton was the chief speaker, and, according to the *Manchester Guardian*, the

[1] Webb, *op. cit.*, pp. 214 ff.
[2] "Representation of the Case of the Executive Committee of the Central Association of Employers of Operative Engineers," London, 1852. Signed by Sidney Smith, Secretary.
[3] The *Operative*, February 14, 1852.

whole meeting rose *en masse* when he finished his address.[1] Newton was the foremost labor leader at that
time in looking to bigger things than merely an isolated
victory here and there. He had the vision of a great labor
party composed of the whole of the working classes of the
country, disciplined and morally strong. But in his view,
this labor organization, instead of avoiding political action,
should seek it and use it. Here he was close to labor leaders
of the next generation. In this speech at Manchester he
appealed to the moral dignity of the men and strove to impress them with the thought that they were fighting the
battle of oppressed artisans everywhere and were helping to
settle the great question of capital and labor. Later, in the
Operative, he exulted in the contest as a means of developing the power of the working classes.

Great solidarity was developed among the working
classes in this struggle. Other trades contributed funds to
the amount of five thousand pounds.[2] The case won much
publicity. Christian Socialists wrote and worked for the
men. They sponsored great meetings to launch coöperative
enterprises on a national scale as a means to defeat capital.
Newton hoped to see these efforts result in a mighty
power "capable of changing the face of the social world."[3]
He at that moment was announcing himself as a candidate
in the interest of labor for the metropolitan constituency
of Tower Hamlets. There can be no doubt that his candidacy was a phase of the profound agitation of organized
labor that accompanied the great industrial conflict.

The strike ended after fifteen months in a defeat for the
men. An indication of the apprehension it aroused, even
among the most friendly of the middle classes, is afforded by

[1] Quoted in the *Operative,* February 28, 1852, which gives a full
account of the meeting.

[2] Webb, *op. cit.,* p. 215; also the *Operative,* March 6, 1852.

[3] *Operative,* March 27, 1852.

a pamphlet by Samuel Fielden, then working to prevent the repeal of the Ten Hours Act. "A mere glance at what must follow upon such a state of things is enough to strike one with terror. . . . From this source every system and theory inimical to the peace and order of society will derive the most effective support."[1]

Scarcely had this industrial war been concluded, when another equally disturbing began to stir the social waters to their depths. This was the lock-out of the Preston cotton-spinners, which lasted seven months and involved thirty thousand operatives in Preston and came to involve as many more in other towns of Lancashire.[2] The manufacturers of Lancashire entered into an agreement to maintain the contest until victory should be complete—a "great cotton-lord conspiracy."[3] The question at stake was not one of wages, the ostensible one, but of mastery. This fact is clear from the report of the committee of the Master Spinners and Manufacturers' Association appointed to handle their defence fund: "To say that Capital is—must—ought to—and shall be the master of Labour, is but to say that civilization shall rule barbarism—foresight, industry—and that frugality shall reign over extravagance, and idleness and waste. . . . It is a law of Providence that the leaders of mankind shall consist of those who are best fitted to the task." As to trade-unions, they had reached a point which demanded "peremptory and effectual" resistance.[4] Such sentiments as these were echoed, more mildly, in other manu-

---

[1] The Turn-out by the Master Mechanics. A letter by Samuel Fielden, Esq. Addressed to the Editor of the *Times*, Bolton, 1852.

[2] A good account from the workers' point of view is in the *Beacon, A Journal of Politics and Literature*, October and November, 1853, and January, 1854.

[3] The *Beacon*, November 16, 1853, and *Britannia*, January 7, 1854.

[4] *Report of the Committee Appointed for the Receipt and Apportionment of the Master Spinners' and Manufacturers' Defence Fund*. Manchester, 1854.

facturing quarters.[1] The masters resorted to the usual device of using the local magistracy to fight their battle, while
influencing the Poor Law Guardians to refuse relief to the
starving men. The *Economist* applauded the latter for thus
refusing to fight the workingmen's battle with the public
money.[2]

Feeling ran high among the men. At monster meetings
labor hymns were sung; the walls were placarded with bills
proclaiming "Labour is the Source of All Wealth," and
with poems beginning, "The Masters will have war! ah, war
to the knife! Well then. . . ."[3] A feeling of solidarity
was stimulated all over the country. Funds poured in to aid
the operatives. The Metropolitan Trades Delegates gave
their active assistance.[4] That all sorts of vague revolutionary ideas and projects were connected with this great
class war is shown by the movement for a Labor Parliament that developed in connection with it. This was, as
West described it, one of the innumerable anticipations of
a general federation of trade-unions.[5] Indeed, it was
similar to the one that had been projected in the course of
the Engineers' strike of a year before. The promoters of
this one, however, were apparently Chartists, especially
Ernest Jones, the uncompromising advocate of social revolution and class war. The Labor Parliament of forty
delegates chosen at public meetings in London, Birmingham,
Manchester, Nottingham, etc., met in March, 1854. Karl
Marx and Louis Blanc were invited, but declined.[6] It was

[1] See an article on "The Folly of Strikes" in the *Woollen, Worsted
and Cotton Journal, a Monthly Magazine of Industry*, November, 1853.

[2] George Howell, *Labour Legislation, Labour Movements and Labour
Leaders*, N. Y., 1902, p. 108; also the *Beacon*, November 30, 1853.

[3] Levi, *Annals of British Legislation*, II. Series A, p. 16 n. Evidence
before the Committee on Councils of Conciliation. London, 1857. Also
English Republic for 1854, p. 224.

[4] *Bookbinders' Trade Circular*, December, 1855.

[5] West, *History of Chartism*, p. 271.

[6] *Ibid.*, p. 271.

decided to organize a "Mass Movement" for the purpose of instituting a gigantic coöperative scheme in manufactures and land as a means to oppose capitalism and prevent unemployment and also for the purpose of demanding a long program of labor legislation.[1] The plans included the collection of five million pounds a year by a levy on wages, to be used to purchase land, to support men on strike, and to promote coöperative efforts. An executive council was appointed. The Preston strike, however, ended within a month after the launching of the project, and it collapsed, just as the similar one that grew out of the Engineers' strike had done.

Such impractical and necessarily abortive schemes possess a considerable amount of significance for the student of working-class thought in this transitional period, who is seeking to determine the intellectual and psychological background of the political developments of the time. Lack of unanimity in analysis of the elements of their problems, the consciousness of their social nature and the need of social remedies, a realization of the necessity of class action verging upon a peaceably conducted class war with revolutionary social aims—these characteristics undoubtedly still clung to the thinking of workingmen. Nor had even the trade-unions yet wholly emancipated themselves from such vague and visionary conceptions. The very months in which the Preston strike was evoking an unmistakable expression of such views were the months in which the question of parliamentary reform was being considered by the Aberdeen cabinet. Among the arguments used freely against all reform at that time were this strike and the opinions it elicited. John Bright's efforts to promote an agitation for the bill

[1] For an account of this project, see Gammage, *History of the Chartist Movement*, pp. 394, 5; also West, *op. cit.*, p. 271; the *English Republic* for 1854, p. 199; the *Britannia*, November 26, 1853; and the *Provident Times*, March 8, 1854, which contains the full program of the Parliament.

were rendered almost hopeless by the aversion of the middle classes to the idea of enfranchising workingmen capable of enunciating such dangerous theories and by the suspicion of middle-class political sincerity aroused in the minds of the working classes by the relentless industrial conflicts. A consciousness upon both sides of industrial antagonism appeared to give the aspect of a hollow pretense to any attempted political alliance. And so, early in 1854, the meager reform bill of the government, which had confessedly aroused no enthusiasm anywhere, was submerged in the rising tide of war sentiment, and the question of enfranchising the working classes was dropped from the program of political possibilities for several years to come.

If the working classes suspected the motives of the middle classes, however, and disdained this bill which the government brought forth, nevertheless the Preston strike was interpreted by many of them as additional proof that the working classes must gain political power. The *Beacon,* for example, gave expression to this argument.[1] In one number it declared there was no hope for labor until it should become politically as well as industrially independent of employers. The House of Commons must be made to represent labor as well as capital.[2] Linton's *English Republic* said: The Preston strike is a war, and a war forever. Victory would mean only a breathing spell. "Political power alone can help the people."[3] So also thought a Chartist and Secularist journal published in democratic Newcastle-upon-Tyne;[4] so also the radical *Sunday Times,* and the *Weekly Times. Reynolds's Newspaper,* the extremist weekly that was rapidly becoming the most widely read paper among the

[1] November 9, 1853. It argued also that the vote was a "right appertaining to every citizen in virtue of his manhood."

[2] October 26, 1853.

[3] For 1854, p. 158.

[4] The *Northern Tribune,* 1854, p. 115.

working classes, denounced the government as the instrument of capitalists, from which danger the people could save themselves only by the acquisition of political power.[1] To all of these arguments, the middle classes retorted with an interminable use of the strike as a text from which to exhort workingmen to learn political economy.[2] The *Times* argued from it the vast danger in enfranchising such a totally ignorant class,[3] and the *Economist* declared that such proceedings had retarded the cause of reform for half a century.[4]

If an understanding is to be gained of all the factors entering into this first phase of that particular political development which has been herein defined as an attempted *entente* between the two great industrial groups in English society, still another question, in addition to expressions of economic and social theories and industrial conflicts in the nature of strikes and lockouts, must be given consideration. This is the question of factory legislation. It was a question of prime concern to workingmen and entered largely into their estimates of political friendships and enmities.

The epoch-making act of 1847, establishing a ten-hour day for women and young persons in textile factories, had been received as an inestimable boon by the operatives. The progress of the measures had been jealously watched, and

[1] All of these quoted in the *Beacon*, November 9, 1853.

[2] A good example is a pamphlet entitled: *The Strike, A Letter to the Working Classes on their present Position and Movement*, by a Lancashire Manufacturer (J. A. Nicholls, F. R. A. S.), London, 1853; also another by the same author in the same vein written in 1856. The author, a mill owner, preached the power, sacredness, and beneficence of unfettered capital to workingmen, telling them they should bless it as the source of life. Strikes and trade unions were anathema. (In vol. of pamphlets on Capital and Labor in Manchester Free Reference Library). Another pamphlet dealing with the question is by J. Frearson, *The relative rights and interests of the employer and the employed discussed; and a system proposed by which the conflicting interests of all classes of society may be reconciled*. London, 1855.

[3] Quoted in the *Beacon*, November 9, 1853.

[4] *Ibid.*, November 23, 1853.

it was seen that Peel's Tory government had allied with the hostile manufacturers in opposition, and that Russell, Palmerston, and Sir George Grey, Whigs, had supported the bill.[1] It was finally passed by Russell's government. Bright and the Manchester School had opposed it, on the ground explained by Bright later when he said, "I was opposed to all legislation restricting adults, men or women.... I could not, therefore, support Bills which directly interfered with and restricted the working hours of women, and which thus were intended to limit the working hours of men."[2]

The manufacturers succeeded to a large extent in nullifying the law by inventing the relay system. Agitation began at once to amend the law to render this impossible. The operatives became convinced that the employers were determined to alter the law so as practically to abolish altogether the newly-won ten-hour day. Excitement in the factory districts became intense, and the operatives renewed their former organization under the title, the Association for the Protection of the Ten Hour Act.[3] By April, 1850, so intense had feeling become that a Chartist paper in Manchester declared that English society was held together only by the last links and that the fate of the Ten Hour Act would determine whether they were to hold.[4] Charges of treason were widely and seriously made against Lord Ashley and others who had formerly supported the measure.[5]

[1] Hodder, *Life and Works of the Seventh Earl of Shaftesbury*, London, 1888, II. 30, 81, 82, 137.

[2] H. J. Leach, *The Public Letters of the Right Honourable John Bright*, London, 1895, p. 253.

[3] For the activities of the renewed organization see the *Champion of What is True and Right and for the Good of All*, December 15, 29, 1849.

[4] The *Champion of What is True and Right and for the Good of All*, ed. J. R. Stephens, April 20, 1850.

[5] See the *Champion*, January 19, April 13, and March 16, 1850. John Fielden, the organizer of the former agitation in the factory districts, had just died, and many workers believed this to be the signal

In the House the debate upon Ashley's proposed declaratory act showed Bright, Milner Gibson, and the Peelite, Sir James Graham, in determined opposition not only to the new measure but to the original one as well, evidently hoping to render it ineffective.   On the other hand, Lord John Manners and Disraeli were leading the Young England group in warm support.[1] The Government soon came forward with their own bill to be substituted for the measure of 1847, increasing the number of hours per week by two, but making relays impossible.[2] Hume, at that very moment the most active middle-class leader in the Association which had for its object the political amalgamation of working and middle classes,[3] straightway denounced the government as "irresolute and weak" in thus assenting to a bill interfering between masters and men.[4] When the government compromise was passed, Bright acted as teller for the opposition and was supported by such political Radicals as Lawrence Heyworth, Trelawney, and C. Villiers.[5]

When a last effort was made to amend the measure still further in harmony with the views of the operatives, by extending it to children, Bright charged that the aim was to force the stoppage of all machinery and thus of adult male labor at six P.M.   Trelawney lamented the harmful doctrines advocated by the supporters of such a measure, yet did not believe that the more sensible workingmen accepted them, but rather felt "confidence in those who were ready to extend to them the suffrage, and who had taught them a

for the desertion of others. Samuel Fielden, son of John, took the lead in the new agitation. Ashley took the accusations against him very seriously.

[1] *Hansard*, 3rd series, CIX. 883 ff. Bright's speech is given on pp. 918 ff.; Manners' on p. 923, and Graham's on pp. 927 ff.

[2] *Hansard*, CX. 1132 ff.

[3] See below, ch. iv.

[4] *Hansard*, CX. 1134-5.

[5] *Ibid.*, CXI. 845. The vote was forty-five to two hundred forty-six. Cobden did not vote.

totally different doctrine."[1]   Then he asked the question:
if workingmen are in favor of this measure, as you say they
are, will you extend to them the suffrage?   His argument
furnishes an excellent comment upon the interrelation of
economics and politics.   The vote upon this amendment
showed the ayes to be almost all Conservatives, with the exception of such trusted friends of the working classes as
Sharman Crawford, W . J. Fox, the Unitarian minister,
Lord Robert Grosvenor, Muntz of Birmingham, Lord Dudley Stuart, Col. T. P. Thompson, and Sir Joshua
Walmsley.[2]

Other amendments of like tenor came on.   In the discussion of one of them Disraeli declared the bill ought to
fix the hours of all labor,[3] while Hume asserted that the
government should scrap all legislation whatever of the nature of this act because such interference was driving capital from the country.[4]   Shaftesbury wrote later in his diary
that in this and similar measures he was constantly supported by a few sincere Whigs and Conservatives and by
the Tories who were angry with Peel.   He was constantly
opposed by Gladstone and Lord Brougham, by Bright,
"ever my most malignant opponent," and by Cobden, who
was "bitterly hostile."[5]

The question of factory legislation thus brings out more
clearly than any other, except perhaps that of trade-unionism, the deep-seated antagonism of the time and reveals the
almost insuperable difficulties in the way of sincere co-

---

[1] *Hansard*, CXI. 849, for Bright's statement, and pp. 853-4, for
Trelawney's.
[2] *Ibid.*, CXI. 855.   For further debates on amendments see *ibid.*,
pp. 1234-1371, CXII, 125 ff. and 1348 ff.   In 1853 Palmerston as home
secretary completed the act by extending it to children, thus confining
all labor in the mills between the hours of six and six.   See Hodder,
op. cit., II. 208, and *Hansard*, CXXVIII. 1251 ff.
[3] *Hansard*, CXI. 1282 ff.
[4] *Ibid.*, CXII. 129.
[5] Hodder, *op. cit.*, II. 209-10.

operation between the working classes and any other. The element in the Liberal party ready to listen to their demands for political recognition were their unflinching industrial opponents, and industrial conflict inevitably diminished their democratic zeal; while those Whigs and Conservatives who could see the justice of governmental interference on the side of the weaker in the industrial world had little sympathy for democracy. Economic interests and political principles cut athwart each other in a manner most disastrous to any strong political cohesion.

That principle was not always the determinant of attitude toward factory and similar legislation, but that interests alone often were, is manifested in connection with the Mines Bill to provide for compulsory inspection and an alteration in the method of payment of wages introduced at the instance of the colliers by T. S. Duncombe, president of the National Association of United Trades for the Protection of Industry.[1] Practically all the members from the mining sections of the country opposed the measure. But Hume, who had lead in opposing the Ten Hour Act, seconded Duncombe's motion. The question arises whether the fact that the Ten Hour Act was an interference with manufacturers and the Mines Bill with landed proprietors chiefly influenced his attitude toward the two measures. Bright consistently opposed both. During the next year, when the question was before the Lords, the landed proprietors, so ready to vote with labor against Manchester, very generally saw danger in a measure which aimed to interfere with the operation of the mines. The Earl of Lonsdale considered it would be a great annoyance to coal owners. The Earl of Malmesbury, while lamenting the loss of life in mines, yet considered it "necessary to have some regard to the interests of the proprietors."[2] A Mines Bill did,

[1] *Hansard,* CVI. 1335 ff.
[2] *Ibid.,* CX. 1162.

however, pass the Lords. When it came up in the House
of Commons Hume supported it. But now Disraeli, who
at that very moment was marshalling Young England behind the Ten-Hour Act on the ground of principle, protested against "this interposition between capital and
labour," explaining that coal owners had represented to
him that such interference with their property would be
seriously injurious.

Another measure in the interest of the working classes
in 1853 occasioned a debate that took a decidedly political
turn; namely, a bill to enforce the law against truck, which
was designed to protect the poor stockingers of Leicester and
Nottingham from being defrauded of the greater part of
their earnings through deductions for frame-rent.[1] Most
of the borough members from the sections involved, representing the employing interests, opposed the measure; the
county members favored it. Hume denounced the advocates
of the bill as the greatest enemies of the working classes,
because they were attempting to do for them by legislation
that which legislation could not do and were using harsh
language about employers, thus causing workingmen to consider themselves tyrannically used. The debate was then
brought into direct touch with the political negotiations going on outside of parliament through the medium of the Association that was attempting to combine the middle and
working classes for political agitation, in an argument which
Sir Joshua Walmsley, member for Leicester, addressed to
Hume. Walmsley, a Chartist in sympathy, was president of
this new Association, and Hume was an active leader in it.
Walmsley now took occasion to contrast the good inten-
tions of Hume toward the working classes politically with
his opposition to their interests in the matter of frame-
rents. G. F. Muntz, one of the most constant democrats and

---

[1] For the debate see *Hansard*, CXXVI. 1079-1117.

a friend of the Chartists, could see no possible good in the proposed measure; while Heyworth, of Derby, another extremist in matters purely political, summed up the Manchester position by declaring that the only possible way to help the wretched frame-work knitters was for parliament to "go on in the glorious course in which they have made such progress; they must make trade free, and remit indirect taxation."[1] It is easy to imagine the sympathetic response to such sentiments among starving weavers, from whom employers were collecting several hundred per cent. profit upon their frames in the form of rent deducted from the already miserable wages. Lord John Manners took the opportunity in the course of this debate to assert anew the Tory-democratic sympathy of country gentlemen with the poor in the industrial centers.[2] The bill was lost on division by a vote of one hundred and twenty-five to one hundred and eighty-six.

If economic ignorance fostered such attempts at legislation as those above described, socialism itself was the parent of the schemes projected by Lord Robert Grosvenor for the protection of the oppressed London bakers. In 1849 and again in 1850 he brought up the question in the House of Commons.[3] Upon the latter occasion Bright, after having read from the pages of the *Bakers' Gazette and General Trades' Advocate* an article on "Wages and Labour," declared that nothing in the schemes of Owen or the Socialists of France was more communistic than the sentiments of that article.[4] Cobden in a previous debate had warned the House that the bill contained an entirely new

[1] *Hansard* CXXVI. 1116.

[2] See discussion in *Woollen, Worsted and Cotton Journal*, June, 1853, from manufacturers' standpoint. It quoted from one speaker as to the identity of the political economy of the Tory country gentlemen and the rabble of the great towns.

[3] *Hansard*, CVII. 481 ff.; CX. 1245 ff.

[4] *Hansard*, CX. 1248.

and dangerous principle, which other trades would not fail to clamor for if enacted into law in this case; let them take warning by the example of France and the failure of the schemes of Louis Blanc.[1] At a working-class meeting in Brighton, in support of the cause of the bakers, the speakers devoted much effort to a denunciation of Manchesterian and Malthusian doctrines, and one speaker cited Cobden's opposition to this measure as a proof that his pretended friendship for the working class was "thin air."[2]

It was in the midst of circumstances such at these, breeding as they did social antagonism of the sharpest nature, that, in the political world, certain leaders of both industrial classes were endeavoring to effect a working *entente*. To these endeavors it will soon be well to turn for a closer examination. There were, however, still other factors in the social and political complexity characterizing this period of transition which must be at least cursorily examined because of their contribution to the confusion of thought and purpose which hampered the attempted political alliance from the first.

First, there were the still vital fragments of the Chartist movement, which for several years played a larger part in the working-class world and hence in the middle-class attitude toward it than is sometimes understood. Chartism had not been extinguished by 1850; it had merely broken into numerous sects.[3] This disintegration of the movement destroyed its immediate menace in the eyes of the upper classes, but the continued adherence of large numbers

[1] *Ibid.,* CVII. 488 ff.

[2] From an account in the *Champion of What is True and Right and for the Good of All,* May 5, 1850. For the division on the bill, see *Hansard,* CX. 1249. The vote was forty-four to ninety-four. On the connection of the protectionist party with this matter see note 2, p. 41 above.

[3] The best account of these bodies is in West, *A History of the Chartist Movement,* chap. v. See also Slosson, *The Decline of the Chartist Movement* and Hovell, *The Chartist Movement.*

of workingmen to the various Chartist interpretations contributed to the perpetuation of a schism between classes.
It is not necessary here to enter into any extended discussion
of these sects and their programs. But it is necessary to
scrutinize them somewhat in the light of their bearing upon
the general political situation.

The central organization continued to be the National
Charter Association.[1] It had so dwindled by 1851 that
W. J. Linton could write of it in his journal that all that
remained was "a handful of men clinging to a forlorn hope
. . . some few believers in the impossible, waiting for
Opportunity to come back."[2] Its shrinkage was the result,
in a measure, of the beginning of a decline in the Chartist
faith, but it was due in a larger degree to the drawing off of
Chartists into other competing bodies, themselves partaking
of some of the nature of Chartism. Several new and vigorous minds were recruited to the cause in this later period.
The programs enunciated were many and various, some
crude and some remarkably penetrating, but the sum total
of them reveals much intellectual vitality. They could not,
however, achieve for long the numerical support which
would lift them out of the position of vain theorizing. The
reasons for this are obvious from the explanations given in
earlier pages of this discussion. Distress was mitigated,
and factory legislation was to a certain extent disintegrating
the lack of confidence in upper-class government. Belief in
coöperation, whether Christian Socialist or other, "went
through the ranks of Chartism and decimated them."[3]
And finally the middle-class overtures for an alliance on

[1] First formed in 1840.

[2] The *English Republic*. An article on the History of Chartism,
pp. 78 ff.

[3] *Freethinkers' Magazine*, December 1, 1850. An article on the
Reasons for Disunion in the Ranks of Democracy.

middle-class grounds possessed an ever stronger appeal for certain groups of workingmen.

This last was, in fact, the wedge that split the National Charter Association in 1850 and brought into leadership a rival to O'Connor in the person of Ernest Jones. At the end of a prison term, imposed for alleged seditious utterances in the Chartist agitation in 1848, Jones placed himself at the ·head of the opposition to the middle-class movement with which O'Connor had by that time become identified.[1] Jones proclaimed in unmodified form the gospel of class war for the achievement of class social benefits and carried the National Charter Association over to a sweeping social program.[2] He denounced attempts to combine with the middle classes as an effort to hand over the Chartists to the Manchester School.

Between 1848 and 1850 several Chartist groups were organized for the avowed purpose, among others, of seeking the aid of the middle classes. The People's League, formed by William Lovett in May, 1848, sought to base this union upon a program of political democracy and social reform. The most unusual of its demands was for the repeal of all indirect taxes and the imposition of a graduated property tax, an item which here, according to J. H. Rose,[3] found its first embodiment in a democratic program. Edward Miall and a few other middle-class leaders gave their adhesion to the project, but Cobden and Hume frankly said that O'Connor had made the very name of Chartist

[1] See below, p. 87.
[2] For this see West, *The Chartist Movement,* pp. 263-5. Upon this program West comments: "Those men, in those unpromising conditions, agreed upon a programme which future generations of reformers spent much time, not in reshaping, but in laboriously rediscovering." See also Gammage, *op. cit.,* pp. 357, 360.
[3] In *The Rise of Democracy,* p. 142. See above, p. 39, for its incorporation in the Trades Delegates' program. For Lovett's account of this organization, see his *Life and Struggles,* pp. 335-341. See also Dolléans, *op. cit.,* II. 392.

distasteful to them.   Hume took the proposal to the Free
Trade Club and got about fifty to agree to financial reform
and household suffrage.[1]   Place remarked to Lovett about
this time, "It will be some time to come before the words
Chartism and Universal Suffrage will meet with favor in
the direction you seem to be looking."[2]   In fact, the middle-
class household suffrage movement was even then beginning
to get under way with the purpose of attracting the Chartists
over to its program as one upon which the two classes might
possibly coöperate.   Hume had begun to advocate in the
House of Commons his "Little Charter" based on household
suffrage.   The League expired after a few months.   The
significance of it, however, is not small.[3]   It revealed the
difficulties that obstructed even the most reasonable and
conciliatory advances of Chartists to the middle classes.
The pivotal point appeared to be the issue of manhood *versus*
a restricted suffrage; in reality it was the issue of working-
class *versus* middle-class control of the government, and
behind this stood questions of a social and economic nature.

Another similar, but in some respects a more fortunate,
organization was the People's Charter Union, formed by
several hundred moderates, including five or six men who
years before had been the organizers of a fight against the
tax on newspapers.   Later they had organized the first
Chartist body.   Among them were Lovett, Hetherington,
James Watson, George Jacob Holyoake, and C. D. Collett.
The aim of this Union was to appeal for middle-class support
for the six points of the Charter and for a free press.[4]
Soon it began to concentrate upon the latter issue.   It opened
negotiations with Cobden, and, at his advice, a council

[1] Lovett, *op. cit.*, p. 335 ; West, *op. cit.*, p. 258.

[2] Lovett, *op. cit.*, p. 335.

[3] The *People* (ed. J. Barker, Wortley) No. 10, 1848, contains an
account of the League.

[4] *Ibid.*, Nos. 30 and 37.   Also, West, *op. cit.*, pp. 258-60.

of ten separated from the main body and started to work independently. It soon gained an influential middle-class support under the title of the Newspaper Tax Abolition Committee. In February, 1851, Cobden, who had been supporting the Committee, formed a new association of his party, but took in as members all of the former Committee. This new body was the "Association for the Repeal of the Taxes on Knowledge," with Milner Gibson as president, Place as treasurer, Richard Moore, the Chartist, as chairman, and Collet as secretary. The executive committee included Cobden, George Dawson of Birmingham, Passmore Edwards, Thornton Hunt, and the Reverend Thomas Spencer. The first legislative victory of the association was the repeal of the advertisement duty in 1853; others were the repeal of the newspaper tax in 1855; of the paper duty in 1861; and of the securities system in 1869.[1] Thus the Chartist group initiated the movement that became the effective agent in abolishing all restrictions upon the press. The movement, therefore, fulfilled an object that had been dear to the hearts of workingmen from the beginning of the century and was a step in realizing their constant policy of bringing education to the working classes. But it must be noted that this Chartist organization succeeded only when it ceased to be Chartist. Radical sympathy was dead to all except its purely Radical demands.

One of the most remarkable programs put forward during this period was that of the National Reform League, formed late in 1849 by Bronterre O'Brien, G. W. M. Reynolds,[2] Lloyd Jones, the Chartist and Christian Social-

---

[1] C. D. Collet, *A History of the Taxes on Knowledge,* London, 1899. I. 136-7.

[2] He had recently become a Chartist. In 1850 he began to publish *Reynolds's Newspaper,* which soon became one of the most widely read by the working classes of all London papers. It was an able but extreme and violent weekly. It still exists.

ist, and others, upon the principles of O'Brien. It sought
political reform, but also sweeping social reforms. O'Brien
lectured constantly in behalf of its principles, "which," says
Gammage, "were speedily embraced by the élite of the
London democracy."[1]   Some students of Chartism seem
to think that this League died almost immediately and that
O'Brien then, in 1850, went into a "National Regeneration
Union."[2]   The fact appears to be that the two organizations were identical, the full title being the "National Reform
League for the Peaceful Regeneration of Society." In
November, 1849, a Chartist paper stated that the followers
of O'Brien were organizing a National Reform League.[3]
Then on March 16, 1850, at a crowded meeting held in
London, certain resolutions were adopted upon O'Brien's
motion which were then printed and distributed under the
title of "Propositions of the National Reform League for
the Peaceful Regeneration of Society, Liberty in Right;
Equality in Law; Fraternity in Industry."[4]   It hardly
seems possible that two such similar bodies in name and
personnel should have been formed, one in November, 1849,
and the other in March, 1850.   March 16 was doubtless the
date of the formal launching of the organization.

The propositions put forward by this association included
manhood suffrage; a reform of the Poor Law so as to
render the poor self-supporting, relief to be considered as a
right; government purchase of lands and the location thereon
of the unemployed; mitigation of the burden of taxation
which had been "vastly aggravated by the monetary and

[1] *History of the Chartist Movement,* ed. 1894, p. 351.

[2] See Slosson, *op. cit.,* p. 108.   Beer, *History of British Socialism,*
II. 174, lists the two as distinct.   West, *History of the Chartist Move-
ment,* p. 261, mentions only the National Reform League for the Peaceful
Regeneration of Society, formed in March, 1850.

[3] The *Democratic Review.*

[4] A copy of this pamphlet is in the Goldsmiths' Library.   The fore-
word gives the facts about its adoption.

free trade measures of Sir Robert Peel"; the adjustment of public and private debts in the interest of the debtor and producing classes, and the charging of the public debt to real property alone; the gradual resumption by the State of its "former proprietorship" over all lands, mines, fisheries, etc., which should be held in trust for the people and rented to them, the rents to take the place of all other taxes. "As it is the recognized duty of the State to support all of its subjects who . . . are unable to procure their own subsistence," there should be a system of national credit to enable men to rent and cultivate the lands. Currency should be based upon real, consumable wealth; public markets should be established for the exchange of products valued according to a corn or labor standard. The government should expropriate the owners of such public utilities as railways, canals, docks, and gas works.

O'Brien, the "schoolmaster of Chartism" and one of its thinkers claimed by modern Marxian Socialists,[1] was able to gather a flock of only about five hundred followers,[2] while the nature of his program itself rendered impossible the acceptance by the middle classes of his tendered alliance. But, contrary to the opinion of most students of this period, his League did not expire soon. It was in existence as late as in 1867. In 1866 it sought affiliation with the Reform League;[3] the year before it had become a branch of the International Working Men's Association, and in 1867 sent a delegate to its congress.[4] O'Brien lived on, no doubt in connection with it, until 1864.

[1] See an article by Bruce Glazier in the *Labour Leader*, January 13, 1919. West, *op. cit.*, p. 72, says of him: "All the theories and most of the shibboleths bound up with Marxian Socialism are to be found in his pronouncements." See also *ibid.*, p. 226.

[2] *Freethinkers' Magazine*, December 1, 1850.

[3] Minutes of the General Council of the Reform League.

[4] Minutes of the Council of the I. W. M. A., November 6, 1866. The association is mentioned as the "National Reform League, founded

And so, with trade-unions both political and non-political in policy, Christian Socialists, Chartists, land nationalizers, currency reformers, social revolutionaries, and advocates of a Radical alliance all preaching their several and sundry gospels to the workingman at this mid-point of the century, small wonder if he found himself bewildered by the multitude of counsels. In order to bring some sort of order out of this chaos of schemes and to redeem the democracy from impotence through schism, conferences were held late in 1850 for the purpose of uniting Chartists, Christian Socialists, the trades, and other bodies in one great "National Charter and Social Reform Union," with a double program as implied in the name.[1] Along with political democracy, reforms to be sought were a system of national education, free speech and press, equitable taxation, land nationalization, and laws to permit coöperative associations. Thus was the attempt made to proclaim frankly the social aims which had been implicit in political Chartism from the first.

But disagreement arose at the very outset, and the scheme was inevitably futile. Only the Christian Socialists, it was said, mustered strongly and evinced a sincere desire for union.[2]

The Chartist world by 1851 was, it is evident, being divided into two factions by the two related questions: should social reform be an avowed object along with political, and

1849," and in the minutes of the Reform League it is referred to by the same name, though the date is not given, and it is called a purely political body. In 1867 A. A. Walton, its president, attended the Congress of the International. (Minutes of the I. W. M. A., August 20, 1867).

[1] A good account is in the *Freethinkers' Magazine* for December 1, 1850 and January 1, 1851. Delaforce, secretary of the Metropolitan Trades Delegates, was a delegate to the Conferences. The committee in charge included Holyoake, Walter Cooper, Harney, Reynolds, Thornton Hunt, and Gerald Massie. O'Connor, Jones, and O'Brien were either hostile or indifferent.

[2] *Freethinkers' Magazine,* December 1, 1850.

secondly, should Chartists abandon a policy of political isolation and seek the aid of the middle classes? Some did not
see the impossibility of pursuing the two policies simultaneously. The manner in which these Chartist developments were related to the Radical movement for a political
alliance with workingmen will be explained later.

Before taking up specifically a consideration of the organization formed in 1848 to secure such an alliance, certain other currents of thought must be noted which, however futile in themselves, were yet appreciable elements in
the political atmosphere in which the new organization was
struggling to live. Ernest Jones in his *Notes to the People*
(1851-2) and his *People's Paper* (1852-8), to which Marx
was a contributor, was setting forth his socialistic analysis
and demanding control of both machinery and land by some
form of nation-wide association.[1] The influence of Jones
upon working-class thought from 1850 to the time of his
death in 1869 was much more profound than is generally
supposed. The chief question before the country, to his
thinking, was the land question. In fact, says Professor
Ernest Barker, it has always been land rather than capital
that English socialists have attacked.[2] About 1850
many Chartist papers and pamphlets were attacking private
property in land.[3] Some of them argued especially for a
policy that soon was advocated by the English working-class
as a whole, that it was the duty of the government to place
the waste lands at the disposal of the unemployed.

[1] *Notes to the People*, May, 1851. Also see F. Leary, *The Life
of Ernest Jones*, pp. 31 ff., for Jones's theories.

[2] *A History of English Political Thought from Herbert Spencer to
the Present Day*, p. 214.

[3] See *Democratic Review*, June, 1849; the *Leicestershire Movement*,
May 25, 1850; *English Republic*, 1851-55, p. 91; the *Truth Promoter*,
1851, No. 30. Some tracts are *Land Common Property*, by Terrigenous
(R. Isham), 3d. edit. London, 1852; *The Land of England belongs to
the People of England*, 1849.

Such attacks upon landed property were the cause of a further confusion of cross-currents in English politics. They furnished a common ground upon which the middle and working classes could stand, at least to the extent of denouncing the landed interests, however much they might differ as to a theoretical justification and the ultimate goal. On the other hand, aristocratic support of working-class extremists, which might be readily enough accorded as long as the object was an attack upon industrial employers or the Manchester School, would be alienated the instant the land system became the object of serious criticism. The land question persisted from that day on as a bond between workingmen and Radicals, the latter laboring persistently with the support of the former to establish "free trade in land" by the abolition of primogeniture and entail. This aspect of the question was pointed out by Shaftesbury in a letter to Russell written in 1851: "Socialistic doctrines and principles are far more rife in the great towns of this country than most people are aware of. They are found principally among the artisans and skilled workmen, and especially in the metropolis. These parties aim at a distribution of all the property of those above them, and calculate on measures to prevent, in the future, all accumulations of wealth in single hands. They do not, I think, look much to physical force; they rely chiefly on the extension of the suffrage. . . . The land is their first object . . . and many who are not disposed to go so far as the Socialist party urge them on to this extent, because they know that a revolution in the tenure, or descent, of landed property must speedily extinguish the House of Lords."[1]

This lengthy survey of working-class thought in its various manifestations in the period of intellectual ferment about 1850—a survey which is necessary in order to render

[1] Hodder, *Life of Shaftesbury*, II. 372-3.

intelligible the background of the contemporary political movement—reveals anything but an acceptance of the opinion reckoned as orthodox among the middle and upper classes. Furthermore, republicanism and internationalism were two other factors in working-class opinion that had to be reckoned with. The former principle exerted but slight influence; the latter was henceforth an important element in working-class politics, and thereby in English politics as a whole.[1] So internationally minded had English workingmen become by 1850 that they found themselves on this point also out of harmony with their would-be allies of Manchester. Cobden and Bright believed in pacifism and economic cosmopolitanism as a concomitant of industrial expansion and free trade. "The best diplomacy is that of commerce, and merchants are destined to become the pacificators of the world," wrote a free-trade journal.[2] Workingmen more nearly concurred in Harney's denunciation of "the 'balmy balderdash' of peace and non-intervention,"[3] or in Linton's declaration that "non-intervention between States is the same as *laissez-faire* between individuals: the liberty of the strongest—the right of ruffianism—Anarchy."[4] This divergence of view on foreign affairs continued to differentiate workingmen and Radicals until the working-class view, in the time of Gladstone, came to displace the Radical as determining the policy of the Liberal party. Not only did this sympathy for Continental liberation movements have a

[1] Slosson, *op. cit.*, p. 96; Beer, *op. cit.*, II. 167; Howell, *op. cit.*, p. 289; West. *op. cit.*, p. 242. Also see Holyoake, *Sixty Years of an Agitator's Life*, I. 90-92, for the influence of Mazzini and other refugees; Linton's *English Republic* (1851-5); Harney's *Democratic Review* (1849-50) and *Red Republican* (1850). The *Operative* occasionally wrote against royalty and in favor of a republic (February 15. March 1, December, 1851).

[2] The *Woollen, Worsted and Cotton Journal; or Monthly Magazine of Industry*, August, 1853.

[3] *Democratic Review*, August, 1849.

[4] The *English Republic*, 1851-5, p. 31.

bearing on the relations between English labor and the Manchester School on the one hand and between labor and Gladstone on the other; it also created a barrier between workingmen and the Conservatives. The Conservative party, in the main, upheld legitimacy on the Continent and would have no dealings with revolution. A final influence exerted by this attitude of the working classes with regard to foreign policy was that it brought them into touch with a group of independent, doctrinaire radicals of the middle class, whose friendship was to prove an element in effecting general class reconciliation.[1]

[1] Among these were George Dawson of Birmingham, Joseph Cowen of Newcastle, T. S. Duncombe, M.P. for Finsbury, P. A. Taylor, later M.P. for Leicester, Joseph Toynbee, Dr. Bowring, M.P. for Bolton, Douglas Jerrold, James Stansfeld, later M.P. and member of Gladstone's government, and Viscount Goderich. On this see R. J. Hinton, *English Radical Leaders*, p. 61, and Holyoake, *Sixty Years*, I. 266.

The nationalist movements in Poland, Hungary, and Italy made a powerful appeal to the sympathies of English working men. In 1846 was formed a Democratic Committee for the Regeneration of Poland; the next year was formed a People's International League, at the suggestion of Mazzini; in 1848 a Central European Democratic Committee was formed. Kossuth's visit to England in 1851 was the occasion of scores of excited meetings in the industrial centers (*English Republic*, p. 375, and *Britannia*, November 22, 1851; also the *Operative*, November 1, 1851). Polish meetings were numerous. See *English Republic* for 1853, p. 264, and *Northern Tribune*, March, 1855. These sentiments, so strongly held among workingmen, had some part in creating a demand for war with Russia in 1854.

CHAPTER III

THE PARLIAMENTARY AND FINANCIAL
REFORM ASSOCIATION

After this somewhat minute dissection of working-class opinion and activities during the first years of that period which was to be characterized by the gradual evolution of the Liberal-Labor alliance, it is now possible with greater understanding to take up for consideration the concrete organization formed in 1849 for the purpose of promoting such a connection. That organization was the Parliamentary and Financial Reform Association. Its promoters were the Radicals. What was sought was in reality a Radical-Labor alliance.

The Radicals at that time could in an undiscriminating classification be reckoned as Liberals in a party sense, but the distance between them and the still predominant Whig element in the party was so wide as almost to constitute them a separate party. Trevelyan, in his life of Bright, describes the period between the repeal of the Corn Laws and the death of Palmerston in 1865 as one of parliamentary confusion, of weak governments, of rapid combinations and dissolution of political partnerships, the most uncertain elements being the Radicals, the Irish, and the Peelites.[1] This confusion was not merely parliamentary and official. It was the result of currents running ever deeper and fuller in English social life, currents whose source and constant augmentation were from the profound industrial and social forces relentlessly at work reshaping external forms to a completer harmony with fundamental realities. The two groups most consciously a part of and affected by these deep-

[1] G. M. Trevelyan, *The Life of John Bright*, London, 1913, p. 178.

moving forces were the employers and the workers in industry. Their response, therefore, to the impelling need of readjustment was more immediate than that of Whigs or Tories, whose ideas and interests were, in the main, more closely related to the system that was passing. On both sides of the House were representatives of old governing families connected with the land or conservative business. The difference between them was more one of degree than of kind. Their domination of English politics had not been immediately shaken by the reform of 1832. So far the governments had all been aristocratic, and, from the point of view of the new aggressive social elements, it mattered little whether they were chosen from Whig or Tory families.

There was in reality, however, a significant distinction between the two parties. The Whigs were only a part of a larger group, the Liberals; and the Liberal party included within its compass the industrial middle class, followers of Bentham and James Mill—the Manchester School. It also included another active political element, Dissent. Liberalism, therefore, was not an integer. Its Whig element drew it close to enlightened Conservatism, but its other elements exercised a contrary attraction. Now Manchesterism, quickly responsive, as has been said, at least to certain aspects of the new economic and social conditions, was drawn to an alliance with the other industrial group, labor. It conceived of the future of England as dominated by industrialism.[1] Consequently the policy of middle-class industrialists consisted of two elements; namely, first, the industrial reconciliation of capital and labor by teaching labor the in-

[1] Several articles in the *Woollen, Worsted and Cotton Journal* set forth clearly the political aspirations of the manufacturers. It declared franchise reform was to be desired only as it would promote the legislative demands of business (April, 1853). It declared against any form of suffrage that would give political control to labor, frankly stating that the issue was the middle class *versus* the aristocracy. (August, 1853).

evitable truth of competitive, *laissez faire* economics,[1] and, secondly, some sort of political amalgamation of the two, for the purpose of taking the political guidance of the country out of the hands of Whigs and Tories and themselves guiding it toward peace, complete civil and religious liberty, and industrial freedom.   Thus the center of social and political power would ultimately be transferred from the land to industry.

What would be the response of Liberalism to the demands of its Radical, industrial wing?   Could it be drawn over to an adoption of their program entire?   Such a change would involve an alteration in the British constitution, based as it was upon classes, themselves based upon a definite recognition of the two types of property, land and business, with the priority given to land through its control of the House of Lords.   Could it open its doors to labor, to democracy?   Herein lies explanation enough of the confusion within Liberal ranks until the question should be answered. The conservative elements in the ranks stood steadfastly by the old order as long as they could, but the steady action of social forces gradually undermined their position.   Liberalism could not live unless it widened its house to admit those whose knocking at the door became ever more imperious, because they knocked with the force that came from the resistless increase of their social weight.

Thus between 1850 and 1870 the Manchester School, powerfully assisted by Dissent, transformed the Liberal party and brought it over to an alliance with labor.   But the Manchester School itself died in the process of creating

[1] As an example of the effort to educate working men in economics cf. certain prize essays, written by workingmen, published by the Leicester Chamber of Commerce in 1849. The preface to the pamphlet stated that the object was to diffuse sound views on labor and wages among workingmen. Note in this connection the comment of von Schulze-Gaevernitz in *Social Peace*, p. 26, "The extraordinary influence of 'Political Economy' springs from the fact that it was merely the industrial, middle class view of life thrown into the form of a theory."

this new political alignment, and its death was as much the result of the operation of social and economic influences as was its victory over Whiggism. The political coöperation of capital and labor proved to be impossible to secure wholly upon capital's terms. Identification of industrial interests, the necessary accompaniment to political identification in the eyes of the Manchester group, could not be realized. The political aims of labor were, therefore, only in part the same as those of capital. The two interests could stand together for civil and religious liberty; their ways diverged appreciably upon the question of international relations, and parted completely upon the issue of the special economic demands of labor.

The most active single figure in initiating and guiding the critical stages of the *entente* was John Bright. In the first few years it was Cobden, and not Bright, who was looked to as the political director of the movement, but the cautious leadership of Cobden, fearful of an approach to democracy, soon gave place to the bolder leadership of Bright. The heir of Bright's labors, who saw the flaws in his policy, was Gladstone. He it was who extricated the vital, or purely liberal, elements from disintegrating Manchesterism and realized the economic incompatibility of the Radical-Labor alliance. He then set himself, however reluctantly, to win the support of labor by a partial recognition of its special interests; and, finally, with labor's approval, he repudiated for Liberalism the Manchester policy of non-intervention in foreign affairs.

In 1848 Cobden, Bright, and their colleagues set about their task of fusing capital and labor into one harmonious economic and political group. We have seen in the preceding chapter that the year 1848 saw tentative steps taken in several different directions to turn the attention of the working classes toward a policy of coöperation with the

middle classes.   Sturge renewed the suggestion of a combined manhood-suffrage movement; leading Chartists set
about forming associations based upon a policy of coöperation; and particularly did Hume in the House of Commons
begin his agitation for the "Little Charter," and Bright project another great national league for the purpose of promoting reform.[1]

The first discussion of Hume's motion drew from
O'Connor a promise of coöperation if the middle classes
should prove to be sincere and from Cobden an open repudiation of O'Connor and all his works.[2] Subsequent debates in
the course of this year and also in 1849 and 1850—for Hume
reintroduced his bill each year—elicited important statements
of opinion.   Cobden stated the objects reformers had in
view in moving for the proposed reform.   It would, he
thought, bring the House of Commons more into harmony
with the wishes and interests of the people, would insure
economy and a more equitable distribution of taxation, and
would, through the redistribution of seats, break the domination of the great proprietors and the small boroughs.   It
would bring to bear upon parliament the virtues and talents
of the middle and industrious classes "to whom the glory
of this country is owing."[3] Bright sounded the keynote of
his whole reform advocacy, to be reiterated persistently until
1867, when he declared that the reform of 1832 had not
placed the middle classes in power.   A further extension of
the franchise was needed to accomplish that end.   So intimate was the relation between the middle and the working
classes, he maintained, that the former could not, with common sense and justice, consent to the exclusion of the latter.[4]

[1] Trevelyan, op. cit., pp. 183-4.
[2] Hansard, IIC. 1307, 1308, 1311.
[3] Ibid., C. 182-94.
[4] Hansard, CV. 1198. The ground of Bright's statement as to the
under-representation of the industrial districts is shown by the fact

These debates revealed that the measure was feared by many as a menace to the constitution, since it sought to divorce the vote from property.[1] Lord John Russell and Sir George Grey, home secretary, opposed the measure as a step toward universal suffrage. A measure introduced in 1850 to assimilate the borough and county franchise was condemned by Disraeli on the same grounds. Members were inconsistent, he urged, who would vote for this measure and yet oppose universal suffrage.[2]

The belief that Cobden and the reformers were aiming at a fundamental alteration of British institutions through an attack on property came out in a debate in this same year upon a motion to assimilate personal and landed property in matters of transfer and inheritance—the beginning of the Manchester agitation for "free trade in land." Newdegate, a Conservative, saw in the proposal a step toward that "organic revolution" in the state, in society, in the tenure of property, "of which Cobden had recently given notice."[3] Three years later a bill was introduced to amend the law regarding inheritance taxes on land. Sir John Pakington declared,[4] "there was in this country a party, which had its representatives in the House of Commons, that was ready to adopt any plan which dealt a blow at the aristocratic institutions of the country, or a blow at the property by which those institutions were supported." The government, he maintained, was yielding to that party because it was not strong enough to resist. It meant a war of classes. It was

that of borough members only eighty-six came from the north, while two hundred forty-eight came from the south. Of county members, thirty-nine came from the north and one hundred twenty-three from the south. (From C. Seymour, *Electoral Reform in England and Wales*, p. 97).

[1] *Hansard,* CIX. 137 ff. This was in 1850.
[2] *Ibid.,* CXII. 1174-80, for this speech.
[3] Quoted in the *Atlas,* March 23, 1850.
[4] *Hansard,* CXXVIII. 65.

upon this occasion that Disraeli declared that a continuance of such attacks upon the landed interest would end "in changing a first-rate kingdom into a second-rate republic." Running through the whole debate was the Conservative fear of democracy, when allied with the manufacturing interests, which was permanently a factor in the Conservative attitude toward an advance on democratic lines. Only as Tory-democracy could democracy ever be accepted.

We must consider now the popular movements toward organization for reform. Bright urged his plan upon Cobden, Villiers, and other Radicals.[1] Finally, in January, 1849, at a large meeting in Manchester, Bright and Cobden explained their plans. Cobden insisted, for his part, upon the adoption by the projected organization of the policy of creating forty-shilling freeholds in urban sections of counties, a policy which had aided the anti-Corn Law agitation. Cobden said afterwards that at this meeting financial reform received more favor than parliamentary reform.[2] The fact is, Cobden was opposed to Bright's scheme from the start, saying that he was not so sanguine as he once was as to the effect of a wide extension of the franchise. To him financial reform was the all-important issue. The forty-shilling freehold policy, he believed, would liberalize the county constituencies sufficiently to destroy Conservative control there, and thus in parliament.[3]

Cobden had, in fact, insisted from the first that it would be impossible to induce the Manchester free traders to join a movement for democratic reform.[4] He saw already that tendency toward conservatism in the upper middle classes

[1] John Morley, *Life of Richard Cobden*, Boston, 1881, pp. 334, 348. Also Trevelyan, *Life of Bright*, pp. 183-4; Garnett, *Life of W. J. Fox*, p. 271.

[2] Morley, *Cobden*, p. 334.

[3] *Ibid.*, p. 335.

[4] *Ibid.*, p. 348.

of Lancashire which became so marked a feature of the politics of the county thereafter. Trevelyan explains that this group, having won free trade, were even then preparing to amalgamate socially and politically with the aristocracy.[1] To Bright Cobden's schemes were wholly inadequate. The result of this division of opinion was that Bright's projected Commons' League came to nothing.

Cobden's plans, on the other hand, were already materializing. In 1848 there had been formed a purely middle-class association to work for financial reform and complete free trade—the Liverpool Financial Reform Association, with Robertson Gladstone as chairman.[2] This association, supported by all the Manchester party, continued to be influential throughout the rest of the century. In the same year the freehold movement was launched at Birmingham with the object of winning the county constituencies.[3] In 1849 Cobden and half a dozen other Radicals formed a similar society for London, which grew with great rapidity under the name of the National Freehold Land Society.[4] The movement was taken up all over the country, and soon Cobden was writing enthusiastically to Bright[5] that they ought to be able to double the county constituencies in seven years and thus secure a better support for reforms than universal suffrage. They might then see the Tories crying out for universal suffrage in order to pit ignorance

[1] Trevelyan, *Life of Bright,* p. 177.

[2] *Reformers' Almanack and Political Year Book,* London, 1849. An advertisement of the Association gives these facts. R. Gladstone was a brother of W. E. Gladstone. See also R. A. Woods, *English Social Movements,* N. Y., 1891, p. 69.

[3] The first annual report of this first organization was published in the *Democratic and Social Almanac for 1850,* London, 1849, p. 11 (in the Goldsmiths' Library). At that time eighteen similar bodies had been formed in such places as Coventry, Northampton, Stafford, and the metropolis.

[4] The *Freeholder's Circular* (organ of the society) contains accounts of the origin of the organization in the numbers for April 13, 1861, and March 15, 1867.

[5] In October, 1849; Morley, *Life of Cobden,* pp. 345-6.

and vice against the "teetotalers, non-conformists and rational Radicals, who would constitute nine-tenths of our phalanx of forty-shilling freeholders." He continued: "The citadel of privilege in this country is so terribly strong owing to the concentrated masses of property in the hands of the comparatively few that we cannot hope to assail it with success unless with the help of the propertied classes in the middle ranks of society, and by raising up a portion of the working class to become members of a propertied order." Even earlier he had written that he believed this scheme to be the "only safe, certain and legal means of effecting those further political changes which are necessary to bring the government into harmony with the wants and wishes of a majority of the people of this country."[1]

Simultaneously with Bright's attempt and failure to organize a great national party under the auspices of the free traders and with the initiation of Cobden's more successful, because purely middle-class, projects, another movement had been inaugurated, which possesses much significance for the historian for two reasons. It exerted some definite political influence in England for several years after it was launched, since it aimed to support Hume in parliament; and, of more importance, it constituted the second experimental stage in the ever-recurring and fundamentally necessary attempt to combine the two industrial classes into one political party. As such, it affords an opportunity to analyze the essential elements in the problem. The first experiment had been Sturge's Complete Suffrage Movement of 1842. Later ones were to be Bright's movement of 1858-9 and the various attempts at organization made during the years of 1864-7.

---

[1] Letter to Scholefield, M.P. for Birmingham. Quoted in *Reformer's Almanack and Political Year Book,* London, 1849, p. 65.

In the very same month in which Bright sought to form
his Commons' League, the National Parliamentary and
Financial Reform Association was formed at a meeting of
several hundred reformers convened by Francis Place at
the Crown and Anchor Tavern in London on January 29,
1849.[1] This organization was formed with the object of
promoting franchise reform as a necessary prerequisite to
securing other reforms, particularly economy in national expenditures.   It also proposed to attend to the registration
of voters and to promote the freehold movement.   Thus its
program sought to attract reformers from all classes, those
who desired organic change and those who looked to practical, middle-class measures.   Sir Joshua Walmsley, a democrat who had loyally advocated the cause of the Chartists in
the House as M.P. for Leicester, was elected president.   In
March its address was published, advocating household
suffrage and the other points of Hume's "Little Charter."
Its first public meeting was held in May, at which, says the
Association's authorized report, for the first time in years
all classes of reformers met upon common ground.   In
August, at a great meeting in Drury Lane Theater, the first
modification of its program took place, making it include the
abolition of property qualifications for members of parliament and the enfranchisement of lodgers.[2] This alteration is significant.   It was a response to pressure by working-class adherents.   The Association held over sixty meetings in the metropolis in the course of a few months and
made its entry into the provinces by a "magnificent demon-

[1] An account of the origin and first year's activities of the Association
is given in the *Reformers' Almanack and Political Year Book*, London,
1850, pp. 33-4.   This publication was issued under the sanction of the
Association.   Place's copy is in the Goldsmiths' Library.   The Association at first took the name "Metropolitan" but in August changed
it to "National."
[2] The *Democratic Review*, August, 1849.   Under the technical term
"lodger" were included perhaps the majority of workingmen in the
metropolis.

stration" at Norwich in October.   By this time it had won at least the outward support of the entire Radical group in parliament and boasted eighteen members of parliament on its council.   Hume was its special spokesman in the House.[1]

But what was the real attitude toward the movement on the part of the middle classes and working men?   Let it be remembered that the active members of the working classes were then Chartists, or Christian Socialists, or trade-unionists, and as such held to the various creeds that were explained in the preceding chapter.   From the moment of the formation of the association the moderate Chartists had looked upon it with favor, though they hoped to induce it to accept the Charter as its platform.[2]   At the Drury Lane meeting in August the association did consent to extend its program, as above described, and it was then that O'Connor's adhesion was given.   Soon O'Connor was described as being enamored of the scheme, even following Cobden to Aylesbury upon one occasion to support him in advocating it.[3]

The more extreme Chartists, however, were of a different mind.   The result was that by 1851 the question of supporting the Association had split the Chartist body into two hostile factions.   The opposition was led by George Julian Harney[4] and Ernest Jones.   Harney wrote:[5] "The object of Cobden with his freehold land scheme, and Walmsley with his 'Little Charter' is, clearly, to so far extend the suffrage as to swamp the House with representatives of the

---

[1] *Ibid.*

[2] Gammage, *History of the Chartist Movement* (ed. of 1894), pp. 347-353, discusses the relation of the Chartists to the association.

[3] Gammage, *History of the Chartist Movement* (1894), p. 351.   Also the *Britannia,* January 12, 1850.

[4] Writing in his *Democratic Review,* and in the *Northern Star* (O'Connor's paper), of which Harney was editor until June, 1850.

[5] *Democratic Review,* February, 1850.

'Manchester School.'   In short, the policy of both is to make use of the proletarians to establish bourgeois supremacy." That they did not mean to help the poor, he said, was proved by their support of the new Poor Law, their opposition to the Ten Hour Law and the bill for the protection of the London bakers. "The feudal lords have scourged the proletarians with whips, but the money lords will scourge them with scorpions." Let the middle classes fulfill their mission to overthrow the feudal aristocracy, but let the people beware lest their dominance shall then follow.

That workingmen were constantly contrasting the political expressions of the Radicals with their opposition to social legislation is certain. During 1850 Slaney, of Shrewsbury, was trying to have appointed by the House a commission to work out schemes for the social improvement of the people.[1] A Chartist journal of Leicester noted that "the professing friends of the working classes, by all sorts of excuses and evasions, contrived to throw cold water upon the motion, which led to its ultimate withdrawal." It continued:

This act tends to show the animus of those who pretend to be the working men's friends. So far as the government is concerned the working classes are to be left in their life-and-death struggle with poverty, pauperism, and the aggressions of capital. Tory, Whig and Radical agree that "let alone" must be the order of the day. Even Parliamentary and Financial reformers do not think that the social conditions of the people can be improved by the appointment of any commission. We trust working men will think of this. Of what use will a reform in Parliament be to them unless they make use of this power by legislating for labour? Working men who move in this matter have this for their object. Then how shallow must be those Parliamentary Reformers, who opposed Mr. Slaney, and who seem to imagine that the working classes are enamoured of their *laissez faire,* free trade, negative notions of government.[2]

[1] See *Hansard,* CIX. 359 ff.
[2] The *Leicestershire Movement,* March 16, 1850.

The *Labour League,* spokesman, it will be remembered, for the National Association of Organized Trades, expressed its distrust of the political movement at the outset because of its skepticism as to the willingness of any party in parliament to effect social reforms, or of the Radical reformers to do more than use the popular force to gain power for themselves in order to legislate according to their own ideas of political economy.[1]   The *League* promised to continue to "unveil the insidious plottings of the heartless Malthusians."   Cooper, the Chartist, in his *Journal* wrote that of Cobden and others prominent in the movement "the masses in the manufacturing districts are now speaking out their opinions with a bitterness which can only increase in strength until it amounts to open hostility."[2]   Without question this bitterness was immediately due to the attempts at that moment being made to nullify or amend the Ten Hour Law, which were causing widespread excitement among the operatives of the North.[3]

Early in 1851 the schism in Chartist ranks was complete.   An unofficial conference was called at Manchester by the O'Connorite Chartists (as distinct from the Jones faction now in control of the regular organization), at which the chief subjects of discussion were the wisdom of abandoning the social aims of their agitation and, secondly, the expediency of an alliance with the middle-class movement.[4]   After heated debates a large body seceded from the Conference and issued an address as from the Manchester Chartist Association, in which they definitely aban-

---

[1] March 17, 1849.

[2] *Cooper's Journal, or Unfettered Thinker and Plain Speaker for Truth, Freedom and Progress.*   London, 1850, January 12, 1850.

[3] See above, p. 59.

[4] The *Northern Star,* January 25, February 1, 8, 1851.   The object for which the conference was called was to consider efforts to convert the middle-class reformers to the justice and expediency of adopting manhood suffrage.

doned all social revolutionary objects and frankly advocated
coöperation with the middle classes, the Parliamentary and
Financial Reform Association in particular, to work for
political reform.[1]   The address concluded by declaring the
Charter to be "a mere political measure."

It was in answer to this pronouncement that the regular
Chartist organization (the National Charter Association),
under the leadership of Ernest Jones, took its stand upon
the wide program of socialistic reform that was noted in
the preceding chapter, thus adhering to the policy of class
war.   Jones denounced the Manchester move as a conspiracy "to hand over the Chartists to the Manchester School."[2]
Thus was the issue squarely joined.   The cleavage among
the working classes was along a line that had been marked
out from the very beginning of the democratic movement
even before 1832.   It was a deep and abiding cleavage;
only partially and temporarily was it bridged over during
the next three decades.   Now, important political developments in England depended upon how great a number of
the working classes stood on the side of the line that meant
an acceptance of middle-class economics and therewith of a
middle-class political alliance.

Many workingmen welcomed the new reform association as a means of class reconciliation and of effecting
parliamentary reform, which, they had learned, the working
classes were not able to effect alone.   But, even among the
adherents of the association, division was rife from the
first.   The middle-class supporters advocated a rate-paying
household suffrage, which would exclude many.   Workingmen, on the other hand, urged the association to come out

[1] *The Council of the Manchester Chartist Association to the Democratic Reformers of Great Britain,* 1851. (Pamphlet from Lovett's
collection in the Goldsmiths' Library).

[2] Gammage, *op. cit.,* p. 360. See above, p. 67.

for manhood suffrage.[1] Lovett individually addressed the middle-class members on "Justice safer than Expediency."[2] Thomas Frost, a Chartist of Croydon, whose memoirs are an interesting comment upon these years, while urging Chartists to support the movement as an instrument to be used against those who opposed all reform, yet understood clearly the limitations which the middle classes tacitly imposed. They desired, he said, to enfranchise the rest of the shop-keepers and exclude workingmen. What they desired was a diminution of taxation; if they could get that without parliamentary reform they would not be for the latter. But now, as in 1832, they needed the workingmen. These, however, he believed could be won only by the adoption of manhood suffrage, which the middle classes would never consent to.

An analysis of the movement from Harney's paper[3] is worth quoting:

Delusion apart, the new "union" amounts to this: the *bourgeoisie* will not unite with the proletarians for the Charter, but they cannot obtain their own pet measure of "reform" without help; they, therefore, make certain concessions, use coaxing language, and talk vaguely of a future when . . . Universal Suffrage, or the entire Charter, may possibly have their support. The Chartists, though unwilling to abandon the measure for which they have so long struggled, are conscious that they have not the strength to achieve their favourite object, whilst struggling by themselves; they, therefore, accept the terms offered by their more moderate allies. The two parties, weak in themselves, acquire strength by their union, and may prove strong enough to carry the "reform" they are agreed to support.

A pamphlet of 1849[4] described the new association as an attempt at "combining the Liverpool with the Notting-

[1] This division appeared at the Drury Lane meeting in August, 1849. See *Democratic Review* for that month.
[2] *Life and Struggles*, pp. 349-50.
[3] *Democratic Review*, August, 1849.
[4] *Prospects of Reform: A letter to Sir Joshua Walmsley, M.P.*, London, 1849 (British Museum). The reference to Liverpool had in mind the Liverpool Financial Reform Association; to Nottingham, the fact that O'Connor was Member for that borough.

ham ethics," and seeking by its title to catch both an economically minded middle class and also those groups whose chief grievance was political degradation. But it charged the Radicals with insincerity. Hume, it declared, gave his motion but little else; Bright, Cobden, and Gibson were secretly opposed. Cobden especially, it believed, had no democratic faith and, under the guise of friendly counsel, was seeking to thwart the efforts of those who had. The pamphlet concluded upon this pessimistic note: "The middle class, as a class, you have not gained over to you, and, whatever your principles, you never will; for that class, as a class, is the most essentially Conservative."

During 1850 the association assumed larger proportions. Public meetings were frequent. Almost invariably a disagreement occurred between the middle class and the manhood suffragists. Cobden and Bright spoke occasionally on behalf of the movement,[1] and others from the former Complete Suffrage Movement of 1842 gave it strong support, among them Miall and the Reverend Thomas Spencer.[2] The agitation was extended to Scotland, while George Thompson (M.P. for Tower Hamlets and Chartist advocate) and Walmsley were campaigning for it in the North.[3] The Executive Council issued another address,[4] in which it urged that the object of the union of classes be kept steadily in view. It stated that the receipts of the association had amounted to five thousand pounds and that in London a series of lectures was soon to be given by such leaders of

[1] At Aylesbury (the *Britannia,* January 12, 1850). At Sheffield Cobden spoke, but only for financial reform and the freehold policy (*ibid.,* January 26, 1850). Bright is mentioned in the Address of the Council for 1850 as having been a speaker for the movement during 1849. See note 4, below.

[2] The *Britannia,* January 12, 1850.

[3] The *Public Good,* 1850-1, p. 32. Also The *Leicestershire Movement,* February 16, 23, 1850.

[4] *Address of the Council of the National Parliamentary and Financial Reform Association,* London, 1850. (In the British Museum).

the "People's Party" as Hume, Fox, Miall, and C. J. Bunting, the "Norwich Operative."[1]

O'Connor's paper, the *Northern Star,* gave the movement much favorable publicity. It approved of its object,
which was not final, but possible, reform. Those who desired more could use this reform as a lever with which to
gain it.[2] "May the walls of exclusion," it fervently exclaimed, "now be thrown down by the united efforts of the
N. R. A. and the Chartists, and the curse of class-legislation
and class-domination be removed from this country!"[3] But
O'Connor considered it wise to urge Chartists to maintain
their strength in order to force an equal alliance with the
Radicals.[4] The *Freethinkers' Magazine,* representing a
certain influential group of workingmen then beginning to
rally around Holyoake and Bradlaugh in the Secularist
movement, approved of the agitation and the association.
but it demanded complete democracy.[5] Another democratic journal[6] besought the association to adhere to manhood suffrage. "The millions in the manufacturing districts must ever form the numerical strength of any great
movement for Reform; these are now waiting to hear
'Manhood Suffrage' pronounced as the true and only watch-
word in your Council." Some reformers, it said, spoke
lightly of the natural right to the franchise; "but this is a
doctrine so firmly fixed in the convictions of intelligent workingmen in this country that they would as soon think of
denying their own existence as of denying its truth."

Such lack of harmony among those interested in the
association obstructed its course with difficulties. An important conference held in April, 1850, revealed the funda-

[1] A workingman who wrote many pamphlets signed thus.
[2] January 5, 1850.
[3] February 17, 1850.
[4] January 19, 1850.
[5] October 1, 1850.
[6] *Cooper's Journal,* January 17, 1850.

mental antagonisms present within the ranks of reformers.[1] One hundred delegates were present, including Hume, Cobden, Bright, Fox, Colonel Thompson, J. H. Tillett, a rising Radical of Norwich, and O'Connor. Cobden, in the discussion, made plain his lack of sympathy with the movement by insisting that political change should be gradual, the only feasible plans being those on foot for liberalizing the counties.[2] The business committee of the association had privately disposed of the question of manhood suffrage, but G. W. M. Reynolds moved it from the floor. The debate aroused grave suspicions as to the possibility of common action by the two factions. The futility of the conference must have been recognized, for on the third day barely fifty delegates were present and no members of parliament except two democrats. Nevertheless, the conference issued an optimistic address, claiming that the movement had the adherence of one hundred and twenty members of parliament, that delegates had come from nearly all the populous towns, and that the proceedings had been most harmonious.[3] It further outlined elaborate plans for agitation, attention to the register, promotion of the purchase of forty-shilling freeholds, and independent action at the polls. The Chartist press declared the conference a failure and lamented its refusal to accept a democratic platform.[4]

The association's official report[5] of its work for 1850 recounted two hundred and twenty public meetings held

[1] A full account was given in the *Atlas,* April 27, 1850.

[2] At this point he gave evidence to show the value of the freehold scheme to the Anti-Corn Law League.

[3] *Address of the National Reform Conference to the Friends of Parliamentary and Financial Reform throughout the Kingdom.* April 27, 1850 (in the Goldsmiths' Library). For Cobden's attitude, see Morley, *Cobden,* pp. 344-5.

[4] *Northern Star,* April 27, 1850; *Cooper's Journal,* May 18; *Freethinkers' Magazine,* June 1. Another conference held late in the year was a reduplication of this one. Seventeen M.P.'s attended. (*Freethinkers' Magazine,* November 1, 1850).

[5] *Address of the Council of the Parliamentary and Financial Reform Association,* London, 1851.

(one hundred and twenty-four in the metropolis), over one hundred and twenty thousand tracts issued, organization of reform associations widely promoted, and the freehold movement advanced by the formation of societies for that purpose. Again it proposed independent electoral action by the great Radical party.[1]

The chances of reform's being taken up seriously in parliament brightened in 1851. Locke King's motion for leave to introduce a bill for the assimilation of the county and borough franchise was carried against the government in a thin house.[2] Though rejected overwhelmingly on the second reading, the first vote had the effect of extracting from Russell a specific promise of a reform bill and from Disraeli a repudiation, in the name of his party, of the idea that they were opposed to all reform.[3] Furthermore, the government was being hard pressed on the protection issue, hav-

[1] Some account of the progress of the freehold movement may here be given. It grew with remarkable rapidity, partly, perhaps chiefly, because it proved to be a good business project. By 1850 there were eighty societies with thirty thousand members; in 1852 there were one hundred thirty societies with eighty-five thousand members; nineteen thousand five hundred allotments of sites worth at least forty shillings a year had been made, and seven hundred ninety thousand pounds had been paid in. (From J. E. Ritchie, *Freehold Land Societies: Their History, Present Position and Claims*, London, 1853). The *Builder*, early in 1854, remarked on the alarm felt lest the movement would lead to "an overwhelming transfusion of the democratic principle." (Quoted in *Provident Times*, March 8, 1854). By this time all varieties of political groups were adopting the scheme, Conservatives, Teetotalers, etc. (*Provident Times*, March 22, 1854. The *Liberator*, September, 1855, shows nonconformists urging its use.) Disraeli saw its political importance as early as in 1850 (a letter to Lord Stanley. Monypenny and Buckle, *Life of Beaconsfield*, III. 238). It had changed the political complexion of the Birmingham district of Warwickshire before the election of 1852 and had influenced Lancashire, West Riding, East Surrey, and Middlesex. In the last two places Conservatives attributed their defeat in 1852 to this cause. (Statement in a Conservative paper, the *Britannia*, August 28, 1852.) The movement was denounced in the democratic press as aiming to "garrison property" and enforce the idea of property as a qualification for the franchise. It "may enfranchise us after many centuries," wrote the *English Republic*, p. 65. Also see *ibid.*, p. 179.

[2] *Hansard*, CXIV. 864-70. Second reading, CXV. 910-940.

[3] G. B. Smith, *Life of Bright*, London, 1889, pp. 135-6.

ing just won ·an important division by a bare fourteen
votes.[1]   Hume suggested later that the need of popular
support thus revealed may have helped Russell to his decision.[2]   Reform had not been mentioned in the Queen's
speech at the beginning of the session.[3]   Later in the session the government was beaten again on Berkeley's motion
for the ballot.[4]   Under these circumstances, Russell began
to approach Bright and the Radicals, even against the
wishes of Palmerston.[5]   Bright thereupon redoubled his
efforts to stir up a combined middle- and working-class agitation, and Cobden now for the first time appears to have
given his formal adhesion to the Parliamentary and Financial Reform Association, on the ground that the question
was now a practical one.[6]   But Cobden was also advising
Bright to wait until the popular cry forced the issue, remarking that he did not see "any indication of a breeze in the
direction of Reform."[7]   It seems that Bright was still hoping to form a reform organization, distinct from the existing one, with the old Anti-Corn Law League as a nucleus.
Cobden insisted the plan was not feasible, because the Manchesterites would not respond.[8]   Sturge apparently was
simultaneously offering to lead in a manhood-suffrage agitation, and Edward Miall, of the *Nonconformist,* was warmly
advocating the principle, because it alone was compatible
with human dignity; it alone would break up the solidarity

[1] This great debate is in *Hansard,* CXIV. 374 ff.

[2] *Ibid.,* pp. 864-5.

[3] *Ibid.,* pp. 2 ff.

[4] *Hansard,* CXVIII. 356-74.

[5] Trevelyan, *Bright,* p. 196.

[6] *English Republic,* June 22, 1851.   Yet he made it clear he approved
only of a "practical, administrative measure."   (National Parl. & Financial Reform Assn. Tracts.   Proceedings of the fourth monthly *soiree*
of the Association.   May 26, 1851).

[7] Morley, *Cobden,* p. 373.

[8] *Ibid.,* p. 376.

of the working class, which was the result of political exclusion.[1]

Thus were all shades of radicalism struggling to find their way amid the maze of contradictions, fears, and hopes of the time. Chartists were increasingly suspicious of the middle-class leaders, and middle-class leaders found it impossible unreservedly to accept political democracy. The relations between the two classes in the industrial world were without doubt having their reverberations in the political. These were the years of the Wolverhampton Tin-plate Workers' prosecutions and of the great Engineers' strike and lockout. Linton scathingly described the Radicals as "the party of financial and parliamentary reformers, the infamous-peace party, the free-traders *in labour,* the mill-owning evaders of the factory-relief bill, the money lords, the comfortable Atheists on 'Change.' "[2] The journal of William Newton of the Amalgamated Engineers expressed its doubt of middle-class leadership; instead, "the people must take their advocates from their own class. No others can so well understand or express their sympathies or feelings—their wants and necessities—their strength and weakness."[3] And again:[4] the conduct of reformers was "open to grave suspicion," and the House of Commons was "a bundle of warring negatives." The Industrial Exhibition had tided them over that year, and "national glorification and commercial ambition have stifled the cries of the people," but now Russell knew only reform could break the parliamentary deadlock. Let the people, therefore, it urged, agitate for as much as they could get, especially for payment of members, "so that the labourers may send those who really have their

[1] A speech of his was published as a pamphlet: *The Franchise Considered as a means of a People's Training,* London, 1851.

[2] The *English Republic,* p. 110.

[3] The *Operative,* July 12, 1851.

[4] *Ibid.,* August 9, 1851.

confidence to parliament"; then they will have the power of "providing by law that capital shall be just to labour," by securing certain measures, such as the amendment of the Master and Servant Law. "And behind these reforms greater ones, affecting society as well as politics, rise up from the darkness of the future, that future which may be the beginning of a bright and glorious end, when those who make the wealth of the world shall be treated as justly as the ox which was not muzzled when treading out the corn."

The spirit in trade-unionism is further revealed by the fact that the cautious *Bookbinders' Circular* broke over its habitual reticence on politics to denounce the "cold, calculating doctrines of Mr. Hume and the Whigs."[1]

With public opinion upon the question of reform in the state that has been described and with apparently general apathy existing toward the question except among a minority of the people,[2] Russell introduced his measure early in 1852. The Radicals opposed it unanimously, though some were willing to accept it under protest as a step in the right direction. Disraeli[3] did not offer any vigorous opposition, because he saw it did not disturb the balance of interests as established by the act of 1832, precisely the feature of it which the Radicals attacked. But the measure never came up for an exhaustive debate, because the government was beaten almost immediately on its local militia bill and resigned. Derby became prime minister and announced his program as consisting wholly of legal and social reforms.

That Russell and the Whigs within the last two or three years had been made more sensible of their dependence

[1] February, 1851. The reference was not specifically to reform, or labor, but to a Contagious Diseases Bill.

[2] Admitted by Hume in debate on this bill. (*Hansard,* CXIX. 268 ff.) He said the people were too well employed to be concerned. The bill provided for a five pound rating franchise for boroughs as well as income tax franchise. It repealed property qualification for members. (*Ibid.,* pp. 261-5.)

[3] *Ibid.,* pp. 303 ff.

upon the Radicals appears in an account of a party conference called by Russell soon after the accession of the Conservatives to office, which Derby and Disraeli detailed in their ministerial statements in parliament. At this conference, it was declared, Cobden, Bright, Hume, and Villiers had been conspicuous, and Russell had promised that in case he were called on again to form a cabinet it would not be wholly Whig.[1] Disraeli said that the Whigs, the Cobdenites, and the Peelites had formed a coalition to force a dissolution of parliament.[2] Derby, in view of this possibility, stated that among the issues upon which the Conservatives would appeal to the country would be that they, while in office, had exerted themselves "to stem with some opposition, to supply some barrier against the current of that continually increasing and encroaching democratic influence in this nation, which is bent on throwing the whole power and authority of the government nominally into the hands of the masses, but practically and really into those of demagogues and republicans."[3]

The prospect of an election seemed to offer an opportunity to the Parliamentary and Financial Reform Association to widen its influence. It did make the attempt. Another conference was held, but the schism between the household and manhood suffragists appeared to be deeper than before. The *Northern Star*[4] declared that workingmen would never support a movement which did not recognize manhood suffrage, to them "a sacred tradition and inexpugnable portion of their political creed." Holyoake and Miall plead for unity, but Ernest Jones pronounced the association reactionary. Thomas Frost, present at the conference, was convinced that the Radicals only meant to use the

[1] *Hansard*, CXIX. 1010 ff. Derby's statement.
[2] *Ibid.*, p. 1063.
[3] *Ibid.*, p. 1013.
[4] March 6, 1852. The *Star* had now passed out of Chartist hands.

working classes in order to gain their own objects.[1] One
of the most persistent working-class advocates of the alliance
represented by the association was Holyoake, who was writing for it constantly in the *Leader;*[2] but he brought down
upon his head many bitter attacks thereby. Linton dubbed
him the "touter in ordinary to the Walmsley incapables."[3]
Charles Murray, a social-reform Chartist of the School of
O'Brien and Ernest Jones, wrote a denunciatory pamphlet[4]
accusing him of treason to his class.

Plainly, the Parliamentary and Financial Reform Association was fast approaching dissolution, even though Hume
was now more active in its behalf than formerly.

The election of 1852 is notable in the political history of
English labor chiefly because it was the occasion of the first
independent labor candidacy—that of William Newton, organizer of the most effective trade-union in England, the
Amalgamated Society of Engineers. The explanation of
this candidacy lies in the bitter war then being waged, as
was described in the preceding chapter, between the Engineers and the Association of Employers of Operative Engineers, in which the masters were seeking to break the union.[5]
The *Operative*[6] had threatened political action as soon as
the dissolution of parliament was rumored, pointing to the
masters' efforts to induce the government to take action in
the strike. "We had rather not use the weapon they are
forcing upon us; but if they will have it so, and that too on
the eve of a threatened dissolution of parliament, we will

---

[1] *Forty Years' Recollections*, p. 207.
[2] J. McCabe, *Life and Letters of George Jacob Holyoake*, London,
1908, vol. I, p. 164.
[3] *Ibid.*, p. 169.
[4] *A Letter to Mr. George Jacob Holyoake, containing a brief review
of that Gentleman's conduct and policy as a Reformer*, etc., London,
1854. (In the Goldsmiths' Library).
[5] See above, pp. 52 ff.
[6] February 14, 1852. It feared an *ex post facto* law against trade-
unions.

not let another week pass over without pointing to the policy which for our own safety we *must* adopt." Soon it began to develop the idea, still somewhat vague, of a great workingmen's party, which it hoped to see emerge from the conference in London on the engineers' strike and lockout—"A great confederation of all those who sell labour for wages."[1] One week later William Newton, editor of the *Operative* and organizer of the amalgamation, announced his candidacy for Tower Hamlets, the second largest constituency in the kingdom.[2] It contained probably several thousand working-class electors.[3]

Newton stood definitely as a labor candidate against both the regular parties. This position was made clear in his opening address,[4] in which he stated that he would try to make the election turn upon questions of labor. There was, he declared, hardly one spokesman for labor in the House now, but workingmen were more conscious than ever before of their need, their power to elect their own members. Middle-class remedies, consisting largely of an increase in trade, were inadequate to solve the paramount problem of unemployment. Direct legislation to legalize coöperative production, amend unjust laws bearing on labor, such as the Master and Servant Law, to take care of unemployment by the use of waste lands and the provision of work by the government, to reform the patent laws—these measures labor could expect only from a parliament in which labor had a voice. As to the political program of the address, it was typically Radical, except for its demand for manhood suffrage.

[1] March 27, 1852. See above, p. 53.
[2] The *Operative*, March 30.
[3] Based on an estimate in R. D. Baxter, *The New Reform Bill*, App. III, London, 1866. The number of working-class electors in each borough in 1866 is given.
[4] The *Operative*, April 10, 1852.

A leading article in the same number of the *Operative*
that carried this address, itself no doubt written by Newton,
argued for direct labor representation, declaring: "There is
a growing conviction that the rights of labour will never be
fairly advocated, nor its wrongs unsparingly exposed, till a
man from the ranks of labour . . . catches the eye of
the Speaker of the House, and in burning words pours
forth the woes, the sympathies, the aspirations of the toilers."

As the campaign progressed Newton's speeches were reported in the *Operative*. He continued to differentiate his
liberal from his strictly labor platform, emphasizing his
unique position with regard to the latter and dwelling particularly upon the problem of unemployment as the fundamental one, to be solved only by wider use of the land. It
is possible to discern in Newton's program his fourfold
character of Chartist, Christian Socialist, trade-unionist,
and Liberal. Portions of his demands can be attributed to
each source of inspiration. Also, in essentials, his program
was a prototype of labor's political program as formulated
and re-formulated during the next half-century, with its two
aspects, the liberal and the labor. The latter portion assumed various guises at different periods, but in it were
constantly to be found, with varying emphasis, of course, the
question of trade-union legislation, the laws of partnership,
patent laws, unemployment, and government interference in
behalf of the weak.[1]

In this contest Newton opposed both the sitting members,
Sir William Clay and George Thompson. His opposition to
the latter is significant, for labor had had no truer friend than
he in its political aspirations during the past twenty-five
years. He advocated all the points of the Charter and sup-

[1] This was never wholly absent, even in labor's most *laissez faire*
period. Witness the demand for factory laws, employers' liability,
and mines regulations.

ported them upon every occasion in the House. But he was a Radical, had been prominent in the Anti-Corn Law League, and no doubt had little eye for the social needs of the time. Sir William Clay, the other sitting member, was a good Radical and supporter of Hume's reform bill and of the Parliamentary and Financial Reform Association. A fourth Liberal candidate was C. S. Butler.

That Newton's contest was a vigorous one is shown by its results. At the hustings he received the largest show of hands, and at the subsequent polling received 1095 votes. Clay and Butler were elected with 7728 and 7218 votes respectively.

During the campaign the *Operative* urged electoral activity on the part of labor all over the country. It advised every town and borough to have its operatives' committee of electors and non-electors, to put forward candidates if possible, and, if not, to demand answers on social questions of those who offered themselves.[1]

One result of the election was to strengthen the ultra-Radical group in parliament. Sir J. Walmsley and W. Gardner were elected for Leicester by large majorities over Whig opponents, who dubbed them Chartists.[2] The ministerialists were also strengthened, but had not a majority of the House.[3] Offers and counter-offers of factional alliances characterized the political situation during the rest of the year. Disraeli tried to strengthen himself by offering an alliance to the Manchester School,[4] which was refused;

---

[1] Ernest Jones contested Halifax. Of the twenty thousand at the hustings the vast majority were for Jones. At the polls he received only thirty-eight votes (Gammage, *op. cit.*, p. 391). At Nottingham the Chartists tried to elect Charles Sturgeon, attorney for the National Association of United Trades. (The *Age,* June 20, 1853).

[2] The *Age,* June 6, 12, 1853.

[3] Their total gain was twenty-two seats (The *Britannia*, July 31, 1852).

[4] Trevelyan, *Bright,* pp. 205 ff.

the Peelites, not to be reconciled with Disraeli, definitely transferred their support to the Whigs.[1]   This coalition overthrew the Conservative ministry at the end of the year and established itself in power under Lord Aberdeen. Overtures to the Manchester School were made by the coalition by offering Bright a place in the cabinet, which he would not accept.[2]

By this time the Parliamentary and Financial Reform Association had well-nigh ceased to function.   The democratic *Vanguard*[3] explained its impotence as the result of compromise.   By trying to make some approach to radical reform, it had antagonized the "millocracy," while, by trying to conciliate the Manchester School, it had alienated the ardent politicians of the working class.   "Cobden, Bright and their confederates do undoubtedly exercise great influence with the middle class, and had they joined heartily with Walmsley and his friends, there can be no doubt that a vast proportion of the middle class . . . would have enlisted under the banner of Parliamentary Reform.   But a veritable, earnest movement for Parliamentary Reform is of all agitations the least likely to serve the peculiar ambition of the Manchester men; *such* a movement could not for long be sustained on the *juste milieu* policy.   The popular passions aroused, and the might of the multitude put forth, the movement would day by day assume a more Radical or even Revolutionary character; and the Manchester liberals, failing to advance, would be submerged by the power they had evoked."   The Manchester men aim to undermine the territorial aristocracy and take their power over, but hesitate to do it by the aid of a popular movement which might go too far.   They, therefore, "have never been more than luke-

[1] Trevelyan, *op. cit.*, p. 208.
[2] *Ibid.*, p. 208.
[3] Ed. by G. J. Harney, 1853, pp. 26 ff. and p. 61.

warm and insincere friends of 'Parliamentary Reform' and now they have inaugurated a new 'dodge' to attract popular attention and support, with the view of rendering any real movement for Parliamentary Reform impossible for at least any (*sic*) time to come." They have got up the Peace Movement and aim to revive the machinery of the League. According to their maxim of one thing at a time, they will give this their whole attention. The money lords "instinctively feel that if the working classes obtained political power their supremacy, social as well as political, would be in continual and imminent danger." And as for Chartism, it is broken and destroyed. "In truth there is not on the soil of the country any party or popular organization willing and competent to continue the struggle for the triumph of pure, unsullied democracy."

Another working class weekly[1] similarly lamented that the working classes were "dead" to political reform, partly because times were peaceful and prosperous; but it believed that, in spite of apparent indifference, the cause of universal suffrage was in a better state than ever before. Much thought was going on about it; workingmen had a settled conviction that the vote was due them and, though momentarily deflected from it, would not rest until it was gained. A few months later this journal, as if forecasting the future, declared that Birmingham, the political teacher of the Midlands, should take the lead in a great new democratic movement in opposition to the Manchester traders.[2] In truth, when next the question of radical reform became an issue in English politics, it was from Birmingham that the movement went forth under the leadership of Bright, the rejected of Manchester.

[1] The *Political Examiner*, March 2, 30, 1853.
[2] *Ibid.*, August 1, 1853.

In 1854 Russell was reluctantly permitted by the cabinet to bring in another reform bill.[1] But in these months a new question was developing that was soon to absorb public attention practically to the exclusion of all other issues; namely, the question of war with Russia. Lord Palmerston, the home secretary, was known to be hostile to reform, and even some of his colleagues suspected him of raising the war cry in order to stifle the demand for it.[2] Disraeli said of the government at the end of 1853 that its alternative was reform or war.[3]

Straightway certain Manchester Radicals and nonconformists began to organize an extensive propaganda for peace.[4] One chief argument against war was its expense. This agitation by the Manchester leaders went far toward alienating from them the support of politically active workingmen. Some considered it a move to shelve reform; others were wholly unsympathetic with pacifism. One of their journals exclaimed,[5] when Bright made a speech disparaging the Turks: "Verily! friend *Bright,* thou art an imposter! thy patriotism is a mockery, thy philanthropy a sham, and thy orations the disingenuous and venomous outpourings of Humbug and Falsehood combined." Another,[6] in giving an account of a great peace meeting at Edinburgh at which

[1] Even this was due to petitions and public meetings engineered by Bright. (See Trevelyan, *Bright,* pp. 209-12). The vast amount of corruption practised in the recent election contributed to the demand for reform. See the *British Journal,* May, 1853; the *Northern Tribune,* p. 33, and the *Political Annual and Reformers' Handbook,* London, 1854, p. 12, for expressions on this matter.

[2] Morley, *Life of Gladstone,* I. 490.

[3] Monypenny and Buckle, *Life of Beaconsfield,* III. 350.

[4] Cobden had been interested in an organization to promote peace since 1847. Bright and other Radical leaders joined. See J. A. Hobson, *Cobden, The International Man,* N. Y., 1919, pp. 36, 56-7, and S. Hobhouse, *Joseph Sturge,* p. 128, note 1. Also *Herald of Peace* (organ of The Peace Society), 1850-3, and *Peace Advocate and Correspondent,* 1851.

[5] The *Beacon, a Journal of Politics and Literature,* November 23, 1853.

[6] The *British Journal,* November, 1853.

were present Cobden, Bright, Miall, and Sturge, declared
that Cobden here "struggled harder to pull down his reputation than he ever did to build it." The *English Republic*
vehemently approved of war with Russia.[1] Meetings were
held in the metropolis in favor of war,[2] and in October a
Conservative journal asserted that Aberdeen had been hissed
as a coward in every public meeting in the provinces.[3]
The Fraternal Democrats pronounced the hesitant policy of
the government to be due to their purpose "to uphold aristocratic domination and suppress the rising influence of
democracy."[4] The *Beacon* called on the people to demand
war in order to give Italy, Poland, and Hungary a chance to
break their fetters.[5] It denounced the mill-owning pacifists who at that very moment were in Preston waging a
life and death struggle with the workingmen of Lancashire,
even while professing peace and liberalism—"tyrants as
rapacious as Nicholas, and a thousandfold more hypocrit-
ical." Secret diplomacy it condemned and demanded, on this
additional ground, that the House of Commons be made representative of the people.[6]

In this fashion did Manchester internationalism, based
upon free trade and peace, clash with working-class internationalism, inspired by a democratic sympathy with all
peoples who were denied political liberty by aristocratic
governments.

The peace party could not carry with them even the
majority of their middle-class allies. Cobden saw the disruptive influence of this fact upon his and Bright's project
of effecting financial reform through a reform of parlia-

[1] November 19, 1853.
[2] *British Journal,* November, 1853.
[3] The *Britannia,* October 8, 1853.
[4] In an address published in the *British Journal,* November, 1853.
[5] November 16, 1853.
[6] November 23, 1853.

ment. He wrote Bright in November that now the Radicals had no good argument for reform, since they were as much in favor of war and war expenditures as the aristocracy.[1]

And so the attempt that had been persisted in since 1848, sometimes half-heartedly, sometimes earnestly, to create a great people's party which should include the body of the working and middle classes, again proved futile. The views of the two industrial groups were still antagonistic, their interests as capital and labor were still unreconciled. Suspicion bred of a consciousness of diverse philosophy and diverse objectives entered into every proposal for political coöperation. Better economic conditions deprived the masses of the one effective stimulant to agitation and left the political movement largely in the hands of the more intellectual elements among the working classes, who would be most conscious of this fundamental divergence of views. Employers' opposition to an extension of factory legislation and to trade-union action reacted upon the political situation in a powerful way. It is no wonder that many workingmen derisively called the whole Manchester group "Cobden & Co.," when Cobden was hostile enough to trade-unions to write as he did in 1856:

So far as the wages question goes, I think the only sound and honest course is to tell the people plainly that they are under a delusion as to their assumed power to regulate or permanently influence in the slightest degree by *coercion* the rate of wages. They might as well attempt to regulate the tides by force, or change the course of the seasons, or subvert any of the other laws of nature—for the wages of labour depend upon laws as unerring and as much above our coercive power as any other operations of nature. There is a desperate spirit of monopoly and tyranny at the bottom of all these trade unions."[2]

[1] Morley, *Cobden,* p. 408.
[2] J. A. Hobson, *Cobden, the International Man,* p. 166, in a letter to H. Richard urging the *Morning Star* to undertake the mission of teaching the people that the middle-class Radicals were their friends.

The whole question of political reform was soon swamped in the excitement of the Crimean War. The working classes considered this war as in a large measure their own. They forgot their own political exclusion for a time in their all-absorbing interest in the struggle against Russia, to them the symbol of all oppression. Or perhaps they sensed the impetus their own cause would receive through the triumph of liberty abroad. When next the question of reform came into the forefront of English politics, it persisted until it received a fairly satisfactory solution.

CHAPTER IV

REVIVAL OF THE REFORM QUESTION AFTER THE
CRIMEAN WAR

The Crimean War, arousing as it did the generous sympathy of the working classes, who saw in it a means of advancing the cause of liberty, and the opposition of the Manchester party and their Peace Society had served to erect another barrier between these two groups. In 1855 the final dissolution of the Parliamentary and Financial Reform Association, whose object had been to cement a political alliance between them, was officially announced.[1] The war had for a time driven into the background all domestic questions. It had, however, furnished certain new arguments for reform, since it had cast discredit upon aristocratic government. Trevelyan estimates its influence thus: "The actual revival of democracy under Bright's leadership from 1858 onwards, culminating in the triumphant winning of the Franchise in 1867, was in no small measure due to the proved incompetence of the aristocrats, even at their own game of war."[2] A further effect of the war that had political bearings was the rise in the price of food which it occasioned, entailing wide-spread distress among the lower orders of society.[3] Ernest Jones found occasion once more to preach his land gospel to ready listeners.[4]

---

[1] In the *Political Annual and Reformer's Handbook for* 1856, p. 12.
[2] *Life of Bright*, p. 236.
[3] By 1855 the price of wheat was ten shillings higher per quarter than the highest price in the years just preceding the repeal of the Corn Laws. (Tables in Levi, *Annals of British Legislation*, 1856, I. 29.) Bread riots were common occurrences. Pauperism in the large towns increased greatly. See *Journal of Progress*, August, 1854, and Levi, *op. cit.*, pp. 17-29.
[4] Lectures published in *Evenings with the People*, 1856.

The conclusion of peace in 1856 made it possible for domestic questions again to assert themselves. It is true that the year 1857 was comparatively uneventful in the more obvious developments of English domestic politics. The single exception was the spectacular fall and reinstatement of Palmerston, and even this was occasioned more by foreign policy than domestic. But a study of the undercurrents of political life in this year reveals an advance in all the related political issues that centered around the pivotal question of enfranchising the working classes. The earlier experiment of an organized party composed of the middle and working classes had followed its tortuous course amid the obstructions offered by conflicting class interests, Chartist intransigence, Radical incoherence and uncertainty. It would have failed had there been no war. The war swept the stage clean of those first futilities. The task of evolving more effective policies concerning the problem of democracy faced all classes. From this year until 1867 the question presents a continuous development. It underwent, however, vicissitudes that are most instructive as to the cross-currents in the politics of the period.

One very significant feature of the decade is the increasing prominence of workingmen, even though unenfranchised, in political activities, both local and national. And these activities partook of a new character; they were not generally Chartist in method, but had more the nature of a considered attempt to constitute an extreme left wing of Liberalism. They were intelligent, perhaps opportunist, and certainly effective to the extent of sharpening the issue of reform. They increased the weight of labor in the Radical-Labor partnership, a renewal of which, after its first failure, was inevitably demanded by the fact that none of the fiscal and political reforms sought had been effected. England was still ruled by Whig or Tory aristocrats; indirect taxation still weighed heavily on industry, while the land remained exempt from bearing its due burden; extravagant expenditure still marked the national finances; religious equality was still to be won; Manchester did not yet prevail over Calne and Droitwich.

In the background of this renewal under changed conditions of the attempt to ally the middle and working classes hovered still the fears and suspicions engendered by differing theories and aims.[1]   Chartism as a class war had disappeared, but Chartist aims could be discerned by the apprehensive manufacturer behind the political demands of workingmen. The class war continued in the industrial field unabated, and the hope of identifying the economic interests of the two industrial groups, which was ever a prerequisite to political alliance for democracy, appeared only less futile than a decade earlier. The middle classes, as a whole, therefore, hesitated to admit workingmen into the enfranchised citizenship, while the Radical wing of the middle classes found their needs and their fears of the working classes running counter to each other. The fact that the former proved stronger than the latter is responsible for their continued efforts to create and guide a reform agitation in and after 1857. And this fact, coupled with two others, is responsible for the Act of 1867. The other two facts were the constantly increasing importance of the working classes politically and socially, which rendered it hazardous to deny them the suffrage; and the evolution of the parliamentary situation to the point where Conservatives and Liberals alike had to yield to the combined pressure of the Radicals led by Bright and the working classes demanding the vote. Entering into every changed aspect of the question was the balancing of fear against necessity. The year 1857, therefore,

[1] See next chapter.

initiated what may be called the final stage in the question
of enfranchising the working classes.

The scattered evidence that can be obtained of the interest of the working classses in politics in this year possesses
great interest. Their activities appear chiefly in connection
with the election. Palmerston had been defeated in the
House upon Cobden's motion condemning the government
for upholding the violent policy of the British plenipotentiary
at Hong-Kong. Against him was formed a coalition of
Radicals, Peelites (including Gladstone), Lord John Russell, Disraeli, and the Conservatives. Palmerston appealed
to the country.

The chief issue in the election was Palmerston's foreign
policy. But it was not the only issue. Another in many
boroughs was parliamentary reform, an issue not pressed
upon the constituencies by candidates as much as upon candidates by the Radicals and the unenfranchised in the
constituencies.

It was unavoidable that this issue should be raised.
Ever since Russell's abjuration of finality in 1848, it had
been universally understood that some amendment of the
Act of 1832 would soon be made. There had been much
talk about the proposal in and out of parliament; there had
been associations formed to promote it; there had been two
government bills to effect it. Very likely no great amount of
sincerity had been felt on any of these points by the ruling
classes. Nor had there been vigorous agitation among the
unenfranchised, due perhaps to the following reasons: it was
a time of ebb in political excitement after the high tide of
Chartist endeavor, and it was also a period of slowly increasing prosperity. Those of the unenfranchised who did not
relax their political interest were restrained from immoder-
ate activity by two convictions: first, that reform, having
been conceded by all classes as necessary, would be a cer-

tainty in the near future, and, in the second place, that when
it came it would inevitably be a middle-class, not a working-
class, measure. This latter conviction was developed in the
course of the prolonged negotiations with the Radicals in
the five years after 1848 and fixed by the limited nature of
the government bills of 1852 and 1854. The question had
been denuded of the features that gave it a democratic appeal, such as natural rights and universal suffrage which
alone was capable of effecting the changes in the existing
order desired by workingmen. The issue had become a
matter of practical bourgeois policy. It was understood
that the reason for its consideration at all was to increase
middle-class power in the government. Confessedly these
advocates of reform wished to exclude great numbers of
the working classes. Other reasons for the lapsing of agitation were foreign politics and the growing absorption of
the upper grades of workmen in trade-unionism and co-
operation.

But the question could not rest at that point, since it had
by this time a fixed status in the political schedule. This
fact had several consequences. As we have noted, it tended
to deter agitation, which obstinate opposition would have
engendered. The question was thus likely to become for a
time a parliamentary annual, which everybody discussed and
nobody acted upon. The time would come at last, however,
when promises would have to become deeds. The lifeless
question, bandied about and tossed from party to party like
a ball in play, would become insensibly charged with a dynamic force capable of shattering the hands that trifled with it.
The source of this latent energy in the question was the constantly increasing importance of the great class concerned.
The Radicals in parliament, daring to evoke this energy
because of their necessity, became the masters of the parliamentary situation. The minority in the House, resting upon

a great democratic support, finally worked their will upon the majority, and reform became a fact. This event began to be foreshadowed in 1857.

As has been stated, the working classes were not a negligible quantity in the election of that year. In fact, it was then that non-electors began definitely and deliberately to take part in Liberal electoral matters, with the result that the question of the franchise was forced more into the open. Reform was certainly a hustings question in this election. Candidates were frequently compelled to declare themselves. In several instances a cleavage over the question appeared among the Liberals, one group allying with the non-electors against the other more conservative group—a forecast of the coming *rapprochement* of the conservative Liberals with the Conservative party, and the closer affiliation of the more democratic faction with the masses.

The most spectacular feature of the election of 1857 was the defeat of the anti-Palmerstonian pacifists. At Manchester, Bright and Gibson were beaten. These two defeats are usually explained wholly upon the ground of opposition to the peace policy of these eminent leaders of the Manchester School. There is evidence, however, of another influence at work; namely, a determined opposition on the part of a Liberal section to the remnants of the Anti-Corn Law League, who were charged with trying still to dominate Lancashire Liberal politics. Bright wrote to his brother after the election that the leaders of the opposition were not moved by the peace question, for they had been just as bitter in 1852, or even in 1847, when his merit or demerit lay in his free-trade policy. On both those occasions they had coalesced with the Conservatives.[1] An illuminating pamph-

---

[1] W. N. Molesworth, *History of England, 1830 to 1874,* London, 1886, III. 90. In a letter to Cobden, quoted in Morley's *Life of Cobden,* p. 440, Bright stressed the peace question, however.

let was published at Manchester at the time of the election of
1857 with the title, *Why the Liberals are Leaving the
League.*[1] It declared that a divergence between the Anti-
Corn Law League and other Liberals had been gradually taking place since 1852. This dissension had been augmented
certainly by the peace issue, but was due also to local considerations, which explained the withdrawal of so many Liberals from Bright and Gibson. The free-trade organization
should have ceased when its purpose was accomplished;
instead, "By means of it, a small clique proposes to hold
this city and some of the neighboring boroughs in their
hands. . . . This degradation were of itself sufficient to
stir up the blood of any body of independent men." The
Leeds Mercury, closely following the contest, declared that
huge sums were subscribed to elect Sir John Potter and
Robert Lowe. A deputation to Lowe told him sixteen
thousand pounds had already been subscribed to fight the
League.[2] This support was transferred to J. A. Turner
when Lowe declined to stand. The *Mercury* later attributed
the defeat of Bright and Gibson wholly to a revolt from the
League, and it saw as a factor in this revolt the growing
alienation of the conservative from the advanced forces in
Liberalism.

It should be remembered that both at Manchester and Salford [a
borough near by] there are many electors whose Liberalism is of a
somewhat antique cast, and who, although they have no love for
Toryism, by no means go so far as the advanced party whose organ
is the League. . . . The Conservative party, too, although weak
relatively to Reformers, is absolutely strong, and its weight seems
to have been thrown into the scale in favor of Potter and Turner,
who approximate much more nearly to its views than do Milner
Gibson and Bright.[3]

[1] *Why the Liberals are Leaving the League: A Letter addressed to
Sir Benjamin Heywood, Bart . . . and Samuel Fletcher, Esq.,* by a
Manchester Liberal. No date, but clearly of 1857.
[2] March 24, 1857.
[3] *Leeds Mercury,* March 31, 1857.

It is a legitimate speculation, in the absence of positive evidence, that the Radical friendliness to democratic reform was a large element in the wide-spread opposition to the Manchester School.   Such was apparent enough in the election two years later, when the non-electors put out a candidate of their own with whom it was feared the Radicals would coalesce.   Liberals and Conservatives united against this contingency.[1]   That in 1857 the non-electors must have given their support to Bright in spite of his stand on the war is indicated by the fact that he received a majority in the show of hands at the hustings.[2]   In two other cases where men of the peace party, but who were also outstanding advocates of reform, went down, the show of hands was in their favor; at Huddersfield, where Cobden was defeated, and at Rochdale, where Edward Miall, editor of the *Non-Conformist* and earnest advocate of democracy, failed of election.[3]

A pamphlet written in 1857 by Charles Sturgeon,[4] attorney for the Association of United Trades and a friend of Chartism and social reform, suggests another cross-current in this election.   It expressed the belief that one reason so many of the Manchester School went down was their attitude on labor legislation.   The evidence substantiating this view in the case of one defeat of a free trader is strong.   At Oldham W. J. Fox was beaten in spite of his known democratic beliefs.   It will be recalled that he had been an orator for the Anti-Corn Law League and was a prominent Dissenting minister.   In 1847 a large Liberal faction, no

---

[1] See below, p. 183.

[2] The *British Standard,* April 3, 1857.

[3] *Ibid.,* April 3, 1857.

[4] C. Sturgeon, *A Letter to John Bright . . . with notes on the first list of friends of the Working Classes, published after the coup d'etat they made upon the Manchester Radicals,* London, 1868.   He listed twenty-seven defeats in 1857 so explained. This pamphlet was a reproduction of one written in 1857.

doubt free traders, had brought Fox forward for Oldham
to oppose the son-in-law of John Fielden, then Liberal member for the borough and the leader in the agitation for the
Ten Hour Law. The operatives of Oldham supported Cobbett (the Fielden candidate) unwaveringly, and his defeat,
said a contemporary, made them "morose, sulky, and vin-
dictive." Fox had been in danger of his life from them.
In the campaign of 1852 the non-electors steadily voted no
confidence in Fox in spite of his democratic political views
and votes. Amid vast excitement, he was defeated by Cobbett, who was a Conservative in politics. Fox's biographer
states that henceforth the operatives abandoned their traditions, while the mill-owners and tradesmen formed the new
Liberal party. Fox was soon elected at a bye-election in the
midst of incredible rioting.[1] It is safe to assume that this
violent partisanship had not disappeared by 1857; it probably
contributed to Fox's defeat at that time.[2]

In the contest at Leeds the difficulty of holding the Liberal sections together and the influence of the non-electors
upon the situation were unmistakable. The action of the
Liberal machine was repudiated by those whom the *Leeds
Mercury* described as "extreme Radicals." They chose W.
E. Forster as their candidate. He declared in his address
that he stood distinctly as the non-electors' candidate.[3]
He promised, if elected, to give a yearly accounting to his
constituents and, if they disapproved of his policies seriously,
to consider resigning. The increasing tendency under democratic pressure for members for large boroughs to consider

[1] An account of these events is in Garnett, *Life of Fox,* pp. 289-294.
[2] A meeting of workingmen in London held after the election
to express sympathy with Bright, Cobden, and Gibson, revealed this
same cross-current in working-class politics. An amendment was
offered that their defeat was a just retribution for their opposition to
measures for the social benefit of the people, such as the Ten Hour
Law. The amendment and the original resolution were reported as
receiving about an equal vote (the *British Standard,* April 24, 1857).
[3] *Leeds Mercury,* March 10, 12, 1857.

themselves as delegates is one significant feature of this whole period. The Liberal organization refused to accept Forster and eventually engineered his withdrawal in favor of one who advocated only a five-pound franchise.[1] The result was the election of a Conservative. This Liberal mishap was explained by the *Mercury*[2] as due to the abstention of many Radicals and workingmen or their casting a Conservative vote because of their disaffection. The Liberal schism in Leeds persisted.

In Newcastle a similar situation developed. Democracy was strong here, and class feeling prevailed widely because of this political antagonism as well as because the employers were believed to be particularly indifferent to the welfare of their men.[3] The largest groups of workers were those in the iron trades and the coal mines. About one half of the population of the town were pitmen. A bitter local strife was going on in 1857 between the Whigs supported by the numerous old freemen electors and an advanced faction calling itself the Rate-payers' Association.[4] It was in reality the beginning of a determined effort to democratize the borough. Many workingmen belonged to the Rate-payers' Association. This group refused to coöperate with the Liberal organization to support the sitting members and brought in a stranger only a week before the election.[5] His meetings were attended chiefly by workingmen. His platform demanded a wide extension of the suffrage with the ultimate aim of universal suffrage.[6] At one stormy meeting the line was drawn clearly between workingmen and others, when

---

[1] *Ibid.,* March 14, 1857.
[2] *Ibid.,* March 31, 1857.
[3] The *Northern Tribune,* 1854, p. 61.
[4] The question involved was the use of certain hospital funds, which it was demanded should be used for the good of all, regardless of class or creed. See *Newcastle Daily Chronicle,* September 11, 1857.
[5] *British Standard,* April 3, 1857.
[6] The *Newcastle Messenger and Advertiser,* March 24, 26, 1857.

the workingmen carried their resolution of support for their candidate, even against one calling for manhood suffrage, but opposing the candidate.[1] At the hustings, with fifteen thousand present, the show of hands was for the popular candidate; the polling placed him at the bottom of the list. But he received 1672 votes, of which a thousand were plumpers,[2] which indicates the zeal of his supporters. The Liberal feud continued until 1865, when the extreme party won an overwhelming and lasting victory.

Another contest that possesses particular interest is that at Kidderminster, a carpet-weaving town which had been much affected by the hard times of the war period. Robert Lowe, its Liberal member, was opposed by William Boycott, a Conservative. On election day, the moment the mills closed a crowd of several thousand operatives gathered at the polling booths and began to attack Lowe's supporters with hisses and blows. When he was declared elected, a furious riot broke out in which Lowe himself was wounded, and which had finally to be put down by the military from Birmingham.[3] The Liberal press explained the fierce Conservative sympathies of the operatives by stating that Boycott had steadily catered to them by denouncing the manufacturers of the town, especially those who introduced steam power, as tyrants and oppressors, and by favoring strikes.[4] Here can be discerned the political significance of the social distress caused by the introduction of machinery into a handloom district. The Conservatives could use it as a weapon against the manufacturers.

An election that revealed other cross-currents in democratic politics was that at Leicester. Sir Joshua Walmsley,

[1] *Newcastle Daily Chronicle*, March 27.
[2] *British Standard*, April 3, 1857. The next highest vote was 2,133.
[3] Account in *British Standard*, April 3, 1857.
[4] *Ibid.*, April 9; *Leeds Mercury*, April 2; *Bell's News*, April 5.

president of the Parliamentary and Financial Reform Association, had been elected here in 1852 despite a Whig-Conservative coalition.[1]   The Liberal schism continued to 1857, when the same coalition succeeded in defeating Walmsley, because of the entrance of another factor.   He was president now of the National Sunday League,[2] a body almost totally composed of workingmen, whose purpose was to effect the opening of museums and art galleries on Sundays.   Because of this, many nonconformist supporters of Walmsley deserted him in this election.[3]   Thus, as social questions were placing obstructions in the way of cohesion between the democracy and middle-class Radicals, so did this question hinder coöperation between the democracy and the nonconformists.   The Sunday question played a large part in several borough elections.

At Bradford the extreme section brought forward Colonel T. P. Thompson, a tried friend of the Chartists in the House, against the candidate chosen by the Liberal party. When the latter withdrew from the contest, the Liberals transferred their support to a Conservative.[4]   Thompson was questioned in his meetings as to his support of such labor legislation as an extension of the Ten Hour Law.   His replies expressed a belief in free contract for labor.[5]   This

[1] *Leeds Mercury*, March 10, 1857.

[2] *British Standard*, March 20, and April 3, 1857.

[3] In 1855 the Sabbatarians had attempted to get legislation enacted to prohibit Sunday trading and the running of trains and steamboats on Sunday and to close all places of refreshment.   The working classes of the metropolis were indignant.   The result of the excitement was three Sunday riots in Hyde Park, which forced the withdrawal of the bill and set the precedent for the use of Hyde Park as a forum for the masses (Frost, *Thirty Years' Recollections*, pp. 257-262).   They also brought Charles Bradlaugh to the front as a democratic champion. A few weeks later a body of workingmen formed the National Sunday League, with Walmsley as president (*Newcastle Weekly Chronicle*, September 14, 1855).

[4] *Leeds Mercury*, March 10.

[5] *Ibid.*, March 19.

election saw the last political stand of Ernest Jones as a Chartist.[1] Toward the close of the year he began an effort to effect a political union of classes, which meant an abandonment of his tenacious class-war policy.

One index of the tendency of working-class opinion is the vote by show of hands at nominations, when non-electors as well as electors could participate. In a number of cases the candidate who won by show of hands lost at the polls. An examination of the programs of these candidates sometimes throws light upon the divergence of working-class opinion from that of the ten-pound electorate. Several significant instances of this have already been noted, as at Manchester, Huddersfield, Kidderminster, and Newcastle. At Sunderland, the largest shipbuilding center in Great Britain, where the shipwrights had just organized in a strong union, an attempt was made to break the grip of the Shipowners' Society upon the parliamentary representation.[2] An extreme Liberal was put out against the candidate of that interest. Much excitement was created, and at the crowded hustings the extremist received the show of hands. He was at the bottom of the poll.[3] The division created here lasted for a decade. Other instances of the defeat of popular candidates who appealed to workingmen in some special way, either by declaring for a very wide franchise or for social legislation, and who received overwhelming majorities by show of hands, were at Hull,[4] Southampton,[5] and New-

[1] He stood for Nottingham, O'Connor's old constituency, and received a great majority of the show of hands, though only 607 votes (*Leeds Mercury*, March 28, and *British Standard*, March 27, and April 3).

[2] *Newcastle Messenger and Advertiser*, January 20, 1857; *Leeds Mercury*, March 17.

[3] *Newcastle Daily Chronicle*, April 3, 1857.

[4] *Leeds Mercury*, March 28.

[5] This was a bye-election a month before the general one. (*British Banner*, February 12; *Newcastle Daily Chronicle*, February 13.)

port (Isle of Wight).[1] In each case a Liberal split was the actual or threatened result. The exact nature of the testimony afforded in this way is hard to determine. Lord Brougham brought the question up in the House of Lords soon after this election and declared that, when the majority by show of hands was in the minority at the polls, it was a majority made up of the lower orders of workingmen, such as day laborers.[2] But if upper workingmen came out at all, as assuredly they did in hotly contested elections, it is probable that they voted with their fellows, except perhaps occasionally, when the latter voted Conservative. The evidence of the vote by show of hands reveals a considerable amount of Conservative sympathy among non-electors. At least one Conservative candidate received the show of hands in 1857 at Leeds, Carlisle, Bolton, Bury, Liverpool, Salford, Kidderminster, Macclesfield, Stockport, Stoke-on-Trent, and Wigan.

Thus far nothing has been said about the metropolis. The contests there developed some interesting features in the way of working-class participation. The most notable instance was that of Greenwich, where what can legitimately be called a local labor party sprang into existence and actually for a short time controlled the parliamentary representation. Within the borough were located the government arsenal and dockyards, employing thousands of workmen. The government influence in the borough was consequently so strong that it usually determined elections through intimidation of voters.[3] Early in 1857 there was a bye-election in which the government candidate was General Sir W. J. Codrington. The workers in the arsenal and dockyards and

---

[1] *British Banner*, February 5, 12. This was also a bye-election.

[2] *Hansard*, CXXXXVII. 910. He was arguing that a six-pound franchise would not alter the representation.

[3] *Christian Weekly News*, January 13, 1857. Also *Borough of Greenwich Free Press*, January 3, 1857.

small tradesmen decided to make a fight for their electoral freedom by demanding a wide extension of the franchise and above all the ballot. They organized the "Greenwich Liberal Association."[1] It held public meetings, interrupted those of Codrington, carried votes of no confidence against him, and placarded the borough with attacks on him. The reports state that at these meetings hundreds of operatives were present.[2] Then the association chose a candidate of its own, Colonel B. W. A. Sleigh, one of the proprietors of the newly established radical *Daily Telegraph,* who declared his belief in manhood suffrage, the ballot, and a single tax on land.[3] Sleigh was denounced by a local Codrington paper as "a Radical and Chartist."[4] Soon cries were heard of the danger of "dividing the Liberal interest."[5] The entire press of the metropolis was against Sleigh.[6] When the nomination took place, the show of hands was in his favor, and on polling day his partisans made great demonstrations, but he received only 1577 votes to 2913 for his opponent.[7]

Within a month after this bye-election the general election came on. At once the Greenwich Liberal Association was in action. One John Townshend, an auctioneer who had been a leading supporter of Sleigh, was chosen as its candidate upon the platform of the ballot and approximately universal suffrage.[8] His candidature was denounced as embodying Toryism, radicalism, Chartism, "and all the other

[1] *Borough of Greenwich Free Press,* August 1, 1857.
[2] *British Standard,* January 16, 1857; *Borough of Greenwich Free Press,* January 3, 14, 1857.
[3] *Bell's News,* January 31; *Borough of Greenwich Free Press,* September 5, 1857; *Newcastle Daily Chronicle,* February 13, 1857.
[4] *Borough of Greenwich Free Press,* January 17, 1857.
[5] *Ibid.,* January 17. Editorial.
[6] *Ibid.,* January 24.
[7] *Ibid.,* February 14. An action for debt was begun against Sleigh during the campaign. It was attributed to government machinations.
[8] *Ibid.,* March 21.

isms."[1] His opponent was Montagu Chambers, the sitting
member, in whose favor it was urged that he had voted for
many bills in the interest of labor, especially the Ten Hour
Act. The "National Association of Organized Trades" sent
out a circular to this effect. But the workingmen continued
their campaign for Townshend, nevertheless, with such success that, to the surprise and disgust of the metropolis, he
was elected.[2]

The triumph of the workingmen was shortlived. Before
six months were out Townshend, like Sleigh before him,
was in the bankruptcy court. His working-class supporters
did not desert him, for they believed his difficulties resulted
largely from his championship of their cause, especially from
his campaign expenses.[3] When his seat was threatened because of a lack of the property qualification, the Association
appointed a committee to raise funds to assist him in fighting
for it.[4] Enthusiastic meetings were held for this purpose.[5]
The whole affair was ridiculed in the respectable press.[6]
Finally his supporters planned to pay him a salary, and by
the end of the year it was announced that all obstacles to
his keeping his seat had been removed by their exertions.[7]

The end of the episode came toward the middle of the
next year, when Townshend was declared bankrupt and his
seat vacant. The London correspondent of the *Newcastle
Daily Chronicle* wrote that feeling was so intense among
workingmen he believed that had it not been for the property

[1] *Borough of Greenwich Free Press,* March 28.

[2] *Borough of Greenwich Free Press,* April 4. One measure he had
advocated was the placing of all taxes on the rich (*British Standard,*
April 3, 1857).

[3] *Ibid.,* September 5, 1857. Also the London letter in the *Newcastle
Daily Chronicle,* August 27, 1858.

[4] *Borough of Greenwich Free Press,* September 12, 1857.

[5] *Ibid.,* September 19. Also *South London News,* October 10, 1857.

[6] *Punch* and the *Standard* quoted in *Borough of Greenwich Free
Press,* October 24.

[7] The *Pancras Reporter,* November 21, 1857.

qualification they would have put forward a workingman for the seat and would have supported him while in parliament.[1] This sporadic effort at political self-assertion ended thus in futility. Nevertheless, it can be safely assumed that it had its part in emphasizing the increasing significance of the working-class factor in the general political situation.

Another noteworthy metropolitan contest was that for Tower Hamlets, where George Jacob Holyoake, ex-Chartist, promoter of coöperation and secularism, and a foremost advocate of a Liberal-Labor alliance—altogether one of the most able and constructive of working-class leaders in the third quarter of the century—stood as a Liberal-Labor candidate. In giving an account of this candidacy in 1868, when trying to repeat it at Birmingham, Holyoake said that in 1857 the idea of labor representation was scarcely conceivable.[2] He was evidently referring to upper-class opinion; he went on to say that John Stuart Mill was the first distinguished person to approve of the idea, having sent him a contribution to his election expenses. His platform[3] was chiefly Radical: residential manhood suffrage, the ballot, triennial parliaments, equal electoral districts, the abolition of Church rates. Its only distinctive features were its proposal to use waste lands in order to extinguish pauperism; security to married women's property; and the opening of museums on Sundays. His biographer states that his chief object was to work for the substitution of affirmation for the oath.[4] The fact is that, in spite of Holyoake's later protestations, this candidature was preëminently a Radical and not a labor candidature. As he himself stated, it was directed against a

[1] August 27, 1858.
[2] "Working-Class Representation. Its Conditions and Consequences." An address to the Electors of Birmingham, October 16, 1868, by G. J. Holyoake, London, 1868.
[3] Ibid. Reviews the earlier campaign.
[4] McCabe, Life and Letters of G. J. Holyoake, I. 283. Also G. J. Holyoake, Deliberate Liberalism, London, 1886 (a pamphlet).

"stationary Liberal," Sir William Clay; consequently when "a more robust Radical" appeared in the person of A. S. Ayrton, he withdrew.[1] Certainly Holyoake's later assertion that this was the first claim ever made to represent Labor in Parliament is not justified.[2] Such a claim was much more distinctly asserted by William Newton in 1852. He was directly connected with the most important trade-union of the day; he stood against both regular parties; he definitely tried to make the election turn on labor, as distinct from Liberal, issues; and he actually went to the poll, receiving a very respectable vote.[3]

Other populous metropolitan constituencies revealed in this election the influence of labor or of democracy. At Lambeth the largest vote polled in the whole election was given to William Roupell, who advocated a residential suffrage, the ballot, educational reform, and the social advancement of the working classes through such means as a shortening of the hours of labor and abolition of the truck system.[4] His opponent's defeat was attributed by a local paper to his having antagonized the working classes by advocating the truck system, opposing the shortening of hours, and the remission of the income tax upon small incomes.[5] Extreme Liberals were elected in Southwark and Finsbury. All the Liberal candidates, in their official advertisements, pronounced for an extension of the franchise.

That the public considered reform to be an issue is proved by comments made during and after the election. The

---

[1] From a pamphlet, *G. J. Holyoake to W. H. Brown*, London and Leicester, no date.

[2] Holyoake, *Sixty Years of an Agitator's Life*, II. 42.

[3] A. W. Humphrey in *A History of Labour Representation*, pp. 2-7, accepts Holyoake's as a labor candidacy, asserting that Mill instigated it. The latter claim is not ever stated by Holyoake himself. For Newton's candidacy in 1852, see above, pp. 100 ff.

[4] *South London News*, March 14, 21; April 4, 1857.

[5] *Ibid.*, April 4.

South London News, exulting in the defeat of Quakerism and the Peace Society, exclaimed: "Let Palmerston bring in a noble measure of Reform and he will be able to defy any coalition so long as he lives."[1] A nonconformist paper remarked, "Now we shall see if Palmerston is really a Liberal by his attitude toward reform."[2] The *Leeds Mercury* wrote:[3] "The growing feeling in favour of Parliamentary Reform, which was checked by the war, has manifested itself in the most unmistakable form during the course of the last month," and Palmerston would not be allowed to sleep on his laurels. The *Pancras Reporter* caustically remarked as to Palmerston's reform projects, "blessed is the man who expecteth little, for he will not be disappointed."[4] During the campaign warnings had been uttered. The Radical *Bell's News* considered that if Palmerston should be swept into power, reform would be shelved,[5] and after the election it declared all mention of progress now mere humbug.[6] The *Christian Weekly News* had urged electors to consider Palmerston's constant opposition to that most vital of all questions, reform.[7] A letter to the *Daily News* urged Liberals to "take guarantees" before electing Palmerston.[8] The Middlesex Reform Association urged support both of Palmerston's foreign policy and of reform candidates.[9] At Huddersfield a large public meeting defeated a motion of confidence in Palmerston "because he is opposed to reform and a determined opponent of the ballot."[10] One London

[1] April 11, 1857.
[2] *Christian Weekly News,* March 31, 1857.
[3] April 11, 1857.
[4] December 5, 1857.
[5] March 21, 1857.
[6] March 29.
[7] March 10.
[8] Quoted in *Leeds Mercury,* March 10.
[9] *West Middlesex Advertiser,* March 14.
[10] *Christian Weekly News,* March 17.

paper,[1] after the election, believed that Palmerston would
not be able to resist the growing demand for reform, and
another[2] expressed the hope that he would bring in a wide
measure.   The *Morning Star*, exponent of Radical views,
was urging the reform issue immediately after the election.[3]
Sidney Herbert wrote that reform was the only subject of
public interest in the next few months, though he did not
believe a large measure was desired by a majority of the
people.   "Palmerston hates Reform as he hates the Devil.
He only dislikes peace because it must lead to it.   But
the country has returned a Parliament to support Palmerston and Reform, and the two must be brought into harmony, or the former will go to the wall."[4]

One other feature of this election should be mentioned;
namely, that this was the first time that nonconformists
attempted to adopt an independent electoral policy.[5]   An
Anti-State Church Association had been formed in 1842, but
the real beginning of their organized political activity was
in 1853, when the Society for the Liberation of Religion
from State Patronage and Control was organized, followed
in 1855 by the formation of an Electoral Committee under
Samuel Morley, a wealthy manufacturer of Nottingham.[6]
Upon the dissolution of parliament in 1857, the Liberation
Society issued an address to electors requesting support for
candidates advocating franchise, administrative, and fiscal
reform, and the liberation of religion.   "No candidate for

---

[1] *Borough of Greenwich Free Press,* April 11.

[2] *South London News,* May 9.

[3] Hobson, *Cobden, the International Man,* p. 208.

[4] Lord Stanmore, *Sidney Herbert,* II. 89.

[5] They were much concerned over the government grant to May-
nooth College, a Catholic institution in Ireland, over the Sunday question, and the abolition of Church rates, for which a bill had passed the
Commons in 1855 and 1856, failing in the Lords.

[6] An account is given in "Electoral Action, with suggestions for its
continuance.   A paper read at the Fourth Conference of the Society for
the Liberation of Religion, etc., by E. S. Pryce, May 7, 1856."

your suffrages who desires these ecclesiastical changes is likely to undervalue the political reforms to which reference has been made."[1] Dissenting journals urged independent action in the election.[2] There appears to be little evidence of such action having been taken, but that the Liberationists were a constantly increasing factor in Liberal politics henceforth is certain.[3]

[1] *Leeds Mercury*, March 12, 1857.
[2] *Ibid.*, March 28. *British Banner*, March 19.
[3] What evidence there is of their influence in this election is chiefly in their opposition to the Sunday League.

CHAPTER V

THE INFLUENCE OF SOCIAL AND ECONOMIC FACTORS UPON THE REVIVAL OF THE REFORM QUESTION

Turning aside from the election of 1857, which reintroduced in an unmistakable fashion the question of an extension of the franchise into English domestic politics and which cast much light upon the cross-currents through which the question would have to find its way, we must now consider certain other features of these years at the end of the decade that affected this and all related questions.

All through the year 1857 there were occurring in the metropolis demonstrations of the unemployed, chiefly of the building trades, that evoked expressions of radical beliefs. These agitations were followed at the end of the year by the dislocation caused by a severe panic, and it in turn was succeeded by the great builders' strike of 1859-60. Thus there were economic disturbances and conflicts of capital and labor, with their attendant theories as to the solution of social problems, that reacted powerfully upon the political situation. Since the Preston strike of 1853-4, there had been no great industrial struggle. As the Webbs express it: "For a brief period it seemed as if peace was henceforth to prevail over the industrial world."[1] But at the moment that the Crimean War ended there began again simultaneously industrial conflict and a movement for enfranchising the working classes. An intimate relationship was bound to develop between the two.

Stagnation in the building trades by the end of 1856 had become distressing and apparently was without prospect of relief. Early in January, 1857, a meeting of about a hun-

[1] *History of Trade Unionism,* p 227.

dred unemployed builders decided to call a meeting of all the unemployed in order to form a "National Association of the Unemployed Operatives."[1] W. J. Macheath, who had taken the lead in the bread riots two years before, organized the meeting, which was convened under the auspices of the Lord Mayor in Smithfield market. About ten thousand were said to have been present; Hugh Pierce, a carpenter, presided.[2] The speeches dwelt on the extent of unemployment[3] and the remedies proposed. They centered their attack upon the system of poor relief, which involved such humiliating conditions as stone-breaking or oakum-picking—the so-called "labor tests"—which they maintained that self-respecting, skilled operatives ought not to have to submit to when out of work through no fault of their own. They insisted that they were entitled to relief at the hands of the national government, that the latter should either provide employment upon the waste land, furnishing loans for draining and tilling it, or assist emigration. The chairman sought to strengthen his argument by the assertion that labor created all the wealth of the country. Resolutions were carried voicing these various demands, and also advising the working classes themselves to seek to abolish over-time and to establish a six-day week as a partial remedy for unemployment. It was suggested that a movement for an eight-hour day be started. The meeting concluded with the formation of a "National Association of Unemployed Operatives" and the decision to hold weekly meetings.

In the course of the discussion, the question of politics was introduced in spite of the contrary wishes of those in

[1] *Bell's News,* January 10, 1857.

[2] *Ibid.,* January 17, and *British Standard,* January 16.

[3] It was said that a quarter of a million were out of work in the metropolis.

charge of the meeting.[1]   A house-painter declared that the
House of Commons was in the hands of men who purposely
caused unemployment in order to keep labor redundant and
wages low.   Would they, therefore, aid emigration and thus
raise wages?   Another speaker, supporting this argument,
moved that "until the people obtain their political and social
rights they can never grapple with the evils under which they
suffer."

The *Newcastle Weekly Chronicle* discussed this meeting
in an editorial of great length under the heading, "Socialism
at Smithfield."   It recognized the fact as serious, that while
peace had given great impetus to business and speculation,
yet in the wealthiest city in the world ten thousand workingmen should meet to consider how to save their families from
starvation.   Nevertheless, it declared, the doctrines there
enunciated revealed

the startling fact that education has as yet done little to remove the
barriers of prejudice and ignorance which separate class from class
in this country.   The old fallacies still hold their ground; capital is
still denounced as antagonistic to labour, and the possession of a
"bit of land" still declared to be the infallible remedy for all the ills
the poor man is heir to.   All men are equal, and no one has a right
to a greater share of the earth than another; this is the popular
theory.   . . .   But this plan of redistribution of property   . . .
is looked upon as a last resource; the workmen's chief complaint is
against their masters.   Capitalists appear to be considered by the
poor as their natural foes; they are supposed to engross all the
profits of industry, leaving it to others to provide the labour for
which so scanty a recompense is given.[2]

The London correspondent to this paper insisted that these
meetings were a more significant sign of the times than mere
party politics.

Other great meetings of the unemployed followed.
Bands of men out of work roved the streets of London.

―――――――――

[1] At the outset it had been announced that the meeting was not to be
diverted toward politics by the agents of Bronterre O'Brien or any such
person.
[2] January 23, 1857.

Conditions in the manufacturing districts were described as even worse.[1] Ernest Jones gathered together an audience of ten thousand men on his own account and preached to them once more his land and Chartist gospel.[2] The *Times* had an editorial on his speech, a column and a half long, in which it adjured the British artisan to "avoid political agitation as he would the plague."[3]

Conditions failed to improve in the course of the year, and in the autumn came a panic that spread distress over the whole country.[4] The increase in the number of paupers in the large towns over the figures for 1857 had by 1858 in one instance reached as high as 160.02%.[5] Wages were reduced in many industries. Though a general recovery began after a few months, the effect of the crisis continued to be felt all through the year 1858.

Those of the working classes who felt the hard times most severely were deeply stirred by the conviction that some means of permanent relief should be effected by government action. In Birmingham the unemployed held several meetings in the spring of 1858 to call upon the government to aid emigration. A memorial to the Queen was adopted and sent to Bright for presentation. He, in his reply, took occasion to drive home once more his argument for fiscal reform by attributing conditions largely to rising taxes and government expenditure.[6] Later in the year the newly formed Trades Council in Glasgow invited Bright to attend a meeting on emigration. In declining, he stated they had no right to

[1] *Bell's News,* February 21, 1857.
[2] Described in a pamphlet, *Evenings with the People,* No. 7.
[3] February 18, 1858.
[4] Beecroft, M.P. for Leeds, stated in parliament that this panic was far more severe than that of 1847. (*Hansard,* CLII. 68.)
[5] These figures are for Preston. In Manchester the increase was 122.87%. See W. R. Callender, *The Commercial Crisis of 1857. Its Cause and Results,* London, 1858.
[6] *Newcastle Weekly Chronicle,* April 2, 1858.

government aid, and to such he would never give his consent.[1]   The meeting was held notwithstanding, and appropriate resolutions were passed.[2]   Thus did economic disturbance stir up from the social depths specters of fallacious theories to frighten those among the middle classes who would help workingmen to political emancipation.

Not only were the unemployed raising the question of poor relief, but in the large cities, especially in London, the question of the area of rating for the poor had become serious, and it too was regarded as possessing dangerous possibilities.   The increasing concentration of the poor in certain parishes owing to improvements made in others lightened the burden of the poor rate on the rich and increased it on the poor as long as each parish was responsible for its own paupers.   Since 1848 proposals had been made in parliament to extend the area of rating, but every time they had been frustrated by the alarm felt lest any change become the first step toward a national system of rating.[3]   In 1857 a serious movement was set on foot in London to extend the area of rating to the whole of the metropolis.   An association was formed for the purpose.[4]   A. S. Ayrton became spokesman for it in the House.   The debates again revealed the fears of the propertied class.   A Liberal Chancellor of the Exchequer compared the whole proposition to the national workshops in Paris, while a Conservative President of the Poor Law Board pronounced the measure communistic, since it aimed to raise money from the rich and give it to the poor.[5]

[1] *Beacon and Christian Times,* September 22, 1858.
[2] *Whitehaven Herald,* September 25, 1858.
[3] See debate on Chas. Buller's bill in 1848, *Hansard,* C. 800 ff.   For the whole question see Mackay, *op. cit.,* III. 342-364.
[4] There is a pamphlet in the British Museum called *The Association for Promoting the Equalization of the Poor Rate and Uniformity of Assessment Throughout the Metropolitan Districts, March 17, 1857. An address.*
[5] *Hansard,* CXLV. 1403 ff.; CL. 509-16.

In connection with this matter of parochial interest, it may be mentioned that there appears to have been a fairly widespread effort in the populous London parishes, as well as in certain large provincial towns, to democratize the local government by abolishing plural voting and property qualifications imposed upon members of certain local boards. In the large working-class parish of Shoreditch, an association had been formed in 1853 to do away with these obstacles to the "rights of the poor."[1] In discussions at the meetings of the association, allusion was made to the existence of similar bodies in other parishes. In 1857 a certain local London paper noted much activity of these associations.[2] In the North similar bodies were numerous by 1857. At North Shields a painter presided over the first meeting of the Parochial Reform Association.[3] In Newcastle the Ratepayers' Association in this year was beginning a vigorous campaign against the ruling cliques, and, itself a radically democratic body, it soon played an important part in democratizing the local government of the borough and in winning parliamentary representation from the Whigs.[4]

Another factor in the social and economic situation, however, was of more importance politically than all others combined. That factor was the builders' nine-hour movement of 1859-61. The influence of this agitation upon all political questions involving the working classes was most important at the time and far-reaching in its ultimate consequences. It was distinctly the starting point of a new phase of the labor question.

[1] *Shoreditch Parochial Reformer,* October, 1853. Only two issues of this are in the British Museum.

[2] *East London Observer,* November 7, 1857. It mentions Wm. Newton (no doubt of the Amalgamated Engineers) as president of the Tower Hamlets Association.

[3] *Newcastle Weekly Chronicle,* September 24; October 2, 1857.

[4] See below, pp. 182 and 249, and above, p. 119.

During the fifties organized labor had been comparatively obscure and ineffective so far as the public mind
judged it.   Beginning with the builders' strike for, a nine-
hour day, the ruling classes realized that the vague, inchoate,
hybrid labor agitations of the forties and early fifties—half
trade-unionist and half Chartist, or here trade-unionist and
there Chartist—had given place to definite programs backed
by strong organization.   The impression made upon the public was profound.   The contest tended also to make trade-
unionists themselves more conscious of their industrial power
and to reveal to the leaders the need of political action in
order to safeguard and promote their organized activities.
Such an epochal conflict served as a flaring torch to reveal
the vaguely known lineaments of social and industrial forces
and enforced a distinct registering of them upon the consciousness of the different social groups.

It was in 1857, the year of the revival of the reform
question, that the carpenters in London renewed their demand for a nine-hour day.[1]   This move on their part was
certainly connected with the stagnation and unemployment
in the building trades, which has been already referred to.
At the beginning of the next year opposition by the master
builders led to the formation by the workmen of a joint
committee of five building trades, known as the Conference
of the United Building Trades.   This committee directed
the movement, which soon attracted nation-wide attention.[2]
Its leading member was George Potter, who for two decades
was to be a conspicuous figure in labor affairs.   By the middle of 1859 negotiations with the employers had completely
broken down, and the Master Builders' Association closed

[1] See Webb, *op. cit.*, pp. 228-32, for an account of the main features
of the struggle.

[2] A history of the movement up to August was given in the *Times*
of August 5, 1858.

down their establishments,[1] throwing twenty-four thousand men out of work.   The masters determined upon an effort to break up all combinations by forcing the men to sign a document renouncing trade societies before being taken back into employment.   A week later the Master Builders sent a deputation to the home secretary to ask that the masters be fortified by an expression of opinion in parliament or by the government.   They suggested an examination of the rules of trade societies to determine wherein they restricted labor, with a view to compelling the removal of such rules.[2]   The home secretary replied that the government could not act.

The moment the struggle took on the character of a war on trade-unionism, workingmen all over the country were concerned.   In London the trades in general took up the cause of the builders.   Conferences of Trades' Delegates were held.[3]   Addresses were issued to the working classes of the kingdom on "Labour in its Trial Time."[4]   The Conference sent a deputation to the provinces to agitate a nine-hour movement among the trades and to collect money.[5] "Trades Committees" were organized in all the chief towns, and money came in in large amounts to aid the builders.[6] The Amalgamated Engineers alone gave three thousand pounds.   A sense of unity was quickened in all the ranks of labor.   George Potter, speaking often through *Reynolds's Newspaper,* uttered doctrines that sounded ill to the watchful and apprehensive upper classes.   The strike was a battle of "the weak against the strong."   The response of the trades with money was "pregnant with the brightest hopes

[1] The men had struck in only one (Webb, *op. cit.,* p. 229).

[2] *Leeds Mercury,* August 11, 1859.   Also the *Builders' Salesman and Mechanics' Advertiser,* August 20, 1859.

[3] *Builders' Salesman,* etc., September 17, 24, 1859.

[4] The *Mechanics' Advertiser,* September 10, 1859.   (This is the same as the *Builders' Salesman.*   The title varied.)

[5] *Builders' Salesman,* August 20, 1859.

[6] The total amount was twenty-three thousand pounds.   Webb, *op. cit.,* p. 230.

of the future union and emancipation of the working classes."[1] When it became certain the masters would have to withdraw "the document," he hailed it as a "triumph of enslaved labour over usurping capital";[2] and when the triumph was assured, he thanked the workingmen of the kingdom for their defence of "the fiercely assailed rights of your class. . . . These sacrifices so cheerfully made, and the triumph which they have enabled us to win, we hail as the earnest of that complete victory of labour over its present oppressors which we believe the future to have in store for us."[3]

The reaction of the upper and middle classes to the great contest, with its accompanying features of class coöperation and class feeling, was for the most part antagonistic. The *Times,* upon the renewal of the nine-hour demand after the withdrawal of the "document," warned trade-unions that persistence in such tactics was making public opinion hostile; that this "was very evident throughout the course of last autumn. It cropped up repeatedly in parliamentary discussions and in the speeches of public men."[4] Adam Black, M.P. for Edinburgh, delivered a set attack upon trade-unions to the operatives of that place, which was answered two weeks later by an address delivered to them by William Newton at the request of the Amalgamated Engineers.[5] The *Edinburgh Review* wrote of the "irresponsible government" of unions, which destroyed the liberty of the English citizen; while the *Times* pronounced trade-unionism "an ignorant and inquisitorial despotism."[6] The Derbyite

[1] *Reynolds's Newspaper,* January 1, 1860.
[2] *Ibid.,* January 22, 1860.
[3] *Ibid.,* March 11.
[4] Quoted in *Reynolds's Newspaper,* May 27, 1860.
[5] *Journal of Typographic Arts,* April 2, 1860.
[6] Both quoted by T. J. Dunning in his defence of trade combinations, *Trade Unions and Strikes; Their Philosophy and Intention.* London, 1860, pp. 8 and 9.

Morning Herald asserted that the success of the nine-hour demand would drive England's trade from the world market.[1]

Frederick Harrison and the Positivists saw deep import in the struggle. Harrison described his impression of a great mass meeting held in the course of it:

What an abyss of social tyranny, wrong, and false witness it opened. One seemed to be living in the midst of an oppressed race bent on their own emancipation and improvement, and yet kept down by the power of wealth and by literary sophistry. How society seems to me to be living over a mine. . . . The little incident of the "Builders' Strike" was, of course, but a drop in the ocean. It opened to me a vision of a great battle going on all around and beneath us.[2]

Professor Beesly, discussing trade-unions in the *Westminster Review*,[3] declared that this strike had such marked features "that it seems to have a chance of standing in the same relation to the coming industrial régime, as the meeting of the States General in 'eighty-nine does to the subsequent history of Europe."

The discussion of trade-unionism became more serious and thorough in all quarters as a result of the light into which it was now brought. The builders had the good sense to seek publicity.[4] Their cause received brilliant defence at the hands of Positivists and Christian Socialists.[5] The National Association for the Promotion of Social Science published a searching report on trade combinations in 1860, contributed to by such friends of working men as Hughes, Ludlow, Maurice, Henry Fawcett, and W. E. Forster.[6] At the same time T. J. Dunning, of the Bookbinders,

[1] Quoted in *Reynolds's Newspaper*, June 3, 1860.
[2] *Autobiographic Memoirs*, London, 1911, I. 252-3.
[3] October 1, 1861.
[4] *Builders' Salesman* and *Mechanics Advertiser* (September 24, 1859) states that this brought sympathy and was the stronghold of the men.
[5] Webb, *op. cit.*, p. 246.
[6] *Ibid.*, p. 227, note 2. Also F. Harrison, *National and Social Problems*, New York, 1908, p. 423; and *Bookbinders' Trade Circular*, July 10, 1861.

published his able discussion of trade-unions in his trade circular, since no "respectable" publisher would handle it.[1]

The nine-hour movement was renewed by the building trades as soon as the first victory over the masters was won. Potter, unquestionably feeling himself about to embark on a crusade for the cause of labor, strove to make the movement national.   A conference of delegates from most of the industrial centers was held at Derby, an association was formed, and plans were mapped out.[2] Builders' strikes were resumed in London and elsewhere in 1861, and they provoked such increasingly hostile comments in the press[3] that the *Spectator* was led to declare that workingmen were justified in believing that their case could not get a hearing, and that this would increase the chasm between classes.[4] So embittered was the antagonism becoming that Frederick Harrison, in a letter to the *Daily News,* said:

Other trades, especially the engineers, are taking up their case—meetings are being held and subscriptions are being raised in the provinces.   The whole apparatus of workmen's associations is being called into full play.   It is creating, in fact, a sort of union amongst unions.   In a word, the contest is becoming the common cause of all working men, and what began in a local dispute is growing into a great class struggle.[5]

The reference here may have been in part to the newly organized London Trades Council, which was an outgrowth of the strike and lockout.[6] Beginning in July, 1860, within a year it had gained the adhesion of the strongest unions. George Howell, who was assisting Potter in organizing the nine-hour movement, became its secretary, and it began to

[1] So stated in the introduction to the pamphlet, in which the articles were soon published (London, 1860).

[2] *Reynolds's Newspaper,* January 27, 1861. Also Geo. Howell, *Labour Legislation,* etc., p. 134.

[3] Many quoted in *Reynolds's.*

[4] Quoted in *Reynolds's,* July 7, 1861.

[5] *Ibid.,* August 1, 1861, quoting the *News.*

[6] Webb, *op. cit.,* pp. 243-5.

participate in London and even national labor questions in such a way as to become a highly important influence. It became an instrument of trade-unionist political activity.[1]

The builders' strike in London eventually ended in a compromise.[2] Potter's attempted national organization came to nothing. Its conferences, however, had contributed not a little to the development of a spirit of coöperation among labor leaders all over the country.[3] This spirit, from 1860 on, was an increasingly important factor in the industrial and political situation. The organization of numerous trade councils between 1858 and 1867 tended toward the same result.[4]

This growing consolidation of the trade-union movement and the greater influence thereby accruing to its leaders undoubtedly struck with consternation the middle and upper classes. So many developments were pointing to the increased weight of organized labor that they indicated an element of effectiveness in the ranks of the working classes that had hitherto been wanting. The student of trade-unionism can see that in those years the movement was advancing toward an acceptance of middle-class principles,[5] but it may well be doubted if the middle classes had at the time a very clear conception of this fact. To them the basic principles of unionism were themselves anathema, not to be palliated by conciliatory explanations. There was on both sides an absence of consistent reasoning. Trade-unionism might argue from the principles of freedom of action, but it was based upon restraint and collectivism; middle-class

[1] One of its first acts was political; it forced the government to withdraw the soldiers it had lent as strike-breakers at the Chelsea barracks. (Webb, *op. cit.*, p. 247. Also *Reynolds's Newspaper*, August 4, 1861.)

[2] Webb, *op. cit.*, p. 246.

[3] So states Howell, *op. cit.*, p. 134.

[4] Webb, *op. cit.*, p. 242 and note 1.

[5] Webb, *op. cit.*, p. 226.

opponents would be bound logically to concede to workingmen the right to combine, but they saw as the ultimate aim
interference with their own control of industry, their own
unfettered enterprise.

In addition, when an attempt is made to analyze the
opinion of those years it must be remembered that opinion
then, as always, was undiscriminating.   Middle-class politicians or journalists could not with the clear eye of the
twentieth-century historian discern the more significant leaders of the labor world from the rest.   They inevitably fixed
their attention upon those who figured most prominently,
and of these in the early 'sixties the chief was George Potter, organizer of the nine-hour movement.   There is no question that to the average member of parliament Potter typi-
fied trade-unionism, and Potter was militant.

In another industrial field than the building trades, developments were likewise taking place that were to be of consequence for the political world as well as the economic.
The miners were organizing and frankly adopting a policy
of political action.   In 1860 the miners' organization secured
the passage of a valuable Act for the Regulation and Inspection of Mines, and in 1863 the National Association of
Miners was formed with a full political program and political
methods outlined.[1]

The middle classes, in their survey of working-class opinion and their estimate of the possible uses to which the vote
would be put, undoubtedly were much influenced by such
evidence as the nine-hour movement, the organization of
trade councils, the agitation for state-aided emigration and
the use of the waste lands by the unemployed, and the wax-
ing power and self-consciousness of the miners with their
belief in state interference.   Cobden in a letter to William

[1] *Transactions and Results of the National Association of Coal, Lime,
and Iron-stone Miners, held at Leeds, November, 1863.* London, 1864.

Williams, M.P. for Lambeth, in 1858 stated that many feared to give the vote to workingmen because of the unsound views on wages which they would try to enforce by act of parliament. For himself, while he doubted the existence of "this monster 'Socialism' " among the workingmen, yet he believed there was "a tendency among many of the working-class to regard their interests as separate from and antagonistic to those of their employers"—a false view, which he believed already showed signs of giving way before experience. That Cobden was surmounting obstacles which he recognized as formidable to many and was abandoning his fear of democracy of a few years before is plain from his concluding words:

The longer I live the greater is my reverence for, and trust in, the mass of humanity. . . . My own opinion is, that if the working classes had votes they would be quite as Conservative in their tendencies as any other section of the community. They would not separate themselves from other classes, but range themselves under influential leaders as they do now.[1]

A description of the conditions prevailing in England about 1860 would not be complete that neglected to take into account, in addition to economic conditions, trade disputes and manifestations of workingmen's interest in politics, their unabated enthusiasm for the cause of liberty abroad as well. This last was a prime factor in keeping alive and developing the political consciousness of workingmen, even though it did somewhat divert their democratic zeal from attacks on political privilege at home. Italy excited their profound interest and sympathy. The election of 1859 turned upon the two questions of Italy and reform, upon both of which the Conservatives stood condemned in the eyes of the people. When Palmerston came back, it was felt that the cause of Italian unification was in safer

[1] Quoted in *Christian Times*, January 24, 1858.

hands than in those of the pro-Austrian Conservatives. The question of Italy, George Howell testified later, had important consequences in the political labor movement, for it was the means of bringing labor leaders together more closely and of interesting them more keenly in politics.[1]

[1] *Labour Legislation,* etc., p. 140.

CHAPTER VI

JOHN BRIGHT AND REFORM

Toward the end of 1857 John Bright, defeated in the general election at Manchester, was returned as member for Birmingham. Just as Gladstone's transference from Oxford to South Lancashire in 1865 was a momentous event in the political history of England, so that of Bright from Manchester to Birmingham was significant in the history of the reform question. Birmingham, parent of the Political Unions of 1831-2, was now to be the center of the Radical movement that was ultimately to mean urban democracy in England. The third and last service of this great city of the Midlands to the cause of Liberalism was to be, still later, the evolution of the caucus as a means to harness and drive this democracy. For two thirds of the nineteenth century the name of Birmingham was as intimately associated with Radical politics as that of Manchester was with middle-class economics. Cobden remarked in 1856 that the people of Lancashire were growing conservative and aristocratic with prosperity[1] and in 1857 that the new democratic appeal in Lancashire had failed. Birmingham, on the contrary, he regarded as much freer from aristocratic snobbery and as possessing a fairer appreciation of democracy.[2] This contrast he attributed to the fact that Birmingham was not a city of great capitalists, as Manchester was, and that consequently there was no such wide gulf there between masters and men.[3] One student of Chartism points out that Engels had declared the work-people of

[1] Hobson, *Cobden, the International Man*, p. 180.
[2] *Ibid.*, p. 193. Also Morley, *Cobden*, p. 443.
[3] Hobson, *op. cit.*, p. 194.

Manchester to be the most thoroughly proletarianized in all England in the forties and hence strongly Chartist, while in Birmingham the artisans were partially independent; hence Birmingham was Radical in politics and not Chartist.[1] Holyoake, in his autobiography, bears witness to the sound Radicalism of the town, saying that the people here had a steadier attachment to independence and liberty than anywhere else in England.[2] Conditions in Birmingham, therefore, accorded well with the basic principles of that advance guard of Liberalism of which Bright was head and chief—the union of the middle and working classes upon a wide basis of political democracy. Hence when, in 1857, Bright was chosen as member for Birmingham, it might have been recognized as a prophecy.

In tracing the history of the reform question in the decade before 1867 it is helpful to observe two lines of development. One is that which had Bright for a leader; the other was more distinctly in the hands of workingmen themselves through the formation of associations and the promotion of reform propaganda. It is of interest to note the various points of approach or divergence between the two and to analyze the contribution of each to the final result.

After the election of 1857 the government promised that the reform question would be taken up the next year. Certain members of parliament, therefore, and other Radicals[3] formed a Parliamentary Reform Committee, with Roebuck as chairman, for the purpose of enlisting all reformers under the banner of household suffrage and the other demands of Hume's "Little Charter," plus the aboli-

---

[1] Slosson, *Decline of the Chartist Movement*, p. 162.
[2] *Sixty Years of an Agitators' Life*, I. 34.
[3] Others who participated were Miall, Fox, and Samuel Morley (the nonconformist). (Duncombe, *Life and Correspondence of Thomas Slingsby Duncombe*, II. 213). The organization was formed in June, 1857.

tion of property qualifications for members of parliament,[1] precisely the program of the now defunct Parliamentary and Financial Reform Association. The movement made little headway, however, until Bright, after a brief illness, placed himself at the head of it in 1858. This, says Trevelyan, marked a new era in the history of the question. Henceforth, until 1867, it possessed a vital significance. Hitherto reform bills had been a matter for the House of Commons rather than the country, and parties had meant little by introducing them. Now the movement was to be outside the House, and Bright was to lead the two industrial classes on a "democratic crusade against the privileged orders."[2]   Says Trevelyan:

The hour had come and the man. The era of Chartism and mutual class suspicion had passed away; far in the future lay the time when "labour politics" would come into collision with "middle-class conservatism." The times were ripe for a union of the Radical part of the middle classes with the working men.[3]

But that this union was not easy to effect, and that class antagonism had not wholly vanished, will appear from a close analysis of the movement begun in 1858.

The reasons for the inauguration of this agitation by Bright were several. The considerations that had weighed with him in 1848 weighed still. The Crimean War had sharply revealed the inefficiency of the aristocratic government and had emphasized the value of peace as an element in the nation's fiscal policy. It is true that the masses had displayed a war spirit that must have shaken Bright's confidence in democracy as a pacifist influence, but he relied on education in the dire consequences of war to act as a corrective. The middle classes were still under-represented in parliament through the preponderance of small boroughs

[1] *Borough of Greenwich Free Press*, November 21, 1857.
[2] Trevelyan, *Bright*, pp. 267-8.
[3] Trevelyan, *Bright*, p. 271.

and agricultural counties in the House of Commons and the monopoly of the House of Lords by the territorial aristocracy. The conflict still presented itself to him as in the days of Corn Law repeal as one between the nation and the landlords. By arousing the nation to a consciousness of the community of its interests and the extent of its might, the work begun in 1846 could be completed. Only then could Bright visualize an England such as the actual distribution of social and economic weight seemed to him to demand. Furthermore, the privileged Church, like the privileged aristocracy, could be forced to surrender only to an all-compelling force such as an effective national party could exert.

Added to these fundamental arguments for an agitation for franchise reform, were others arising from considerations of party tactics. Three times within the decade had a government promised a bill, only to abandon the project each time. Palmerston had just resigned under a pledge, which the Derby government had renewed. The situation appeared to reformers to be critical. Unless they were vigilant, Disraeli might effect an alliance with the Whigs to redeem the pledge by passing a wholly inadequate bill. On the other hand, the Conservatives, a minority in the House ardently desirous of retaining office, might be coerced by the Radicals, if supported by a popular agitation, into conceding a large measure of reform. A Tory surrender to an agitation such as had occurred in 1829 and 1846, and was to occur in 1867, was not an impossibility in 1858. The Radicals wished to avoid above all things a collision with the Derby government, lest Palmerston be returned to office and reform be postponed indefinitely. They believed that Derby would concede much in order to keep office.[1]

[1] *Newcastle Weekly Chronicle,* April 2, 1858, and *Whitehaven Herald,* April 17, 1858, in an account of a Reformers' Conference.

A final inducement to Bright to enter upon this movement was the fact that the working classes themselves were interested in the question. A sense of betrayal would certainly possess them if the issue were trifled with much longer. They were speaking out already in their meetings and associations. It was essential for the welfare of the state that the question should be dealt with in a statesmanlike manner, in the interest of all classes, and not in response to an angry class demand. The Chartist movement had fixed this latter danger indelibly in the minds of politicians as a possibility, in the event of another conjunction of severe commercial depression with an active feeling of resentment and distrust toward the ruling classes. To concede what was just because it was just was a wiser policy than grudgingly to concede it to threats of violence. Bright hoped to bring parliament to the point of making such concessions as should have the appearance at least and the effect of concessions to justice. In reality, as his inauguration of a popular agitation shows, he knew the concessions, if made, would be in response to the hint of the reserve power residing in the nation that this agitation would furnish.

Another part of Bright's tactics was for reformers to embody their demands in a reform bill of their own, as an illustration to the government of what they would expect, and to organize a vigorous agitation for it, which should threaten the independent action of reformers unless the government measure should satisfy them.

The campaign opened at Birmingham in October, 1858. Bright, having warned his hearers of the danger of a "country gentleman's Reform Bill," demanded why reformers should not have their own reform bill, have it introduced into parliament and "supported with all the strength of the great national party; and if it be a bill sensibly better than the bill that is being prepared for us in Downing Street, why should we not, with all the unanimity of which we are capable, by public meetings, by petitions, and when the proper time comes by presenting ourselves at the polling booths, do everything in our power to pass that measure into law?"[1]

The vital point in the program, which was to serve as a basis of the "great national party" which Bright hoped to call into being, was now, as in 1850: how far should the suffrage be extended? Bright pronounced for a rate-paying household suffrage. He had been urged by Joseph Sturge, still true to his platform of fifteen years before, to champion manhood suffrage, but Bright had replied: "I am not working for failure, but for success, and for a real gain, and I must go the way to get it. I am sure the putting of manhood suffrage in the Bill is not the way."[2] To this Birmingham audience, many of whom he admitted believed in manhood suffrage, he declared: "I have not the smallest objection to the widest possible suffrage that the ingenuity of man can devise," yet such a measure could not then be wisely advocated.

A week after the public launching of the movement, a step was taken to organize it. A conference of reformers was held in London, called by the Parliamentary Reform Committee, to deliberate on the plan Bright had outlined at Birmingham, by which private members were to prepare their own bill and attempt to force it upon the government by calling into play agitation out of doors. Anti-Corn Law League tactics were to be furbished up anew. The hope doubtless was not so much to pass their own measure as to use it as a basis for a new political party or as a lever to

[1] *Mr. Bright's Speeches at Birmingham*, etc., London, 1859. (A pamphlet corrected by Bright), p. 6; also, *Speeches on Public Policy by John Bright*, ed. Rogers, London, 1868, II. 3-30.
[2] Trevelyan, *Bright*, p. 270, note 1.

force a good bill from Parliament. The conference conferred upon Bright the task of drawing up the bill and introducing it. Its provisions were not declared, for Bright
requested the fullest liberty in his conduct of the matter.[1]

Bright continued to multiply his public utterances. His
speeches struck the conservative portion of the people as
radical in the extreme, even as republican. They appeared
to threaten the foundations of the constitution. Thus his
speech at the conference had attacked the House of Lords
as incompatible with free institutions. His next address,
before an enormous crowd in the Free Trade Hall, Manchester, where the old Leaguers were present in force with
George Wilson in the chair, reiterated this belief. "We
know, everybody knows, nobody knows it better than the
Peers, that a house of hereditary legislators cannot be a
permanent institution in a free country."[2] And as matters
then stood, he declared, even the House of Commons was
little better than a deputy of the House of Lords, an organ
of the great territorial interests. It hated equality of taxation; it shielded real property from bearing its share of the
public burdens; it passed no measure because it was just,
but because of popular restlessness or the exigencies of
party.

The Glasgow speech[3] of a week later sought to show
workingmen what they would gain by reform. They
would profit by an extension of free trade even to the land
and by an economical fiscal policy which an enlightened
foreign policy would do much to insure; everything the

[1] Report of the Conference in the *Beacon* and *Christian Times*, November 10, 1858. One hundred twenty delegates were present, including
about a dozen M.P.'s; also Miall, S. Morley, and P. A. Taylor. No
workingmen were recorded as present, but doubtless a few leaders were.

[2] *Mr. Bright's Speeches at Birmingham*, etc., London, 1859 (account
copied from the *Manchester Guardian*).

[3] *Ibid.* (from *Morning Star*); also, *Speeches on Questions of Public
Policy*, II. 53-79.

government spent, he declared, diminished the fund out of which wages were paid.

It was not until the fourth great meeting, at Bradford in the West Riding in January, 1859, that Bright finally made known the terms of his bill—household suffrage for boroughs, a ten-pound suffrage for counties, redistribution, and the ballot.[1] Here he emphasized the importance of redistribution: "Repudiate without mercy any bill of any government, whatever its franchise, whatever its seeming concessions may be, if it does not distribute the seats obtained from the extinction of small boroughs mainly amongst the great city and town populations of the kingdom. The question of distribution is the very soul of the question of reform." His own proposals on this point were sweeping. He would take one hundred and twenty-five seats from small boroughs and give them to large towns and industrial counties.[2] He answered the charge of unfairness to the land by asserting that the House of Lords represented it almost exclusively.

The clauses of Bright's proposed bill were a disappointment both to those who had hoped and to those who had feared that he would go farther. The *Leeds Mercury*[3] summarized the press comments: the *Times* was surprised at the moderation of the proposals, after the speeches; the *Globe* declared it would enthrone the manufacturers and was neither a liberal nor a national measure; the pro-Bright

[1] *Ibid.* (from *Manchester Examiner* and *Times*). Also *Leeds Mercury*, January 18, 1859, and H. J. Leech, *Public Letters of John Bright*, pp. 82 ff.

[2] A report called *Information for Reformers respecting the cities and boroughs of the United Kingdom, classified according to the schedules of the Reform Bill proposed by John Bright. Prepared at the request of the London Parliamentary Reform Committee*, etc., by Duncan McLaren, London, 1859, gives an excellent analysis of population, property, amount of taxes paid, etc., and reveals the middle-class nature of Bright's proposals.

[3] January 18, 20, 1859.

Daily News and the radical *Morning Advertiser* praised it;
while the *Morning Post* declared that Bright's reputation
as a public man had been so completely destroyed by his four
addresses that the public would not now credit his seeming
moderation as due to conviction.   Bright further explained
his ideas in the course of the next few weeks, by saying
that he did not mean to propose even complete household
suffrage.   He would fix a three-pound rating line, above
which all would be enfranchised, and below which those
could gain the vote who would personally pay their rates.
Practically all houses below a three-pound rating were then
compounded for, the landlord paying the rates.   Bright
hoped thus to exclude "such as are not likely to have any
independence and such as are utterly careless as to the
possessing of a vote."[1]   Since Bright also advocated only a
ten-pound franchise for counties, it was conceded by many
that he had receded from the advanced position taken in his
first speech.   One journal[2] declared that after having
done his utmost to excite the people by promising every man
a vote, he turned round and shut the door in the face of
four-fifths of the "raging multitude."   "Dost thee think,"
it asked, "the mob will cease to howl, or that Ernest Jones
will not come behind and say of thee all that thou hast said
of the shortcoming Whigs?"   A pamphleteer appealed not
to "the Bright of the embryo Reform Bill, which would
bring all England under the rule of Cotton Lords, but the
Bright of the Glasgow oration."[3]

Attempts were made at once to give the new movement
an organized form.   This was the beginning of a series of

[1] *Newcastle Chronicle* supplement, April 16, 1859. Also Leech, *op. cit.*, pp. 82 ff.
[2] *The Beacon and Christian Times,* December 15, 1858. It had learned before the Bradford speech what it was to propose.
[3] *Who is the "Reformer," John Stuart Mill or John Bright?* London, 1859. It approved Mill's recent *Thoughts on Parliamentary Reform,* which pronounced universal suffrage right, though not yet expedient.

political associations that appeared and disappeared, or grew in strength, or shifted position, constantly up to 1867. A careful scrutiny of them will be found to yield important results for an understanding of the inner workings of English politics in this critical decade. Now at Birmingham was formed a Reformers' Union, which set itself the task of organizing the Midland towns.[1] A similar one was the Lancashire Reformers' Union, which included many of the Corn Law Leaguers. George Wilson, who had been president of the League, was president of this Union. Early in 1859 it held a conference to which a thousand delegates came,[2] and which resolved to support Bright's bill. A West Riding Association was formed for the same purpose.[3]

Bright's agitation served in more ways than one to define the issues involved in the central question. Especially did it draw from the Conservatives expressions which prove their fears of reform and at the same time their realization that in the support of the working classes perhaps lay the key to future power. They tried, therefore, to sow dissension in the ranks of reformers and to bid for democratic support for Conservatism. In this vein, Henry Drummond, M.P., wrote his pamphlet, *A Letter to Mr. Bright on his Plan for Turning the English Monarchy into a Democracy.* A characteristic bit reads:

Your chief panacea is, that the members of the House of Commons should represent men, and not property. Now since property always was, always is, and always must be in the hands of a few, and distress, poverty, starvation, wretchedness, suffering, cold, hunger, sickness, improvidence and desperation, the lot of the many, your plan, which you take from the Socialists and Chartists, is that the members of the House of Commons should represent poverty and not wealth. The necessary and inevitable consequences of this

[1] *Beacon and Christian Times,* November 3, 1858.
[2] *Birmingham Daily Post,* February 2, 1859.
[3] *Leeds Mercury,* January 20, 1859.

must instantly be that the poor will take possession of and divide the wealth amongst themselves—a feeling that this ought to be done has been growing up amongst all classes of labourers in this country for several years.

Then, going on to taunt the Manchester party with their steady opposition to social legislation, he said:

Of all the organized hypocrisies which were ever formed, none has equalled the pretext that Democracy is sought for as a means of improving the conditions of the operatives. . . . You build greatly on the ignorance of your auditors when you imagine they have forgotten Lord Shaftesbury's labours in this matter and your opposition.[1]

In this fashion did Conservative leaders envisage the conflict precipitated by Bright. They believed him to be setting class against class, and they proceeded to oppose him by the same sort of appeal. The new Liberalism was projected by Bright; Tory-democracy, by Drummond.

The charge was constantly made that Bright aimed to "Americanize" English institutions, by which was meant republicanize. In fact, even avowed republicans saw a fellow-worker in him. C. C. Cattell, later president of a republican club in Birmingham, declared, "Paine never had an abler exponent than John Bright."[2] Many lamented that he was arousing class antagonism. One paper feared that the old cry of "confiscation" would be heard again to the detriment of improved relations between capital and labor.[3] Bernal Osborne, a Radical member of parliament, declared Bright had been injudicious in frightening people out of their wits and in setting class against class.[4] Even Cobden cautioned him in December, 1859:

There is an *apparent* tendency in your speeches to advocate the interest of the working class as apart from the upper classes.

[1] Third edition, London, 1858.
[2] *Mr. John Bright and Labour Representation* (no place of publication and no date, but apparently 1859).
[3] *Whitehaven Herald,* November 6, 1858.
[4] *Reynolds's Newspaper,* April 20, 1860.

Now I am sorry to say that whenever the case is so posed, there is a tendency in the middle class to range themselves with those above them to resist a common danger.[1]

The *Times* commented upon the campaign: "But, somehow or other, the more Mr. Bright talked of reform, the less the country seemed to desire it. He frightened and disgusted the upper classes without conciliating the lower."[2] That the feeling of distrust of Bright was strong enough to be used by Palmerston as an excuse for keeping Bright out of the cabinet upon the defeat of the Conservatives in 1859 is certain. He said to Cobden, "it is his attacks on *classes* that have given offense to powerful bodies, who can make their resentment felt."[3]

The fact that the Financial Reformers at Liverpool, of whom Bright was one, were spurring up their campaign simultaneously with this franchise agitation seemed to give point to the latter in the minds of the propertied classes. Bright, addressing a public meeting called to launch this renewed effort, discoursed at length upon the injustice of taxation, which was heavy on industry and light on the land.[4] At the same time other Radicals were moving for changes inimical to the land. Locke King moved in Parliament for a law to enforce the equal division of the real, as well as personal property of intestates. Palmerston declared this would destroy primogeniture and lead to the establishment of a republic.[5]

The agitation produced a numerous crop of pamphlets, which attempted to discuss various theories of representation and the danger or desirability of various proposed

[1] Morley, *Cobden*, p. 543.

[2] Quoted in *Reynolds's*, April 22, 1860.

[3] Morley, *Cobden*, p. 465. Bright's version of the matter was that it was his attack on certain English institutions (speech at Birmingham in 1865. *Newcastle Weekly Chronicle*, January 19, 1865).

[4] *Leeds Mercury*, December 3, 1859. Also Morley, *Cobden*, p. 543.

[5] The *Christian World*, March 11, 1859.

amendments of the existing system. One of the most discerning was written by Holyoake under the title, *The Workman and the Suffrage*.[1] Remarking upon the widespread fear of universal suffrage, he declared it unfounded:

So many of the people are uninformed, prejudiced, and indifferent upon politics, that ignorance, animus and bigotry may be relied upon to vote for "things as they are." And were votes given to all means would exist, and means would be used, for limiting any "dangerous" operations against established influences. For myself, I doubt the wisdom of carrying universal suffrage by popular force—if it could be so carried—so long as the influential classes deem it "dangerous"; because it would generate on their part, or through them, new elements of corruption and intrigue in the state in their endeavours to circumscribe the operation of the dreaded franchise . . . Universal suffrage, if adopted frankly by the governing classes, would work well in this country, where reverence for law, for rank and wealth, is the religion of the streets and lanes.

Regarding the fear often expressed that workingmen would be elected to Parliament in great numbers, he said:

Do not think that members of the working class will very soon find their way into the House of Commons. . . . The whole thing is so absurd that nobody but a Tory could imagine it, and nobody but a Whig of antique faith could believe it.[2]

It is evident that behind the outward aspect of the reform question, now made a practical issue by Bright, appeared the likelihood of transformations in the political and economic system that were even more to be feared than Chartist schemes, because of their greater likelihood of success. A consciousness of the imminence of political realignments in relation to this question found frequent expression from 1858 on. The *Press,* a new Conservative organ, declared

[1] *The Workman and the Suffrage. A Letter to the Rt. Hon. Lord John Russell and the Daily News,* London, 1858. (2nd edit., 1859, is in the British Library of Political Science.)

[2] Another excellent tract written by a workingman is *A Working Man's Dream of Reform,* London, Manchester, 1859. One pamphlet advocating labor representation to the extent of forty or fifty members was *Reform. Fingerposts and Beacons,* London, 1859.

that there were only two parties, the Conservatives and the Manchester School, and that the Whigs would have to choose between them. It declared that Disraeli was striving to unite Whigs and Tories "upon the broad understanding that reforms are to cement the foundations of the monarchy, and not attempt the anomalous paradox of uniting democratic institutions to a defenceless throne."[1] Disraeli considered that only two leaders occupied intelligible positions, Derby and Bright.[2]

It is remarkable that in those years, when attempts were so numerous at discovering the basic principles upon which party lines could be redrawn, Gladstone took no constructive part. Within a decade he would reap where Bright had sown, yet at the time of the initiation of Bright's final effort to construct a "great Liberal Party," the man who was to lead it, almost to personify it, had not emerged from Conservatism far enough to see any need of reform[3] and was ardently defending nomination boroughs.[4] He whose first government was to pass the Ballot Act voted against the ballot in 1858. In fact, so close was he to the Conservatives then that Derby offered him a place in his cabinet.[5] Gladstone refused, but accepted missions to the Ionian Isles and Corfu. He voted in favor of Disraeli's reform bill in 1859 and against Russell's resolutions meant to encompass the defeat of the government. Yet, strange comment upon the devious ways of politics, when that event had taken place, and Palmerston was making up his cabinet, Gladstone accepted a place in it, though it was pledged to a reform bill

---

[1] Quoted in Monypenny and Buckle, *Life of Beaconsfield,* III. 496. (The article was by Bulwer-Lytton.) The author comments that Palmerston saved the Whigs from having to make the choice, which did not come until 1886.

[2] *Ibid.,* p. 500.

[3] Morley, *Gladstone,* I. 631.

[4] *Ibid.,* p. 521.

[5] Monypenny and Buckle, *op. cit.,* IV. 116.

along the lines of Russell's resolutions. One consideration that helped to make this apparent inconsistency possible was that of Italian freedom, of which Gladstone was the ardent champion, and upon which he suspected the Conservatives. As Trevelyan puts it, "Gladstone had begun to travel by way of the Neapolitan prisons toward the Liberalism of his later years."[1] In fact, says one writer, this question even altered his views on the franchise. "Parliamentary Reform, when accompanied by a sympathetic attitude toward Sardinia, seemed to him a far more tolerable thing than it had appeared to be shortly before."[2]

This issue of foreign policy was a powerful influence upon domestic questions in these years. It set up a barrier between Bright and democratic workingmen, and it was the cause of the first sympathy between anti-democratic Gladstone and the democracy. It made it possible for democrats to accept the return of Palmerston with a fairly good grace.

Turning aside for the moment from the middle-class phase of the reform movement, we must pause to inquire to what extent the working classes responded to middle-class overtures thus tendered.

Workingmen had demonstrated their interest in reform during the election of 1857 in several boroughs, as has already been explained. During the next year a working-class franchise movement of some importance was launched in London. Its leading spirit was Ernest Jones. It will be remembered that in the period of severe unemployment in 1857 he had sought to bring the old Chartist message to the lower strata of the working classes. The failure of that appeal for class action to secure political and social reform determined Jones upon a reversal of policy. In the autumn

[1] G. M. Trevelyan, *British History in the Nineteenth Century*, London, 1922, p. 274. See also Stanmore, *Sidney Herbert*, II. 180, 196, for some evidence of interest upon Gladstone in 1858-9.

[2] Stanmore, *op. cit.*, II. 180.

of 1857 he began to advocate a union of Chartists and the middle classes. This is the beginning of a revival of the political importance of this earnest Chartist leader, which was to continue until his death in 1869.

The new movement took shape at a conference called by Jones as head of the Chartists in February, 1858. It was proposed to invite leading middle-class reformers and to submit to them as a basis of union a proposal to adopt manhood suffrage and the abolition of property qualifications for members of the parliament.[1] It was to be a test, said Jones, of middle-class sincerity.[2] Those reformers who were interested in the Parliamentary Reform Committee were approached, but without avail. When the conference met, therefore, no men of eminence among the middle classes attended regularly, and the total number of delegates was small.[3] The failure of the parliamentary reformers to respond to the overture led Jones almost to the point of renouncing his policy of coöperation. The conference debated the matter. Washington Wilks, a democratic journalist, and Holyoake plead for union. A compromise motion was carried to agitate for manhood suffrage, the ballot, triennial parliaments, equal electoral districts, and the abolition of property qualifications, but not to attempt to interfere with other reform efforts.[4]

The confused account of the Conference in Jones's *People's Paper* leaves many points in doubt, but it seems clear that, aside from Radical members of parliament, there was considerable interest evinced by a number of middle-

[1] *People's Paper,* January 2, 1858.
[2] *Ibid.,* February 6.
[3] West, *History of the Chartist Movement,* p. 274, quoting from *Reynolds's Newspaper* (hostile to Jones) says only forty delegates attended, representing a constituency of about five hundred. This must mean forty Chartist delegates. A short biography of Jones, authorized by him, stated there were three hundred delegates (*Ernest Jones. Who is he? What has he done?* March, 1867).
[4] Full account in *People's Paper,* February 13, 20, 1858.

class Radicals and democrats, whose alliance with working-men was to be fruitful in the subsequent agitation in the sixties. In fact, a glance at these names proves the conference to be what Jones claimed it to be, one of the antecedents of the great Reform League of 1865-7. Among them were Joseph Cowen of Newcastle, Passmore Edwards, Professor Newman, Washington Wilks, George Dawson of Birmingham, A. Trevelyan, Thomas Aveling, W. P. Roberts, the "pitmen's attorney," John Watts, Charles Gilpin, J. Baxter Langley, Alderman Livesey of Rochdale, a noted temperance leader, E. Hooson of Manchester, prominent in the coöperative movement, Charles Bradlaugh, Merriman, and Nicholay, later on the executive of the Reform League. Among ex-Chartists present were Holyoake, Harney, Linton, and a younger man, Benjamin Lucraft. Mention is made of the presence of a William Newton and a William Allan, probably of the Amalgamated Engineers. It is important to note that an invitation to the conference had been extended to the trade societies. Delegates were sent by the West End Boot and Shoe Makers, Operative Masons (of Westminster), Painters and Glazers' Society, City Operative Plasterers, and Operative Stone Masons (Sun Lodge). It is significant that the trades responding were the shoemakers—always radical—and the building trades, then occupied with their nine-hour movement and suffering much from trade depression.

The net result of the conference was the formation of a Political Reform Union,[1] with an executive committee of thirty and a managing committee of twelve, three each of Chartists and trade-unionists, and six middle-class men.[2]

[1] *People's Paper*, February 27, 1858.
[2] *Ibid.*, February 20, 1858. This account does not accord with that given in West, *op. cit.*, p. 274, which says there was an Executive of one. In *Ernest Jones, Who is he*, etc., p. 11, it is stated that Jones was president.

J. B. Langley[1] was made treasurer. The program was to be union with the middle classes, but with special agitation for registered manhood suffrage and the other points mentioned above.[2]

Throughout 1859 the Political Reform Union seems to have been active. It held enthusiastic meetings for its program at the time that Bright was launching his household suffrage movement.[3] The London correspondent for the *Newcastle Weekly Chronicle* reported that Bright's scheme was not accepted by the people themselves, that the working classes in their meetings were speaking out for a union with the middle classes, but only on their own terms of manhood suffrage.[4] Early in 1859 Jones held a meeting of several thousand in the Guildhall, presided over by the Lord Mayor himself, at which Bright's bill was rejected and a resolution for manhood suffrage adopted.[5] An intelligent working-class contemporary wrote in his recollections concerning the attitude of workingmen toward reform at that time that the appearance of apathy on their part toward Bright's measure was not an indication that they were apathetic toward the possession of the franchise. The fact was that there was "not much in any of the measures of Parliamentary reform successively produced by Lord John Russell, Mr. Bright or Mr. Locke King to prompt the working men of

[1] He was editor of the *Newcastle Weekly Chronicle* for its Radical owner, Joseph Cowen. Later he was an officer of the Reform League and parliamentary candidate for Greenwich.

[2] It seems that Jones's Chartist organization did not give up its identity, but became a component part of the new Union. (See evidence in the *Investigator*, December 1, 1858.) Also some Chartists refused to recognize the new move in any way, but formed a "National Political Union for the Obtainment of the People's Charter." It put out its own monthly sheet, the *National Union*. See this for May for an account of the organization. It denounced Jones's new move.

[3] See the *Investigator* for November and December, 1858.

[4] November 19, 26, 1858.

[5] *Newcastle Weekly Chronicle*, February 12, 1859. Also, *Ernest Jones. Who is he? What has he done?* p. 11.

London and the large towns which led the van in such movements, to shout and throw up their caps. Every measure
that made rating a necessary preliminary to registration
could be regarded by working men as only an exemplifica-
tion of 'how not to do it.' "[1] Again, this writer said more
specifically of Bright's utterances on reform in 1858-9 that
they were too undecided to gain the confidence of workingmen. "He never seemed to know whether he advocated
manhood suffrage, or household suffrage, or a suffrage
limited to householders who paid a certain amount of
rent."[2] The *Birmingham Daily Post* early in 1859 expressed regret at Bright's failure to explain away criticisms
of his bill for its restrictiveness. It declared that the rate-
paying clauses made the measure worse than Russell's; that it
would not add half a million voters.[3] A nonconformist
paper testified to the rejection of more moderate proposals
in public meetings, where workingmen insisted that the union
of classes should be upon the basis of complete democracy.[4]
A Conservative member asserted in parliament early in
1859 that a workingmen's club in Birmingham had recently
carried by a bare majority of one a motion that Bright really
represented them.[5]

The formation of manhood suffrage associations on the
model of Jones's in London spread over the country. In
Salford a meeting requisitioned by over a thousand citizens,
chiefly operatives, carried a manhood suffrage resolution
overwhelmingly.[6] In Manchester an important movement
began in 1859 under the leadership of Alderman Abel Heywood, a bookseller and publisher of radical literature who

[1] Frost, *Thirty Years' Recollections,* pp. 273-4.
[2] *Ibid.,* pp. 272-3.
[3] February 3, 1859.
[4] *Beacon and Christian Times,* November 17, 1858.
[5] *Hansard,* CLIII. 705. Statement by Adderley.
[6] *Christian Times,* April 5, 1859.

had risen from poverty by his own efforts, a man of high character and unwearied zeal for democratic principles. After Bright's agitation had begun and after Disraeli had promised a bill, the Manchester Manhood Suffrage Association was formed at a meeting of four thousand persons.[1] This organization had much vitality. In the very next election it brought Heywood forward as a candidate, and he polled the amazingly large number of 5420 votes.[2] Other organizations based upon the same democratic program were formed at Renfrew in January, 1859;[3] at Wednesbury at about the same time;[4] at Dudley in March;[5] at Rochdale;[6] and at York.[7]

In London, later in 1859, after Palmerston had returned to office, several political unions were formed that soon achieved a fairly large membership and a fair amount of influence among workingmen. The relation of these bodies to Jones's Union is not clear. The leading spirit in these later associations was an ex-Chartist, Benjamin Lucraft, henceforth a significant figure in London labor politics. The first, the North London Political Union, was followed by others in South London and Westminster. A tone of earnestness combined with moderation pervades the accounts of the activities of these bodies. The best notices of them are in the *Ballot*[8] and in *Reynolds's Newspaper*.[9] These Unions were the immediate forerunners of the Reform League formed in 1865.

[1] *Newcastle Weekly Chronicle,* November 19, 1858, quoting from *Manchester Guardian.*
[2] See below, p. 183.
[3] *Christian Cabinet,* January 12, 1859.
[4] *Birmingham Daily Post,* February 1, 1859.
[5] *Ibid.,* March 9, 1859.
[6] *Newcastle Weekly Chronicle,* October 29, 1859.
[7] *Ibid.,* October 22, 1859.
[8] See issue of August 4, 1860, for annual report of the N. London Union. See also January 21, February 4, March 17, May 5, 1860.
[9] See May 6, 1860.

Perhaps the most vigorous of all such bodies, however, was that formed at Newcastle in January, 1858, under the leadership of Joseph Cowen, Jr.[1] The occasion of its formation was the disappointment felt by the non-electors over the defeat of their candidate in 1857, as described above.[2] The Chartists in the borough now agreed to abandon the six points on condition of a united agitation for manhood suffrage, the ballot, and the abolition of property qualifications. These three points were adopted as the program of the Northern Political Union. Its secretary was R. B. Reed, an active iron-worker.[3] Its manifesto was Chartist in tone, but it concluded with the statement that the association would accept any obtainable measure of reform "as an installment."[4]

The Union carried on a vigorous campaign for membership in the towns and villages of Tyneside. The response was hearty everywhere, especially from workingmen. The movement received assistance from a few democrats of the middle class, such as P. A. Taylor, Washington Wilks, and James Stansfeld. On the day of the introduction of Disraeli's reform bill in February, 1859, the Union presented petitions for manhood suffrage from forty-two towns and villages of Northumberland and Durham. The total number of signatures was 34,676, estimated at one half of the total adult male population of the places represented. About two thirds of the signers were non-electors.[5] The Union brought out P. A. Taylor for Newcastle in 1859.[6] It continued its activity in the face of the Palmerstonian reaction

[1] *Newcastle Weekly Chronicle,* January 8, 15, 1858.
[2] Pp. 119-20.
[3] See William Duncan, *Joseph Cowen,* p. 20.
[4] *Newcastle Weekly Chronicle,* March 12, 1858.
[5] Ibid., March 5, 1859. Also a pamphlet in the Howell collection, *Petitions for Manhood Suffrage and Vote by Ballot.*
[6] See below, p. 182.

till 1862, when it dissolved, only to be revived in 1866 as a branch of the Reform League.[1]

Before continuing an examination of the popular reform movement, we must pause long enough to glance at the party situation that was developing in parliament in order that the two may be related to each other. The Conservative reform bill of 1859 introduced new factors into political relationships and programs.

[1] Duncan, *Cowen,* p. 21.

CHAPTER VII

THE PUBLIC AND THE REFORM BILLS OF
1859 AND 1860

Reference has been made to the reform bill Bright was to introduce whenever he deemed the occasion fitting. He never did introduce it. Instead, two successive governments brought in measures. The first was Disraeli's bill in 1859, the second Russell's in 1860. It is instructive to consider briefly the progress of those measures in parliament and, more especially, to note the response of the people to them. The object of the inquiry is to discover, if possible, the inter-relation of several factors—the tactics of parliamentary parties, Bright's group and their agitation in the constitu-encies, and the workingmen themselves.

Derby announced upon his accession that while he saw no need to amend the act of 1832, yet it was dangerous to the country to have the question perpetually "dangling before the legislature" and perpetually postponed.[1]

The Conservative party, like the Liberal, was in the fifties and sixties passing through a period of transition. With the abandonment of protection as a platform in 1852, it found itself in urgent need of another as soon as the coming of peace in 1856 again turned public attention to domestic questions. Buckle describes the party as broken and dispirited in 1856-7, in part because of the personal unpopularity of Disraeli, but in part also because liberal ideas were fermenting within the party.[2] Lord Stanley, Derby's son, was a foremost exponent of this spirit, but it was Disraeli who was to interpret it to his party and guide

[1] *Hansard,* CXLIX. 42.
[2] Monypenny and Buckle, *Life of Beaconsfield,* IV. 58-63.

its policies into at least a partial acceptance of it. He too, since his earliest political views were expressed, had aimed at founding a "national party," but his national party was to be a union of the aristocracy and the masses of the people, excluding the manufacturers, not, like Bright's, a union of the manufacturers and the masses against the aristocracy.[1] His constant hostility to the manufacturers was due to the fact that he saw in them the enemy of the territorial interest, and hence of English institutions.[2]   In an attack on the Anti-Corn Law League, he had said that rather than see them in power he would entrust political power to the people: "if we must find new forces to maintain the ancient throne and immemorial monarchy of England, I for one hope we may find that novel power in the invigorating energies of an educated and enfranchised people."[3]   Disraeli's willingness to call in the aid of the nation in government had presupposed an alliance of the nation with the aristocracy against the manufacturers.   From 1850 he was confronted with the prospect of an alliance of the nation with the manufacturers against the aristocracy.   Either of two opposed policies the Conservatives might adopt with advantage.   They could stand as a bulwark for English institutions against the threatened advance of democracy and possibly attach to themselves all the conservative elements in the state; or they could accept the imminence of democracy and declare themselves ready to welcome it as widening the basis of national institutions and affording a firmer foundation for aristocracy, church, and throne.   In other words, they could counter

[1] *Ibid.*, II. 82 (debate on the Chartist petition in 1839). Also, on this, see Beer, *History of British Socialism*, II. 80. For other statements of his views see Monypenny and Buckle, *op. cit.*, II. 88; also Disraeli's *Coningsby* and *Sybil*, which his biographers state represent his "permanent conception of what may be called the Tory Idea, and of the background of history in which he found that idea" (II. 267).

[2] Monypenny and Buckle, *op. cit.* II. 83.

[3] *Ibid.*, p. 369.

John Bright's "American" democracy, aimed at a political levelling, with an English democracy, devoted to Tory ideals.

The fact that the Conservative party in the next two decades followed neither the one policy nor the other consistently, but deviated from one to the other, was the result of the fact that it was not itself a unit as to principles and program. The first of the above mentioned policies was attended by the danger of proving to be an impossibility; in that case, the democratic flood, opposed, would break the barriers and sweep away the ancient landmarks and with them the Conservative party. The second policy might also fail. It might merely serve as an auxiliary to Bright's efforts. The Conservatives might assist at the creation of a democracy only to find it hostile to English institutions and the confessed guardians thereof, the Conservative party. The dilemma found expression in that working of liberal ideas within the party, to which reference has already been made, and efforts to combat them. A consistent policy was impossible for this party as well as for its opponents, who were divided upon the same issue. The position of party leaders on both sides was difficult because of the rapidly shifting aspect of the entire political situation. And let it be remembered that, with political parties and their chiefs, power is often as potent a consideration as principle, especially when the prospect of power is immediate and the validity of principles obscure.

In 1857 Disraeli and Derby had outlined in their correspondence the two possible lines of action the Conservatives might follow, now that the question of reform had been raised again. Disraeli thought that the party might even take the initiative in reform and thereby build an enduring power for themselves. "Our party is now a corpse, but it appears to me that, in the present perplexed state of affairs, a *Conservative public pledged to Parliamentary Re-*

form, a bold and decided course, might not only put us on our legs, but greatly help the country and serve the State."[1] But when he proceeded to sketch the measure of reform he had in mind, it proved to be very slightly in the direction of democracy and designed in the frankest manner to strengthen the county interest.   Derby, in his reply,[2] outlined the contrary policy of resistance to reform.   Pointing to the schism among Liberals, the closer approach of Russell to the Radicals and his hostility to Palmerston, Derby declared it perhaps the best course for the Conservatives to encourage such dissensions and attract those of conservative tendencies into the lobby with themselves as often as possible in opposition to Radical moves.   He added that he was afraid his own followers would oppose taking the initiative on the question of reform.   He and Disraeli agreed as to the extent of reform they would countenance in any case; they would not lower the qualifications for the franchise in boroughs.   But events were soon to force the hand of the Conservatives.

When Derby took office in 1858, Palmerston's pledge to introduce a reform bill that year was fresh in mind.   The public, explains a journal of the day, was "strongly though quietly" in favor of reform.   To introduce a bill was the only way to save the government from expulsion at the will of Palmerston; if they did not take up the question, they would be compelled to resign themselves to opposition for the rest of their existence.[3]   Buckle says that Derby, Disraeli, Lord Stanley, and a large section of the party realized this.[4]   Consequently, the government promised a bill for the next session.

---

[1] Monypenny and Buckle, *op. cit.,* IV. 78-9.
[2] *Ibid.,* IV. 80.
[3] Analysis of the situation in the *Universal Review of Politics, Literature and Science.* (London, 1859, 60), May, 1860.
[4] Monypenny and Buckle, *op. cit.,* IV. 120.

From the moment of this announcement, the independent Radicals in the House gave fairly steady support to the ministry in the hope of winning from them a satisfactory measure. Certain of them openly declared they preferred to keep the present ministers rather than to reseat the Whigs.[1] But when the government brought in a bill early in 1859, it was a grievous disappointment to reformers. It did not propose to lower the qualification in boroughs, but only to create certain "fancy franchises," such as one based upon the possession of sixty pounds in a savings bank, or one for paying twenty pounds a year as a lodger. It would enfranchise the ten-pound householders in counties, but at the same time it would make many of them voters in boroughs rather than in counties by extending the area of boroughs to take in those now large urban populations living outside the boundaries of existing boroughs. This would prevent these industrial groups from influencing the counties. Also, with a similar purpose, the bill would compel those possessing forty-shilling freeholds in boroughs, for which they had formerly voted in counties, to vote only in boroughs. This would operate to remove an already large urban influence from the counties. The bill was, therefore, plainly what Bright had warned it might be, a "country gentleman's bill."

[1] Cox (Finsbury) and Roebuck so stated in debate on Disraeli's bill in 1859 (*Hansard,* CLIII. 350, 333). It was stated in parliament that the government's India Bill was saved by Radicals and that in many instances they received aid from Bright (*Hansard,* CLIV. 153). Lord Granville gave similar testimony (*ibid.,* p. 47). An instance of Conservative concession to the Radicals is in their permitting Locke King's bill to abolish property qualifications for M.P.'s to pass practically unopposed—one point of the Charter. For the debate, which revealed opinions upon democracy of much interest, see *Hansard,* CL. 1426-2094. Also Rose, *The Rise of Modern Democracy,* p. 170. An interesting pamphlet on the Tory-Radical alliance of these two years is called *The Contrast; or John Bright's Support of the Present Government Justified.* By a Liberal M.P., London, 1859. It describes the shortcoming of the Whigs and their snobbish attitude to the unaristocratic elements in the party.

Disraeli defended his retention of the present borough franchise by declaring that if they resorted to the "coarse and common expedient" of lowering the qualification the result would be a monotonous constituency of one class, one mind, "the predominance of a household democracy."[1] The object of the government was to confer the vote upon "all of those to whom we thought that privilege might be safely entrusted." To workingmen two new avenues to the franchise would be opened by means of the sixty-pound savings clause and the freehold clause.[2]

It is clear enough that for the Liberals to accept this measure would have been to consent to the eradication of two important Liberal elements in the counties—the freeholders in boroughs, of whom it was estimated that there were ninety-five thousand voters in counties out of a total county constituency of five hundred and four thousand,[3] and those in the urbanized sections of counties. They themselves would not be compensated by any large increase of the Liberal strength in boroughs through a generous enfranchisement of workingmen. The bill was consequently attacked by all shades of Liberals on one or both of these two grounds—the freehold clauses and the failure to lower the franchise. The Radicals took up particularly the latter argument. One declared in the debate on the second reading that in the three weeks following the introduction of the measure it had been condemned on every platform in the kingdom.[4] Francis Crossley, of the West Riding, who had supported

[1] *Hansard*, CLII. 985; for the whole speech, pp. 966 ff.

[2] The fact is that the freehold clause proposed no additional qualification.

[3] Statement in a pamphlet, *Speech of C. N. Newdegate, M.P., at the Annual Meeting of the Rugby and Dunchurch Agricultural Association, November 26, 1858*, London, 1859. Newdegate was a prominent Conservative member for North Warwickshire. It was said that a quarter of the electors of the Liberal West Riding were of this class (*Leeds Mercury*, April 9, 1859).

[4] Alderman Salomons (Greenwich), *Hansard*, CLIII. 442 ff.

Derby in office in the hope of a good measure, condemned
the bill in a speech filled with commendation of the working
classes.[1]   W. J. Fox, the democratic member for Oldham,[2]
and Ellice,[3] of Coventry, likewise pleaded the cause of workingmen.   Bright declared that the bill, offering the people
nothing, could create only anger and disgust.[4]   Gladstone,
sitting on the Conservative side of the House, defended the
government and condemned the concerted Liberal attack
upon it, but he admitted the borough suffrage should be lowered and the spirit of reform should be that of trust toward
the people.[5]

The debate[6] elicited the expression of much doubt or
fear of democracy.   Horsman, a Whig member for Stroud,
declared[7] that the Liberals, by their attack, were making it
impossible to pass this or any moderate measure, and this
would render agitation inevitable; eventually a period of distress would come, and then even Bright might be looked to
as a preserver and his bill accepted as a compromise with
angry passions.   Several members referred to the great
meetings being held over the country, which were universally demanding either household or manhood suffrage.   Lord
Robert Cecil declared that Nottingham, Manchester, and all
the metropolitan boroughs "had spoken in favour of every
principle advocated by Mr. Ernest Jones."[8]   E. Bulwer-Lytton, colonial secretary, stated that opinion lately expressed
in local public meetings required something no Whig government could propose and no conceivable government at that

[1] *Hansard,* CLIII. 574 ff.
[2] *Ibid.,* CLIII. 729.
[3] *Ibid.,* CLIII. 950.
[4] *Ibid.,* CLII. 1024.
[5] *Ibid.,* CLIII. 1046-67.
[6] The whole debate is in *Hansard,* CLII. 966-1618, and CLIII. 330 ff.
[7] *Ibid.,* CLIII. 459. ff.
[8] *Ibid.,* CLIII. 479-80.

time could carry.[1]   Judging by these popular expressions
of opinion, it would not be possible, he said, to stop short of
manhood suffrage, if they began to transfer power to the
working classes.   The Solicitor General testified to the
"singular unanimity" of public meetings in demanding either
manhood or household suffrage, triennial parliaments, and
the ballot.[2]   Another speaker declared the point at issue to
be numbers versus property.[3]   Drummond declared that
the debate had been the making of the member for Birmingham; all he had to do now was to sit still, and in five years
they would all have swallowed his bill.[4]   Lord Elcho, a
Whig opponent of reform, having described the dangers
that would threaten property, called upon the House "to
resist the democratic tide which was setting in" while there
was yet time.[5]   Finally, Disraeli, in concluding the debate,
summed up the terrors of democracy in words that were remembered against him less than a decade later.

If you establish a democracy you must in due season reap the
fruits of a democracy. You will in due season have great impa-
tience of the public burdens combined in due season with great
increase of the public expenditure . . . you will in due season
have wars entered upon from passion, and not from reason, and
you will in due season submit to peace ignominiously sought and
ignominiously obtained, which will diminish your authority and
perhaps endanger your independence. You will, in due season, with
a democracy find your property is less valuable and that your freedom is less complete.

As to any reduction of the borough franchise, he declared:

I cannot look upon what is called reduction of the franchise in
boroughs but with alarm; and I have never yet met with any argument which fairly encounters the objections that are urged to it.
You cannot encounter it by sentimental assertions of the good qualities of the working classes. The greater their good qualities the
greater the danger.

[1] *Ibid.*, CLIII. 546-559.
[2] *Ibid.*, CLIII. 621.
[3] *Ibid.*, CLIII. 702 (Adderley).
[4] *Ibid.*, CLIII. 849-50.
[5] *Ibid.*, CLIII. 943-47.

He believed the national constituency "ought to be numerous enough to be independent, and select enough to be responsible." This the government bill had sought through a variety of franchise rather than by "the introduction of the mere multitude, which, if once we began the reduction of the borough franchise, would ultimately and speedily be accomplished," for, "if you enter upon it again you will be forced not only to adopt the numerical suffrage . . . but at once to go down to household suffrage, and introduce democratic elements, the consequences of which I have slightly traced."[1]

One other significant aspect of opinion manifested itself in the debate on this reform bill; namely, the frequent reference made to the attitude of workingmen on industrial questions. The two preceding years, it will be remembered, had seen a resumption of industrial conflicts. The miners were restless and were forming trade-unions and demanding legislation; in 1858 there had been a fierce contest in the flint-glass industry; the builders' nine-hour movement had reached a critical stage by the close of 1858 and, at the time of this debate, strike and lock-out were in full operation. Reverberations of the industrial war sounded in the halls of parliament and weighed in the opinions there expressed concerning the desirability of granting the suffrage to the working class. One member declared workingmen to be unsound on political economy.[2] Another pointed to the danger of socialism because of the wrong conception workingmen had

[1] *Hansard,* CLIII. 1245-55. Many speakers made reference to the evidence then being gathered by a committee of the House of Lords secured by Earl Grey to investigate the municipal franchise since compound householders (the poorest class) had been admitted to it. It was believed the evidence was damaging to the cause of workingmen in politics, but an examination of the report, published in 1860, reveals little of such evidence. It is a valuable source for both the attitude of the upper classes toward the working classes, and the activities of the latter.

[2] Ker Seymer. *Hansard,* CLIII. 435.

of the functions of capital.[1] Bright declared that the trade-union movement would become revolutionary if wage-earners were condemned to remain "a separate and suspected order in our social system."[2] Drummond contended that if workingmen got votes they would have to have the ballot to protect them from trade-unions, and Lord Elcho protested against handing over the government to the tyranny of trade-unions, "which of all tyrannies was the most grinding and intolerable."[3]

Russell, with the support of all the Liberal factions, introduced certain resolutions setting forth the principles upon which reform should be based. Those resolutions were carried, and the government resigned. Derby dissolved parliament. He would appeal to the country, he declared, upon two issues—the difficulty of carrying on the government created by the opposition of small factions which could "combine to attack but not to govern," and, secondly, the danger in leaving reform to the Liberals, who had made their peace with Bright and thus had embarked upon his "wild and visionary" schemes. As for the Conservatives, they felt themselves free to take up the whole question of reform anew; a policy of "no-policy," as Granville described it.[4] But upon whatever grounds the ministry hoped to base the election, the main question upon which it turned was reform.[5]

Turn now from parliament to the country;—an examination of public opinion as expressed in public meetings and the press during the debate upon Disraeli's bill and the subsequent election reveals a mounting tide of interest among workingmen. Never since the waning of the political ex-

[1] Beresford Hope. *Ibid.*, CLIII. 739-40.
[2] Quoted by Trevelyan (*Bright*, p. 280), who says trade-unions were much feared because of strikes.
[3] *Hansard*, CLIII. 943.
[4] Derby's ministerial statement. *Ibid.*, CLIII. 1266 ff.
[5] The other issue was foreign policy, especially as regarded Italy.

citement of the preceding decade had there been such wide-spread expression of that interest. The *Newcastle Weekly Chronicle,* now the property of Joseph Cowen, who was the leading figure in the recently formed Northern Political Union, condemned the government bill as designed to deprive the masses in perpetuity of political power. Statesmen of all parties, even Bright, would, it declared, give the vote to bricks and mortar, not men.[1] The Northern Political Union held numerous meetings in Northumberland and Durham. One number of the *Chronicle* listed fourteen meetings in these counties in a few days, of which only five passed resolutions in favor of a more moderate reform than manhood suffrage.[2]

In Yorkshire, Lancashire, and the Midlands, the *Leeds Mercury,* carefully feeling the pulse of the country, recorded in every number in January, just prior to the introduction of the bill, meetings that demanded household suffrage, though at most of them manhood-suffrage amendments were offered, and at some it was made clear that the more moderate measure was accepted because it alone would gain middle-class coöperation.[3] These meetings of January can be credited to Bright's agitation undoubtedly, and were meant to influence the government; but in March the meetings were for the purpose of expressing opinion upon the bill itself. The middle-class reform associations condemned it unanimously.[4] At Birmingham Bright called upon an audience of eight thousand to enter upon such an agitation as would "make the tottering monopolies of aristocracy tremble to their very foundation."[5] At Bradford, in a

[1] March 5, 1859.
[2] March 26.
[3] *Leeds Mercury,* January 20, 1859 (Rochdale meeting); January 29 (Halifax).
[4] See *Leeds Mercury* for March; many meetings.
[5] *Ibid.,* March 10.

meeting of twenty-five hundred, resolutions condemning the government bill as an insult to workingmen and approving Bright's were put by workingmen.[1]   At Todmorden a manhood-suffrage motion was carried enthusiastically.[2]   At Huddersfield a workingman moved a manhood-suffrage resolution, but, said the *Mercury,* it was overwhelmingly lost.[3] At Preston, scene of the great strike of five years before, the motion approving of Bright's bill was made by George Cowell, the organizer of that strike.[4]   In Leeds, meetings were held by wards.   Workingmen appear to have participated quite generally and usually to have supported a rating franchise, though not always.[5]   Workingmen at Barnsley supported a manhood-suffrage amendment in an excited meeting.[6]   Norwich held a great and harmonious meeting, concerning which one paper says that there had been no such political excitement there in years.[7]   At Derby a crowded meeting was held in the Town Hall.   A workingman presided, and most of the audience the *Birmingham Post* described as "of the Chartist body."[8]   The same paper states that at Coventry, in a meeting of four thousand, the manhood suffragists made it impossible to carry either their amendment or the original motion.[9]

Most of these meetings appear to have been under middle-class auspices—a part of Bright's agitation.   The accounts of them reveal the efforts of the middle-class chairmen to secure a united expression from the middle and working classes, but in practically every meeting a manhood-suffrage

[1] *Ibid.,* March 12.
[2] *Ibid.,* March 12.
[3] *Ibid.,* March 17.
[4] *Ibid.,* March 17.
[5] *Ibid.,* March 10, 17.
[6] *Ibid.,* March 19.
[7] *Christian World,* March 11.
[8] March 18.
[9] March 17.

amendment was proposed and often carried. The available reports of these meetings are in the middle-class press, animated by the same desire to produce the impression of harmony among all ranks of reformers. In consideration of this fact, it is necessary to attribute added significance to those expressions of working-class opposition to the program of the promoters of the meetings that found their way into print. An admission of any large amount of dissension would have weakened the effect of the anti-government agitation. Many meetings limited themselves to negative resolutions of condemnation, and on these middle-class orators could declaim unchecked upon the insults offered to the working classes by the "landed party." Petitions against the bill were rapidly signed. In Birmingham forty thousand signatures were obtained in one week.[1] At the end of the first week's debate the petitions altogether had received over one hundred eighty thousand signatures.[2]

In the metropolis working-class demonstrations were numerous. It will be remembered that Ernest Jones had launched a union to unite the two classes upon a program of registered, residential manhood suffrage and that it had been promoted by Passmore Edwards, Bradlaugh, P. A. Taylor, and others. This union was probably still functioning at the time of this agitation; certainly its leaders were vigorously at work. Numerous working-class meetings against the bill were held in Hyde Park, at which Jones and Bradlaugh were favorite speakers.[3] "Much Chartist oratory" was heard in Islington and in Bonner's Fields.[4] A meeting called by the Radicals at the Guildhall under the Lord Mayor's chairmanship clamored for Bradlaugh, but he was

[1] *Leeds Mercury,* March 22.
[2] *Christian World,* April 1.
[3] Bonner, *Life of Bradlaugh,* I. 81. *Birmingham Daily Post,* March 22, 1859. Jones condemned both Disraeli's and Bright's measures.
[4] *Beacon and Christian Times,* March 20.

refused permission to speak.[1]   In Lambeth, at a "very large meeting" with the two borough members present, Ernest Jones's manhood-suffrage resolution was carried unanimously "amid tremendous cheering."[2]   In Shoreditch, with the members for Tower Hamlets present, manhood suffrage and all the points advocated by Jones's Union were adopted.[3]   At a similar meeting in Marylebone, which the local members attended, manhood suffrage was overwhelmingly approved.[4]   Such were the proceedings in Finsbury, Southwark, and Westminster.[5]   At two Greenwich meetings manhood suffrage failed of adoption.[6]

Thus was extremist opinion, whether of the middle or working classes, making itself known.   One nonconformist journal that had followed events closely asserted in the middle of March that a genuine agitation was in progress, due more, however, to anger than to interest in reform as such.   The people felt themselves insulted and tricked, and the Radicals felt keen disappointment after their hopes of the government.[7]

In April came the election.   The two issues over which the people were concerned were reform and Italy.   The Liberal factions in parliament had coalesced to defeat Derby. Bright understood that the Liberal compact called for a bill embodying a six-pound franchise for boroughs and a ten-pound qualification for counties.   He stated at the opening of the new parliament that his so-called alliance had been secured on such an understanding.[8]   Thus did Bright

---

[1] Bonner, *op. cit.*, I. 812. Also *Beacon and Christian Times*, March 16.
[2] *Birmingham Daily Post*, March 9.
[3] *Ibid.*, March 15.
[4] *Christian World*, March 18.
[5] *Beacon and Christian Times*, March 16.
[6] *Leeds Mercury*, March 17, 19.
[7] *Beacon and Christian Times*, editorial, March 18.
[8] *Hansard*, CLIV. 226 ff.

abandon his own measure, which even then was being agitated for over the country.   The explanation of this step may be that the failure of this agitation to arouse an enthusiastic and united response may have convinced him of the futility of the Radicals' attempting to act alone, if he had ever had any such intention.   Yet the agitation had revealed enough of parliamentary and popular strength to enable the Radicals to put a price upon their alliance.   It may at least be pondered whether the signal evidence of the loyalty of workingmen to the principles of manhood suffrage afforded at public meetings may not have rendered the Radicals themselves more inclined to harken to the voice of the more cautious elements in the party.

A brief examination of this election with the purpose of discovering the part played in it by workingmen is of interest. They had before them two concrete proposals, Disraeli's and Russell's for a six-pound suffrage.

The Northern Political Union under Cowen, with its manhood-suffrage program and large working-class constituency, brought forward P. A. Taylor for Newcastle against the two Whig members.   Taylor canvassed the workingmen in their places of employment and was so active generally that the Liberals raised the cry that he would let a Tory in.[1]   The Union had declared that Taylor's candidacy was as much for the purpose of propaganda as anything else.[2]   The polling gave him only 463 votes to 2680 for the next highest competitor.[3]   Immediately, the workingmen of the borough formed a "Non-electors' Association," distinct

[1] *Newcastle Weekly Chronicle,* April 23, 1859.

[2] *Ibid.,* April 9.

[3] *Ibid.,* May 7.   There were about fifteen hundred workingmen electors in Newcastle, but most of them were freemen, corrupt and allied with the Whigs (figures from a carefully compiled table in Appendix III of R. D. Baxter's *A Reform Bill,* London, 1866; he gives the number of working-class electors in 1866 as 1559, and of freemen, not ten-pound electors, as 1433).

from the Union, with the purpose of bringing out a manhood-suffrage candidate at every borough election.[1]

In Manchester workingmen appeared as an independent party. The leaders of the old Anti-Corn Law League had formed the Lancashire Reformers' Union, and it now, confirming the charges made against the League rump that it was still attempting to dictate Manchester politics,[2] selected as its candidate Thomas Bazley, recently successful in a bye-election. The other sitting member was Turner, who had been put in office by the anti-Bright forces in 1857. But the workingmen would have none of either. They wanted a manhood-suffrage candidate and found one in Alderman Abel Heywood, who had organized their Manhood Suffrage Association two years before. He was acknowledged by the press everywhere as the workingmen's candidate. The Bazley group was friendly toward his candidature; the Turner group did all it could to defeat it. Bazley and Turner were elected, but Heywood received the surprising number of 5420 votes, the lowest successful vote exceeding his by less than two thousand.[3] It is worth noting that the number of workingmen electors in Manchester, according to an estimate for 1866, was 5822.[4] They considered that in this election they had won a signal triumph.[5]

In Leeds, Forster stood again, but this time not as a candidate of the non-electors definitely, as in 1859. He stood for no broader reform than that proposed by Russell.[6] The

---

[1] *Newcastle Weekly Chronicle*, May 28.

[2] F. P. Rickards, *Manchester and John Bright*, London, 1859,—a pamphlet which speaks of the tyranny of the League, able to make and unmake M.P.'s at will. Also *Leeds Mercury*, May 7, 1859.

[3] Full account in *Leeds Mercury*, May 3.

[4] R. D. Baxter, *A New Reform Bill*. Appendix III.

[5] So stated in a pamphlet, *Manchester Reform and Manchester Reformers. . . . In a letter to Mr. Alderman Heywood, by Wm. Stokes*, 2d edit., Manchester, 1859. (In Manchester Free Reference Library.)

[6] *Leeds Mercury*, April 28, 30.

Conservative candidate here, who was elected, apparently had a large working-class support.[1]

A few other significant features of this election may be noted. At York, A. H. Layard, beaten by a small margin, was strongly supported by workingmen.[2] At Bramley, party unity could be secured only by allowing both electors and non-electors to participate in the choice of the candidate.[3] At Huddersfield great excitement attended the canvass of E. A. Leatham, a relative of Bright. His speeches were strong pleas for workingmen's rights. When his victory was threatened after the polling by a petition to unseat him, the non-electors met in central and district committee rooms to raise funds with which to defend his seat. They marched through the town with banners bearing the words, "Leatham the friend of real reform and champion of the people's rights."[4] An equally warm support seems to have been given to a brother, who was elected for Wakefield in the West Riding.[5]

At Oldham, an interesting situation developed. Two years before, Fox, a democrat, but of the Manchester School in economics, had been defeated by Cobbett, a Conservative advocate of the Ten Hour Law and other factory measures.[6] Now Cobbett was in turn condemned for his vote in favor of Disraeli's reform bill.[7] His seat was secured by T. H. Hibbert, who possessed both keys to the sympathy of the working classes. He believed in manhood suffrage and the ballot and also advocated legislation with regard to hours

[1] A body of five hundred workingmen accompanied him to the hustings.
[2] Layard testified to this in 1860. See *Reynolds's,* December 9, 1860.
[3] *Leeds Mercury,* April 7.
[4] *Ibid.,* July 21, September 13.
[5] *Ibid.,* August 2.
[6] See above, pp. 117-18.
[7] *Leeds Mercury,* April 9, describes a meeting to condemn Cobbett and pronounce for manhood suffrage.

of labor, and sanitary and legal reform.[1]   Kidderminster, scene of working-class riots against Lowe in 1857, had now forced him out, and popular favor was centered upon the man who had defended the rioters upon the former occasion.[2]

In the metropolis few contests took place. Those boroughs which had established their name as ultra-radical— Finsbury, Tower Hamlets, Southwark, Marylebone—maintained their reputation. A few gains were made at the expense of moderate Liberals. A Conservative journal remarked on the question of "playing to the mob" in democratic constituencies: "a conscientious man does stop somewhere but a metropolitan member will promise anything you please."[3]   That non-electors played a big part in electoral campaigns there is beyond question. In the hearings before the Lords' Committee,[4] then sitting ostensibly to investigate the working of the municipal franchise, with special regard to corruption and intimidation, but in reality to throw light on the probable operation of a democratic franchise for the nation, an electoral agent in the metropolis testified that about eighty per cent. of those present at political meetings there would usually be non-electors and that their interest was as great as that of the electors.

That the prospect of a six-pound franchise was not calculated to create enthusiasm among the metropolitan working classes is apparent upon a consideration of facts brought out by Gathorne Hardy, a member of the government, in the debate upon the Conservative bill. Eighty per cent. of the houses in the metropolis already conferred a vote under a ten-pound qualification. Furthermore, even straight house-

[1] See *Birmingham Daily Post*, April 21, 1859, for his platform.
[2] *Christian World*, April 15.
[3] The *Constitutional Press*, June, 1859, p. 194.
[4] See above, p. 176, note 1.

hold suffrage would not there enfranchise the body of artisans, because they were technically lodgers, not householders. In Marylebone, for instance, a household franchise would benefit not more than one per cent. of the artisans.[1] This situation in London and a few other large towns must be borne in mind always in considering the attitude of workingmen in those places toward the various reform proposals.

Simultaneously with the debate on the reform bill and the election, the Austro-Sardinian question reached a crisis. This question increased the pro-Liberal sympathies of workingmen, for they believed the Conservatives to be unfriendly to Italian national aspirations. Thus, on the two counts of reform and foreign policy, the people found against the Conservatives. Again Palmerston's shortcomings in domestic affairs had to be set over against his popular attitude toward Italy.

When the new parliament met, Disraeli, in his speech on the address, admitted that the Conservative reform bill had been rejected and that the election showed that the borough franchise would have to be altered to admit the working classes.[2] In view of that fact, he declared the Conservatives to be "perfectly prepared to deal with that question . . . by lowering the franchise in boroughs, and by acting in that direction with sincerity" so as to effect a real settlement.[3] To this facile adoption of the "coarse and common expedient" of lowering the franchise, Bright rejoined with a declaration of no confidence and a proclamation of the Liberal reconciliation on the basis of Russell's proposed six-pound measure.[4]

[1] *Hansard*, CLIII. 1104-5.
[2] Disraeli was much disappointed in the way the boroughs voted (Monypenny and Buckle, *op. cit.*, IV. 233).
[3] *Hansard*, CLIV. 139.
[4] *Ibid.*, CLIV. 226 ff.

One other aspect of the election of 1859 should not fail of notice. There is some evidence that it was the occasion of the initiation of Disraeli's policy of improving the party organization in populous centers, which was to contribute so effectively toward securing to Conservatives some of the fruits of their democratic measure of 1867. The *Constitutional Press*[1] discussed this problem after the election with reference to the metropolis in such a way as to indicate that efforts had been started to rescue certain of these boroughs, which never were known to "return a gentleman." Tower Hamlets was to be wrenched from its "desperate Liberalism," Westminster cleansed of its "reputation of a self-seeking democracy." The article stated that Marylebone and the City had already been successfully influenced through revision in the registration courts. The Constitutional Party, it declared, intended to set up a registration society in every borough to continue these party efforts. Charges of unprecedented use of money by Conservatives were widely made. *Punch* sketched Derby parodying Peel: "The Battle of the Constitution must be *bought* in the Registration Courts."[2]

Palmerston's coalition ministry did not include Bright, who, men had professed to believe, held the key to the Liberal situation.[3] His exclusion was an ominous portent for reform. The Whigs would not go beyond Russell's six-pound franchise, nor would they go even so far if they could find a loophole of escape. The European question permitted them to postpone the matter for a time; then Palmerston and the *Times* whipped up a French panic, as many believed, to divert attention from reform.[4] Bright declared that the

[1] November, 1859.

[2] Quoted in *Leeds Mercury*, May 5, 1859.

[3] It did include Milner Gibson, however, and Cobden declined a place in it.

[4] Trevelyan, *Bright*, p. 284, and W. N. Molesworth, *History of England*, 1830-1874, III. 146, 169.

oligarchy would consider a war with France a cheap price to pay for a few years' respite from the question.

Finally, when, in March, 1860, the government introduced its bill for a six-pound borough franchise, it met with scant favor, was encumbered with obstructions that the government made little effort to prevent, and was withdrawn in June.

And yet the whole tone of the debate on this measure was different from that of any preceding debate on the question. It possessed at once a character of indifference and of deepest concern. Members knew that this particular bill was not to be taken seriously, but they also knew that the whole question was approaching a critical and more dangerous stage. An intense and newly augmented dread of conferring political power upon the working classes is evident throughout the debate. The reason, beyond question, was that the builders' and other recent strikes had made trade-unions for the first time a reality for conservative England. Their power, their efficiency, their apparently easily aroused sense of solidarity, and their heterodox opinions on wages and hours, miners' legislation, and the like, were all staggeringly manifest to the world in 1858-60. A *laissez faire* England, a hitherto middle-class and aristocratic England, was called upon to enfranchise workingmen, who were carrying on a conflict which was regarded as a class war as truly as Chartism had been, and far more ominous, because more efficient. Furthermore, the coöperation between workingmen and Bright's followers, chiefly with the object of fiscal reform, was not reassuring. To the propertied classes it meant only the class war from another angle. The conservative reaction to the situation, as it thus revealed itself, was to stiffen the ranks of opposition, to draw closer the cordon of property against the threatening advance of democracy, and thereby to save English aristocratic institutions based upon property. An overwhelming majority of the House of Commons, by tacit consent, set themselves to hold the line for as long a period as they might be able.

Much evidence can be adduced to substantiate these observations. In the first place, it is enlightening to examine the debate in parliament for the purpose of discovering the attitude toward trade-unionism there revealed. Disraeli's opening attack on the bill pointed to recent events as proving the power of combination and discipline possessed by the working classes who were now to be admitted into the constitution in a body. They would act as a unit, because their "opinion, feelings and habits are identical." If they were admitted, counterpoises reckoned on the basis of the payment of direct taxes were an absolute essential.[1] Ker Seymer, of Dorsetshire, declared it impossible to forget recent events in the building trades and the constant strikes; Potter had recently actually addressed his "poor dupes" in the language of triumph. Such unintelligent action on the part of workingmen, he said, struck many with uneasiness.[2] Another member quoted at length from a pamphlet by Potter on the builders' strike and deduced similar evidence of false economics from Dunning's pamphlet on trade-unions.[3] Lord Robert Montague used the late strikes as damning evidence; workingmen, he said, had much to avenge against capitalists.[4] Lord Robert Cecil referred to the strength of trade-unions and to Bright's recent advice to them to act politically,[5] which Lord Robert was confident they would

[1] *Hansard,* CLVII. 842-6.
[2] *Ibid.,* CLVII. 1085.
[3] Rt. Hon. J. Whiteside, *ibid.,* CLVII. 1103-5.
[4] *Ibid.,* CLVII. 2200.
[5] Noted in *Reynolds's Newspaper,* January 22, 1860.

do by combining to throw off the burden of taxation, which Bright also condemned.[1]

Adam Black, a Liberal of Edinburgh, whose name was henceforth anathema to workingmen, denounced their passion, their ready acceptance of such delusions as the possibility of receiving ten hours' pay for nine hours' work, and their tyranny over each other, as demonstrated by Potter's influence. Trade-unions would ruin English manufactures. In the recent election, he stated that he had been asked if he would favor an eight-hour bill. "I told them to their faces that the putting of such a question only showed the danger of giving them the franchise." He doubted if members were aware of the number of trade-unionists—six hundred thousand, said Potter—and all under the command of a small, energetic executive.[2]

From a Liberal member for Salisbury came a similar argument. If this bill passed, no man could hope to be elected who would not promise an eight-hour law.[3] A Berkshire member predicted that if workingmen were sent to parliament time would be wasted in discussions of wages, capital, and labor, and "the grievances of journeymen bakers, who disliked night work," and other matters "which did not lie within the province of legislation."[4] Du Cane, of North Essex, read an article from the *Weekly Dispatch* which cited the builders' strike as evidence of the close understanding that existed among trade societies and all working-class organizations.

Some of them possess an organization so perfect that in a few hours the Central Council could set in motion every affiliated branch throughout the empire. It is on these classes the franchise is about to be conferred. Who or what can stand before them? They will

[1] *Hansard,* CLVII. 2213.
[2] *Ibid.,* CLVIII. 137 ff.
[3] *Ibid.,* CLVIII. 166 ff.
[4] *Ibid.,* CLVIII. 352.

poll to a man—will they not all poll one way? It is notorious that the middle classes do not possess the cohesion and spirit of union which support the power of the working classes. Henceforward, for weal or woe, the Democratic element reigns in England.[1]

In the House of Lords, Derby pointed to the simultaneous introduction of a reform bill and of Gladstone's budget, which was based on the assumption that taxes were too heavy on the lower classes and too light on the upper, and which involved a deficit to be met *after* reform. He believed the new voters would follow agitators and were themselves unable to form correct political judgments. The existing electorate, he declared, were filled with the "utmost apprehension" over the prospective effects of the measure.[2]

If these debates afford a revelation of a sharper fear of an extension of the franchise than had been felt before and of trade-unions as the cause, testimony of the same kind can be added from other sources. A pamphleteer of Manchester would have allowed no trade-unionist a vote.[3] The *Economist* in August, 1859, asserted that the strike then raging proved the wisdom of admitting a portion of the working classes to the franchise, but the danger of their predominance.[4] The *Westminster Review,* commenting upon the report of the Executive Committee of the Master Builders' Association, expressed its fear that trade-unions would act politically for such objects as a reduction of hours. "It becomes a grave question how far we may safely give polit-

[1] *Hansard,* CLVIII, p. 406.
[2] *Hansard,* CLVII. 1961 ff. In 1865, in a debate upon a reform bill introduced by Baines, Horsman pointed to the change in the attitude of members of parliament toward reform that was manifested from 1860 on. Only in that year, he declared, did members begin to look upon a reform bill as a practical business question, and as such to oppose it. This attitude had been much intensified by 1865, he said. (Quoted in an editorial in the *Times* of May 10, 1865.)
[3] "Reform: Look before you Leap," quoted in *Newcastle Weekly Chronicle,* February 12, 1859.
[4] Quoted in *Leeds Mercury,* August 30, 1859.

ical power into the hands of those who entertain views so erroneous respecting fundamental social relations. . . . Men who are ready to render up their private liberties to the despotic rulers of trade-unions, seem scarcely independent enough to exercise political liberties." They would try to gain by political power what they now seek to gain by private organization. Furthermore, it declared, the mischievous activities of reformed municipalities of late, in providing at public expense baths, parks, libraries, etc., thereby increasing the burdens on the rich, should act as a warning.[1] The editor of the *Newcastle Weekly Chronicle* remarked a few years later:

When the working men of the metropolis showed their skill in combination during the great strike in the building trades, the Tories frightened the timid occupants of the opposition benches by conjuring up a spectacle of terror and anarchy.[2]

Perhaps the most valuable evidence is that brought out by Earl Grey's committee on the elective franchise in 1860. Many inquiries were put as to the actual or probable political activity of trade societies or their members. R. D. Baxter, an authority on electoral statistics and those pertaining to the working classes, testifying as to Sheffield, said he believed that if matters arose specially affecting artisans, or in case trade-unions were to attempt to send one of their own number to parliament, the electorate, if increased by a six-pound franchise, would be in the hands of a "knot of men in a public house" like those who were directing the builders' strike in London. Also, the working classes, he stated, had "entirely different objects in view as regards restrictions on labour, from what the educated classes have."[3] A solicitor of Leeds believed trade-unionists would act together in a

[1] April 1, 1860.
[2] September 16, 1864.
[3] *Report,* pp. 176-8.

time of excitement or disputes with masters, and could and would control elections.   He admitted, however, that they never had acted politically in Yorkshire.[1]   A Conservative witness feared workingmen would, without question, elect "factory delegates" to parliament.[2]   Henry Ashworth, cotton-spinner of Bolton and close student of labor problems, after testifying to the intense interest the operatives and miners of Lancashire took in politics, declared that even now, when employment became scarce, they talked of Feargus O'Connor and universal suffrage, believing their condition to be an affair of government.   He believed they would make the question of wages and hours a political one.[3]   Edward Baines, M.P. for Leeds and a leading nonconformist, feared the same danger.[4]   So also did a Liberal election agent of London, who pointed to the attempt of the builders in their strike to influence members of parliament.[5]

Trade-union political activity was a possiblity, then, to be feared on its own account; add to it the fact that trade-unions and Bright appeared to be in political alliance, and the situation became ominous indeed.   It did not matter that the alliance was not wholly successful.   Many did not realize that.   Most of the upper and middle classes saw in the situation a menace to property.   One contemporary declared that Bright's agitation had changed the whole aspect of affairs; that he had "frightened into sincerity many a man whose Democratic theories were merely Bunkum" by boldly disclosing that his aim was to dethrone one class and install another, thereby shifting the basis upon which the Constitution rested.[6]   In the debate in parliament one

[1] *Ibid.*, pp. 217-8.
[2] *Ibid.*, p. 130.
[3] *Ibid.*, pp. 455-466.
[4] *Ibid.*, pp. 446-453.
[5] *Ibid.*, pp. 227-230.
[6] *Bentley's Quarterly Review,* March, 1859.

member considered that Bright's taxation agitation por-
tended a graduated property tax.[1]

In view of the amount of evidence to that effect, it is
not a hasty assumption to declare that in 1859-60 the reform question in parliament and among the majority of
electors took on a new aspect of danger to property and
institutions that stiffened the resistance offered to it by the
moderate and the propertied classes. A common sentiment
of antagonism to any reform, as dangerous in itself and as
likely soon to lead to a wider extension of the suffrage,
possessed the great body of the politically significant classes.
In 1861 Russell stated in parliament his opinion that for
two or three years past—"especially last year"—the middle
classes had radically altered their view of reform; "they are
not in favour of the admission of the working classes into
the number of those who hold the franchise, and that opposition given the bill last year proceeded far more from the
middle classes than from either the House of Lords or from
any portion of the upper classes of this country."[2]   Late
in 1860 Gladstone remarked in a letter to Graham upon
"how much the tone of ultratoryism prevails among a large
portion of the liberal party."[3]   And Lord Stanley wrote to
Disraeli that business men generally were afraid of Russell's
bill and that the country was full of Conservative opinion
disguised as moderate Liberalism.[4] Bouverie, Liberal
member for Kilmarnock, explained the defeat of Russell's
bill as due to the following causes: lack of a favorable public opinion; alarm at the prevalence of strikes and a widely
held belief that trade-unions were going beyond their legitimate sphere by interfering with the natural laws of trade;

[1] *Hansard*, CLVII. 1088.
[2] *Ibid.*, CLXI. 1922.
[3] Morley, *Gladstone*, II. 37.
[4] Monypenny and Buckle, *op. cit.*, IV. 272, note 2.

and, finally, John Bright's speeches, in which he put forth the idea that social inequalities and inequalities in wealth were the result of political inequality, and in which he treated reform as an issue between classes.[1]

The situation in parliament and in the country, therefore, for a few years after 1860, made possible, even demanded, an interregnum like that during Palmerston's last ministry. Because his face was set against all change in existing institutions, Palmerston reigned over acquiescent Conservatives as well as Liberals. For the next five years, he personified the House of Commons, elected to enact reform, but killing it with neglect. Factions had for the time ceased, and the majority opinion was more honestly expressed than when Conservatives fought Whigs, while both knew that they were as one upon the chief issue of domestic politics.

But an agreed and harmonious parliament could have only a momentary existence. The great forces out of doors were not agreed and not harmonious. The issue that had meant parliamentary chaos during the decade of the fifties was in 1865 to break up the calm waters of a Palmerstonian régime. Again men had to take up in all seriousness a position toward the question of democracy. The age of Gladstone was ready to succeed to the age of Palmerston. Only when the new factional strife in parliament had resulted in a settlement of the question could the old parties come back into their own as the embodiment of genuine principles and policies.

The unenfranchised had evinced little interest in Russell's bill. It is significant that from this time on workingmen leaders, especially in London, took a more decided stand for manhood suffrage as the only suffrage adequate to enfranchise their class. They organized manhood-suf-

[1] *Reynolds's Newspaper,* November 4, 1860.

frage associations that continued active until they were absorbed by the national manhood-suffrage Reform League, formed in 1865. In fact, political agitation among working-men, both trade-unionist and non-trade-unionist, continued at an accelerated pace from 1860 on. The strictly trade-unionist phase was inaugurated by the builders' strike and the formation of trades' councils. All phases were stimulated by contact with foreign workmen and interest in liberation movements in other lands. To these developments let us now turn our attention.

CHAPTER VIII

TRADE-UNIONS AND POLITICS IN THE SIXTIES

The nine-hour movement among the building trades and the struggle that it precipitated in 1859-60 proved to be the beginning of a new era in the history of trade-unionism. From that date to the date of their great political victory of 1875-6, the history of trade organizations is one of constantly widening influence in both the industrial and the political sphere. This chapter is an effort to describe the growth of this influence during the sixties with special reference to its political aspect and its contribution to the development of the particular political situation out of which the Reform Act of 1867 came. Along with trade-union activities are considered also any significant similar movements among the working classes at large. The proportionate part played by trade organizations or their members was noticeably larger than at any period since the middle of the century.

It is well first to survey briefly the social and intellectual condition of the working classes in order to be able the better to judge of them as factors in society and politics. First, as to their wages.[1] Conditions in Lancashire may be cited as an example. David Chadwick[2] in 1860 estimated that the wages of nearly all classes of factory operatives in Lancashire had risen from ten to fifteen per cent. in the past twenty years. Quoting Henry Ashworth, he says that in 1850 an

[1] Statistics compiled from various sources can be found in Park, *English Reform Bill of 1867*, ch. ii.

[2] D. Chadwick, *On the rate of Wages in Two Hundred Trades and Branches of Labour in Manchester and Salford and the Manufacturing District of Lancashire during the Twenty Years from 1839 to 1859*, etc. Read before the Statistical Society of London. 2nd edit., London, 1860. These figures were used by Bowley in his *Wages in the United Kingdom in the Nineteenth Century*, but there is a slight variation. See table for Manchester after pp. 118 and 122.

average spinner's wage was nineteen shillings; in 1859 it
was twenty-five shillings a week.   In the silk trade, the
average rise had been ten per cent. since 1849.   In such unskilled trades as calico printing, dyeing, and bleaching, however, there had been a decrease.   Among the building trades,
bricklayers' wages had risen about ten per cent. since 1849
(with a slight decrease in hours) ; stonemasons' about seven
per cent.; plasterers' and painters' slightly more; and joiners' wages had not risen at all.   In the mechanical trades,
reckoning since 1839, wages had risen from six and one-half
per cent. to fourteen per cent. in some branches, and to nearly
fifty per cent. in the case of boiler makers, but had decreased
as much as fifteen per cent. in others.   Chadwick's figures
show no increase in the ten years before 1859 for screwers,
drillers, tin-plate workers, millwrights, moulders, wire workers, cabinet makers, coach builders, printers, engravers,
clockmakers, leather workers, paper makers, paper hangers,
glass makers, bakers, tailors, coopers, wheelwrights, and gas-
men.   In fact, many had suffered a decrease.   Miners'
wages in the Lancashire district had fallen very low in 1849
and by 1859 had been restored practically to what they had
been in 1839.

Chadwick's discussion also included an estimate of the
decrease since 1839 in the price of food, which he calculated
absorbed nearly two thirds of the weekly wage of a skilled
workman with a family of three.   This decrease he placed
at twenty per cent., or a saving of fourteen per cent. of the
income.   Most of this decrease, however, had taken place by
1850.   During the decade of the fifties prices had been
steadily rising.

None of these figures take into consideration periods of
unemployment.   Another statistician figures unemployment
percentages in the leading organized trades as 1.61% of the
membership in 1860, 4.28% in 1861, 7.81% in 1862, 5.74%

in 1863, 2.56% in 1864, and 8.51% in 1868. At that point there was a steady drop until the lowest point was reached in 1872.[1]

As to London, Bowley gives the weekly wage of an artisan as 36s in 1867, having risen from 28s in 1833.[2] The provincial artisan received about 27s in 1867; the town laborer, 20s; and the agricultural laborer, 14s. Baxter estimated the amount of national income that went to a skilled worker in 1867 as £50 a year; to a lower grade of worker as £33 and 10s.[3] Taking the wages of 1890 as 100, Bowley gives the index figures for 1840-50 as 60, for 1850-60 as 65, for 1860-70 as 75.[4] All of these figures show an improvement, though not to a great extent.

Savings bank deposits had increased between 1842 and 1857 by £9,290,405, and the number of depositors by 485,-268. In 1862 there were a hundred thousand members of four hundred retail coöperative societies.[5]

The advance of workingmen in social and intellectual conditions had been considerable since 1850. The first workingmen's college had been established at Sheffield in 1842. Others had followed, and in 1867 about half of their students were estimated to be genuine workingmen.[6] In 1861 there were ninety schools of design with 15,483 pupils, largely of the working classes.[7] In 1867 it was said that the pupils of two hundred and twenty schools of science were all from

[1] G. H. Wood, *Some Statistics of Working Class Progress Since 1860*, London, 1900.

[2] A. L. Bowley, *Wages in the United Kingdom in the Nineteenth Century*, London, 1900, p. 70.

[3] Quoted in Bowley, *op. cit.*, p. 65. Unskilled workers' share was twenty-four pounds ten shillings.

[4] *Op. cit.*, p. 126.

[5] S. and B. Webb, *The Consumers' Coöperative Movement*, London, 1921, p. 16.

[6] J. M. Ludlow and L. Jones, *The Progress of the Working Classes*, 1832-1867, London, 1867, p. 177.

[7] *Ibid.*, p. 160.

these classes.[1] As to elementary education, the proportion
of day scholars to the population in England and Wales in
1851 was one in 8.36; in 1858 it was one in 7.7. The average
daily attendance at schools rose from 531,210 in 1857 to
901,750 in 1865.[2] Between 1841 and 1862, the proportion
of men who signed the marriage register with a mark fell
from 32.7% to 23%, and of women from 48.8% to 28.5%.[3]
Chadwick, however, tells a worse story for the cotton districts. Of fifty thousand Lancashire operatives examined
by Factory Commissioners in 1856, 83% could read, but
only 38% could write.[4] Ludlow and Jones concluded their
careful study of conditions in 1867 with the assertion that
"the testimonies to the improvement in the character of the
working population generally by means of education are so
abundant that in reference to them it is puzzling to know
where to begin, or where to leave off."[5]

Public libraries maintained out of local rates had been
authorized by law in 1850, and since then had been established in practically all large towns. Certain trade societies
maintained libraries of their own. Newspaper circulation
had greatly increased since the removal of the newspaper
tax in 1855.[6] The number of newspapers in the United
Kingdom by 1861 had increased by four hundred. In one
hundred and twenty-three towns papers had been established
where none had existed before 1855. Of the two hundred
and fifteen newspapers in London, seventy were in 1861
selling at two pence or less. In Derbyshire, Lancashire,
Nottinghamshire, Worcestershire, and Leicestershire, the

[1] Ludlow and Jones, *op. cit.*, p. 162.
[2] *Ibid.*, p. 149.
[3] *Ibid.*, p. 149.
[4] *On the Rate of Wages,* etc., p. 7.
[5] *Op. cit.*, p. 151.
[6] All of the following figures are taken from a pamphlet: *Newspaper Press Census for 1861,* London, 1861.

number had doubled since 1855.   In the midlands all the
newspapers were cheap except one.   In the northern counties ninety-eight papers had been started since 1855, and all
were cheap (selling for two pence or less).   Of the total
number of two hundred and four papers in the North, one
hundred and thirty-five were of this class.   As to politics,
there were in all England two hundred and eighty-five
Liberal papers, one hundred and twenty-six Conservative,
eighty-five independent, and three hundred and thirteen
neutral.

Mechanics' Institutes, of which there were probably one
thousand two hundred in 1861, with a membership of two
hundred thousand, were especially numerous in Lancashire
and Yorkshire.   In 1860 the "Yorkshire Union of Mechanics' Institutes" had one hundred and twenty-seven constituent bodies.   In Leeds it was said that one out of every
eighty-four of the population belonged, and in Huddersfield
one out of every twenty-one.[1]   These Institutes had tended
everywhere to become tradesmen's or middle-class clubs.[2]
Yet their influence upon workingmen was attested by Reverend Henry Solly, a lifelong worker among the working
classes, who said that in his experience invariably the
mechanics of superior education and aspirations proved to
have received much from these institutions.[3]   A new type
of organization, the workingmen's clubs, chiefly for whole-
some amusement, was becoming an important social influence by 1865.

A modification of the wretched living conditions in
populous sections of large cities had been begun by the
Public Health Act of 1848, which set up a central Board of
Health to advise and assist local boards whose creation was

[1] *Working Men's College Magazine,* October 1, 1860.
[2] Henry Solly, in *These Eighty Years,* II. 157, London, 1893, describes
how operatives were shouldered out.
[3] *Ibid.,* II. 161, note.

empowered.[1] By the end of 1853 one hundred and eighty-two local boards had been set up, and the central board, in spite of constant obstruction by vested interests, was able to accomplish some slight good. The housing problem received its first grudging attention in 1851 with Ashley's Common Lodging House Act. In 1855 overcrowding was prohibited in a valuable Nuisance Removal Act, which was extended in 1866 to compel local authorities to condemn unfit buildings and build new ones for working-class dwellings. The Public Works Loan Commission could lend money for this purpose, secured by the local rates.[2] But until the passing of the legislation of 1875, only the barest beginning had been made in the direction of rendering the poorer sections of cities fit for decent habitation.

A survey of the conditions prevailing in the early sixties discloses a limited amount of improvement and a more hopeful outlook for the future. But it would be an error to overrate the amelioration wrought by the two decades since the hungry forties. Available statistics apply chiefly to the upper ranks of labor. The vast majority, unorganized and subject to each slight variation of economic conditions, could not yet sing paeans to English prosperity. These facts must be borne in mind as the background against which to sketch political developments.

We may now resume the narrative of working-class political activities between 1860 and 1867. Special emphasis should be placed upon their most significant aspect, the participation therein of trade-unions and their members.

---

[1] G. Slater, *The Making of Modern England*, pp. 166 ff.

[2] E. R. Dewsnup, *The Housing Problem in England*, Manchester, 1907, chapter vi; table of these Laws, p. 89. The extension of the Nuisance Act in 1866, and further amendment in 1867-8, created much alarm. The *Morning Star* said it proposed a revolution (February 22, 1866). In parliament one member called it a leaf from the book of Louis Blanc, and feared it would end in *ateliers nationaux* (*English Leader*, February 23, 1867).

The chief reason for this increasing participation was the legal restrictions under which trade societies rested. Particularly obnoxious were the Master and Servant Law and the application to trade disputes of the common law of conspiracy. Furthermore, trade-unions could claim the rights of legal bodies only by a falsification of their rules so as to be brought under the Friendly Societies' Act. And constantly they rested under the apprehension that hostile legislation might at any moment place trade-unions under such restrictions as to destroy them completely.

The builders' strike was the opening of a new political movement on the part of the trades. Out of it grew the London Trades' Council, whose rules declared its duties to be "to watch over the general interests of labour, political and social, both in and out of Parliament."[1] Within four years the council had become the organ of the small group of national trade-union officials with headquarters in London, who from 1860, in coöperation with certain provincial leaders and councils, guided the political action of trade-unions.[2] These men—the Junta and their allies—turned to this method of emancipating the worker, rather than to a sole dependence upon industrial strife.

They believed that a levelling down of all political privileges, and the opening out of educational and social opportunities to all classes of the community, would bring in its train a large measure of economic equality. Under the influence of these leaders the London Unions, and eventually those of the provinces, were drawn into a whole series of political agitations, for the franchise, for amendment of the Master and Servant Law, for a new Mines Regulation Act, for National Education, and finally for the full legalization of Trade Unions themselves.[3]

For these purposes, they used the trade councils, which they made "the political organs of the Trade Union world."[4]

[1] C. Richards, *A History of Trades Councils from 1860 to 1875* (introduction by G. D. H. Cole), London, 1920, p. 11.
[2] *Ibid.*, p. 15.
[3] Webb, *History of Trade Unionism*, p. 241.
[4] *Ibid.*, p. 242.

The London manhood suffragists had, in 1859-60, endeavored to enlist the trades in their agitation. One chairman declared that if they would act "they would no longer have need for any strikes . . . for they would be enabled to have justice done to them by their employers."[1] Passmore Edwards and Benjamin Lucraft repeatedly attempted to organize conferences of delegates of trade and other working-class organizations to further political reform.[2] But the trades were unresponsive. The membership was fearful of the disrupting influence of politics and was absorbed in the daily struggle for a living and in frequent contests over wages. The one exception seems to have been the shoemakers who, says Howell, often joined in political movements by vote of the members.[3] There was in 1859 a "Reform Society of City Boot and Shoe Makers" with two branches;[4] in 1861 the First Trade Union Directory listed a "Boot Makers' City Reform Association" with four lodges, and a "Boot and Shoe-Makers (strong) Reform Association" with three lodges.[5] It was the task of the leaders of trade-unions to win them away from their non-political attitude. Of these leaders, Howell says, many had been associated with Chartists and with international democratic movements and were, therefore, prepared to form new combinations to advance the old cause of political freedom.[6]

Certain incidents testify to the interest of trade-union leaders in the subject of a reform of the franchise at the opening of the decade. The Amalgamated Engineers officially protested against permitting Lord Robert Montague, M.P.,

[1] Reynolds's Newspaper, January 22, 1860.
[2] Ibid.
[3] Labour Legislation, Labour Movements, etc., p. 140.
[4] Builders' Salesman and Mechanics' Advertiser, September 17, 1859.
[5] United Kingdom. First Annual Trades' Union Directory, London, 1861, p. 42. (In the Goldsmiths' Library.)
[6] Labour Legislation, etc., p. 140.

to preside at a meeting of the building trades called for the purpose of reopening the nine-hour movement. Their protest was based upon the fact that Montague had opposed Russell's reform bill of 1860. They even sent an officer to the meeting in question to demand that Montague apologize in the House of Commons for words used in that debate. A lively controversy over the incident was carried on in the press and elsewhere for some time.[1] Another incident points to a similar interest in reform. In March, 1861, the *Journal of Typographic Arts* repudiated a scheme proposed by Mackinnon, Liberal member for Rye, to establish councils of conciliation, partially on the ground that Mackinnon's speeches on the reform bill proved his utter inability to understand the character or the requirements of the classes for whom he proposed to legislate.

The building trades continued through 1861 to be the center of trade-union interest. A struggle with employers as desperate as that of the preceding year took place. In the course of it, the new London Trades Council won its first parliamentary victory by forcing the government to recall soldiers it had lent to replace men on strike at the Chelsea barracks.[2] The profound influence these great contests were having upon the trades involved is evident from an examination of the reports and trade journal of the Operative Bricklayers. A report of their executive committee upon the dispute over the hour system of payment, signed by E. Coulson, G. Howell, C. Shearman, and H. A. Noble, reveals as Chartist a tone as any document of ten years before. It declared, "Labour is the primary source of all

[1] *Reynolds's Newspaper,* July 22 and August 5, 1860.

[2] An account of the whole builders' movement to date is found in the Report of the London Operative Bricklayers' Executive Committee, November, 1861, on the Dispute relating to the Hour System of Payment. (Appended to the Society's *Trade Circular and General Reporter,* for July 1, 1862.)

wealth," yet the "idlers" enjoyed the most of it. They
made the laws and had thus been able to keep down the
real producers. On the question of hours the committee
quoted Owen and Comte.[1]   At the same time its *Trade
Circular* was advocating the union of all trades in a Labour
Parliament to "legislate for labour" and to exercise influence
"upon all social and political questions affecting their common interests."[2]   It published a letter from Charles Neate,
Professor of Political Economy at Oxford, in which he
used the case of the Chelsea barracks to point the lesson of
the need of political power, saying it ought to show them
their mistake "in appearing, as you have done, indifferent to
the extension of the suffrage."[3]

In December, 1861, the *Circular* carried a long letter
arguing for the political use of trade-unions. Strikes for an
increase of wages or shorter hours, it stated, only touched
the surface. "The machinery of trade-unions . . . might
be turned to raise millions of men in social position and
thereby lay for centuries of years the foundation of national
freedom and power."   The vote was not to be sought for
political reasons, but "purely as a measure for the advancement of the respectable working classes in their social position, and as a guarantee for their industrial rights and privileges."   The editor of the *Circular* approved the policy here
outlined and suggested the formation of a great political
trade-union committee of five hundred members. He admitted, however, the existence of much difference of opinion
among trades upon the whole question.[4]

Not alone were the building trades and the London
Trades Council projecting political action.   In November,

[1] See above, p. 205, note 2.
[2] *Operative Bricklayers' Society's Trade Circular and General Reporter*, October 1, 1861.   It began publication in September, 1861.
[3] *Ibid.*, September 1, 1861.
[4] *Circular*, December 1, 1861.

1861, the Glasgow Trades Council, representing over thirty trades of the west of Scotland, issued an address favoring such a policy. It continued to urge this until action was taken on it in the matter of the Master and Servant Law in 1864. The address[1] is important enough to quote from at length. Declaring the belief of the council in manhood suffrage as the ultimate goal of reform, it yet advised the expediency of accepting whatever could be obtained and of using that as a vantage ground from which to work for greater victories. It continued:

We would respectfully, yet confidently, declare that the various trade societies of the country are the best existing machinery for carrying out a successful movement of this kind. We are aware that many are opposed to trades' meetings being mixed with politics; we cannot coincide with such views so long as trades societies are amenable to the law. There are several matters in law that affect them, such as those relating to combinations of working men, and the inequality of the law of master and servant; also how many times have they been baffled in the attempt to establish councils of conciliation and arbitration? By what means are these measures to be rectified or obtained but by the possession of political power?— the want of which affects the whole labouring class. If these things be true, how can it be that working men, in their associated capacity, ought not to entertain politics? . . . We conclude by submitting our plan of action, which is that all trades' councils, trades societies and such like associated bodies at once memorialise the government to fulfill their pledge in the ensuing session of Parliament; after which let a monster national petition be got up for presentation to parliament on the day of its opening, in favour of a comprehensive measure of reform.

This proposal, declared Bradlaugh's *National Reformer*, secured wide discussion, but the general attitude toward it was hostile.[2] One notable exception was the favor shown to the project by Bright. He wrote the Glasgow Trades Council that he approved such a movement on the part of

[1] Contained in *Reynolds's Newspaper*, November 10, 1861.

[2] C. F. Brand, in the *American Historical Review*, January, 1925, in an article on "The Conversion of the British Trade-Unions to Political Action," shows that the proposition was discussed in the London Trades Council, but rejected because the trades disapproved (p. 252).

the unenfranchised.[1] In fact, Bright in a speech at Birmingham over a year before had advised trade-unions to agitate for reform.[2]

The industrial struggle between employers and employed continued unabated. In parliament a prominent Conservative was led to declare that the great social question of the day was the growing alienation between middle and working classes as shown by strikes and trade-unions.[3] A new and sinister aspect was being given to the conflict by what have been labeled the Sheffield outrages. As early as in 1861 came the first reports of violent measures adopted by Sheffield trades to terrorize workers into joining the unions and submitting to their dictation. Those guilty of the outrages were, says one authority, with a single exception, small societies with occupations purely local and very destructive of life. The men knew they could not live long and so acted recklessly in attempts to secure high wages.[4] Early in 1862 the large unions were denouncing the proceedings at Sheffield.[5]

The reaction of the outrages upon the political situation was immediate. Holyoake pointed to the use at once made of them as an argument against enfranchisement;[6] so did Bradlaugh.[7] Charles Kingsley, whose words had just weight with workingmen, declared that if unions did not drag to punishment their offending members they would prove themselves "incapable morally as well as politico-economi-

[1] National Reformer, November 23, 1861.

[2] Reynolds's Newspaper, January 8, 1860; Quarterly Review, April, 1866, p. 545.

[3] Newdegate, in a debate on the Country Franchise bill. Hansard, CLCI. 603.

[4] Ludlow and Jones, Progress of the Working Classes, 1832-1867, pp. x-xv.

[5] See Bookbinders' Circular, January 21, 1862; Reynolds's Newspaper, January 26, 1862; the National Reformer, February 8, 1862.

[6] National Reformer, February 8, 1862.

[7] Ibid., January 25.

cally" and would have to be put down, leaving capitalism to reign unrestrained. "I, and others, have been seeing with dread the growing inclination of the governing classes to put down the Trades' Unions by strong measures."[1] Unfortunately for the labor movement, these outrages continued throughout the decade, spreading eventually to Manchester and other cities. Their effect in hardening resistance to reform was great, but eventually they served to enhance by contrast the peaceful and disciplined methods of trade-unions as a whole, by forcing an exhaustive investigation of the whole question.

Meanwhile, leading trade-unionists were increasingly becoming politically-minded. By 1862 the London Trades Council had been joined by the large national societies and had come under the control of their officials. George Odger, the foremost working-class politician of two decades, had become its secretary, and the council was entering into correspondence with similar bodies elsewhere. Thus began a nation-wide coöperation among leaders, which, with other influences, was to lead before long to the formation of the Trade Union Congress.[2] The council continued its policy of parliamentary agitation in behalf of measures it favored, and in 1862 entered into communication with the working-men of Naples—a step which was one of a direct succession of events that resulted in the International Working Men's Association.

The large societies had by this time a regular organ in the press in George Potter's *Bee Hive,* which continued to serve this purpose for nearly twenty years.[3] In April,

[1] *Ibid.,* January 25.

[2] Members of Parliament as early as 1860 were much interested in the growing consolidation of the trade-union movement, as evinced in the builders' strike. The Select Committee on Masters and Operatives questioned George Potter closely on the subject. (See *Report* of this Committee, 1860, p. 67.)

[3] C. Richards, *History of Trade Councils,* p. 15.

1862, in an article on "Purposes of Reform," it declared:

We do not seek an extension of the suffrage, etc., for abstract reasons, nor for party purposes, but as a social necessity to combat the deteriorating influences of society, the diminishing earnings of the great body of the people, and their gradually increasing outlay on the necessaries of existence.[1]

Then, touching upon a matter in which workingmen were intensely interested—emigration and the land as a solution for unemployment—it declared: "Parliament will not place the people on the colonial lands, so long as it is composed exclusively of members whose interest it is to keep wages low." Such a procedure on the part of the government would be reckoned as revolutionary now, but "that is the description of revolution that we expect from Universal Suffrage, equal representation, and a Parliament reflecting the people."

The importance of the leaders who assumed control of the labor movement in the sixties cannot be over-emphasized. Foremost were those included in the so-called Junta— George Howell and E. Coulson of the Bricklayers' Society, William Allan of the Engineers, George Odger of the Shoemakers, and Robert Applegarth, who became secretary of the new Amalgamated Society of Carpenters and Joiners in 1862. In addition, there were others who, while playing a less effective part industrially, were as important as the Junta in politics up to 1867. Among these may be mentioned W. R. Cremer and T. G. Facey, carpenters, and William Stainsby, of the tailors.

Outside of these groups and at times at war with them was George Potter, the organizer of the builders' movement and editor of the *Bee Hive*. Alternately denounced and accepted by the officers of national societies who com-

[1] Quoted in *Barker's Review*, April 26, 1862.

prised the London Trades Council and the Junta,[1] Potter moved as an erratic force in the working-class world. He wielded, nevertheless, a great amount of influence both in the political and the industrial field. It is perhaps safe to state that up to 1867 he loomed larger in the minds of the middle and upper classes as a leader and exponent of labor than did any other man. In the provinces his influence over trade societies was extensive. The feud that developed between him and the Junta did not succeed in injuring his position until after the passage of the franchise act; and even after that his position in working-class politics was important. The nature of the feud itself is significant. It developed out of the opposition between Potter's aggressive trade policy and the more cautious policy of the Junta.[2] In a certain sense Potter embodied the spirit of the "new unionism" of the last of the century, which was to rise up against the policy of the Junta, which had by that time become traditional, and call it a betrayal. Fortunate was it for trade-unionism, however, that the more bourgeois-minded Junta made good their leadership in the critical decade of the sixties.

All of these leaders, except perhaps William Allan, believed in political action by trade-unions. Applegarth, for instance, declared at the moment of assuming office in his society that he was going to try to induce it to go into politics.[3] This purpose common to the leaders crystallized in the autumn of 1862 in the formation of an organization of trade-unionists, called the "Manhood Suffrage and Vote by

[1] See the MS minutes of the conference of Amalgamated Trades (The Junta), 1867-1871, in the British Library of Political Science, for evidence of these relations.
[2] See account in C. Richards, *History of Trade Councils*, pp. 20-22, and Webb, *op. cit.*, pp. 254-5. Personal animosity and jealousy had much to do with the feud, no doubt.
[3] A. W. Humphrey, *Robert Applegarth*, London, 1913, p. 26. This author says Allan deprecated such action, and certainly his political activity is very slightly evident before 1867.

Ballot Association," for the purpose of agitating the trades. It issued an address to them signed by Applegarth, Howell, Odger, Cremer, Facey, and others,[1] which asserted that "all the evils under which we suffer have a common origin, namely, an excess of political power in the hands of those holding a higher social position." Now, they believed, the organized workers should undertake to advance the interests of the "toiling masses" by political action. Their intention was not to convert trade societies into political organizations and thus divert them from their social objects, "but we must not forget that we are citizens and as such should have citizens' rights. Recollect, also, that by obtaining those rights we shall be able more effectually to secure our legitimate demands as unionists." In these sentences they phrased the two reasons for the political agitation by workmen for the next five years. The association intended to try to draw together the many members of unions who were already active in various political societies and to invite the coöperation of all trade-unionists of the United Kingdom, either as corporate bodies or as individuals. It deprecated all violent measures. "Let our advocacy be firm, intelligent, and persistent; not a sowing of the seeds of discord, but a promotion of the growth of union; not an exciting of class against class, but an endeavor to extend the welfare of all." The preamble to the rules of the association based its demand for manhood suffrage upon the double ground of natural right and the payment of taxes.

George Howell, writing the history of working-class politics up to 1867, stressed this association as an important link in the development of public opinion that finally forced

[1] Humphrey, *op. cit.*, p. 57, says Applegarth wrote the address. Howell says in a MS letter of September 24, 1867, in the Reform League Letter Book, that he wrote it. For the Address see *Reynolds's Newspaper*, November 23, 1862, and Humphrey, *Applegarth*, pp. 57-9.

the measure of that year.   He states that the association continued its work quietly up to the time of the formation of the all-embracing Reform League in 1865, whose program was identical with that of this association and in whose formation and activity the members of this association had a prominent part.[1]

The interest in Continental politics, which English workingmen had shown since Chartist days, persisted undiminished throughout the decade of the sixties.   It led to important results in their own political history.   Intermittent intercourse with foreign workmen, soon to lead to the formation of the First International, went on during 1861 and 1862.   But it was in 1863-4 that events in foreign lands came into close touch with English domestic politics, largely through the interest therein displayed by English workingmen.   In this year three conflicts served to reveal the deep international sympathies of the English working classes.   So engrossing were these questions that they alone would account for the barrenness of this year in the organization of the democratic movement in England.   But if America, Italy, and Poland absorbed for a time the thought of the English people, those three conflicts, in which the central issue was human liberty, hastened England only the more swiftly toward her own democratic goal.   Let us consider somewhat carefully how this came about.

The American Civil War appeared to all classes of Englishmen as a conflict between aristocracy and democracy.[2]   As this issue became clear to them, the social groups in England became partisans of one or the other of the contestants in America, according to their attitude toward the

[1] Reform League Letters (MS). Letter written September 24, 1867,
[2] E. D. Adams, *Great Britain and the American Civil War*, I. 26, states that America had had this significance for England since the early nineteenth century.   See also II, ch. xviii, for a careful discussion of this aspect of the Civil War.

same question in their own country.   Workingmen almost
unanimously became ardent advocates of the cause of the
North as the cause of freedom ;[1] opposed to them stood the
conservative elements in society, both Whig and Tory,
chiefly, says Trevelyan, because they knew if democracy
triumphed in America it could not long be delayed in England.[2]   The aristocratic influence controlled press and parliament, and, had it not been for Bright's party and the workingmen, their views might have determined the action of the
government.   Again the Radicals appealed to the masses, as
in 1832, 1846, and 1867, and helped form the national policy.
"The working men throughout the country, instructed by
Bright, saw in the Southern Confederacy the men who
would degrade labour to a chattel of the capitalist, and in
the great Northern Republic the central force of democracy
whose fall would involve the baffling of their own hopes of
enfranchisement."[3]   John Morley said that partisanship on
the American issue veiled a sort of English civil war, and
the triumph of the North "was the force that made English
liberalism powerful enough to enfranchise the workmen,
depose official Christianity in Ireland, and deal a first blow
at the landlords."[4]

In 1862 the Radicals set to work to counteract the alleged
pro-Southern sympathy of England.   They formed an
Emancipation Society for this purpose, among whose mem-
bers were P. A. Taylor, John Stuart Mill, James Stansfeld,
Professor Cairnes, E. A. Leatham, M.P., Abel Heywood of
Manchester, Thomas Hughes, G. Lushington, George Wil-

[1] One writer states that only in London, Liverpool, and Glasgow
were workingmen divided—in London because never united, in Liverpool because of close touch with the South, in Glasgow because of block-
ade runners.   (Hinton, *op. cit.*, p. 63.)

[2] *Life of Bright*, p. 303-4.

[3] Trevelyan, *Life of Bright*, p. 306.

[4] Article in the *Fortnightly Review*, October 1, 1870, on "England
and the War" (Franco-Prussian).

son, E. Miall, Prof. Beesly, Joseph Cowen, Edward Dicey, Edmond Beales, and Jacob Bright.[1]   All of these middle-class men from this time on were in increasingly close relation with workingmen.   Lincoln's proclamation of emancipation at the close of 1862, which was soon interpreted in England as placing the issue squarely on slavery, gave such vigor to the pro-Northern forces that thereafter, wrote Cobden to Sumner, it was impossible for the government to intervene.[2]

The working classes pronounced in no undecided tone upon the question.[3]   The operatives of Lancashire, in their great distress caused by the stoppage of the cotton supply, remained staunchly loyal to the North, although government intervention for the South would have meant cotton and work.   In the midst of their deepest distress, they met to congratulate Lincoln upon his proclamation.[4]   In London the trades were aroused to action and thereby impelled further along the road of participation in politics.   In March, 1863, a great meeting of trade-unionists was organized by members of the London Trades Council.[5]   It was held in St. James's Hall with John Bright in the chair.   His address described the United States as the land where "Labour is honoured more than elsewhere in the

[1] From a pamphlet called *The Emancipation Society* (no date) in the British Museum.

[2] Hobson, *Cobden, the International Man,* pp. 368-9.   Trevelyan explains that this placed the Southern sympathizers in the position of defending slavery (*Bright,* p. 305).

[3] For an analysis of their attitude see an article by J. H. Park in the *Political Science Quarterly,* September, 1924, on "The English Workingmen and the American Civil War."   Also, Adams, *op. cit.,* II. ch. xviii, and pp. 107-111 and 132-3.

[4] Ludlow and Jones, *Progress of the Working Classes, 1832-1867,* p. 99.

[5] Adams, *op. cit.,* II, p. 291 and 292, note 1, gives some evidence to the effect that Karl Marx brought about this meeting, and that he was trying to impress the class nature of the American struggle on British workers.

world."[1]   A few days after the meeting a deputation from the Trades Council waited upon the American Ambassador to present an address to Lincoln adopted at the meeting. Bright, in introducing them, stated that this was, he believed, the first occasion upon which trade-unions had expressed their opinion as a united body upon any political question, adding his wish that they would do it oftener in their own behalf.[2]

The influence of this event upon the politics of the government was important.   In the political history of English workingmen, it was of great significance.   Howell wrote to Bright in, 1867 that it did much to awaken the political interest of trade-unions and "aided us greatly in our endeavor to bring them into the political arena."[3]   Upon another occasion, Howell declared that it thoroughly committed trade-unions to politics.[4]   Furthermore, it brought Bright and the workingmen into close and harmonious relations for the first time.   Never since he undertook in 1848 to create a national party by a union of the middle and the working classes had Bright been able to secure the unreserved confi-

[1] Smith, *Life of Bright*, p. 229.   Trevelyan, *Bright,* pp. 306-7.   Note that *Reynolds's Newspaper* called the American government the only workingman's government in the world (February 22, 1864).

[2] *Reynolds's,* May 10, 1863.

[3] MS Letters and Articles 1867-9.   Letter written October 7.

[4] MS Reform League Letters.   A letter of September 24, 1867.—The move did not meet with unanimous approval from the London trades, however.   T. J. Dunning, astute and influential secretary of the book-binders and editor of their *Circular,* stated his belief that it was a political move by wirepullers to serve the Federal cause; that no trade was consulted or authorized the meeting, and he believed it did not express their sentiments.   They did not trust Lincoln, because his proclamation, which extended only to disloyal states, was not to benefit the Negro but to destroy the Confederacy. This, he declared, was the opinion of nine tenths of the workingmen he had heard speak on the matter. *(Bookbinders' Trade Circular,* March 2, 1864).   The *Circular* was making war upon the Trade Council steadily.   This may have been a phase of Potter's opposition to it, since Dunning was a loyal follower of Potter.   This article says the action taken in connection with the American war was not taken by the Council *as such,* but the effect upon the public was the same and was meant to be so.

dence of the latter. His attitude on factory legislation, his opposition to their proposals for state-aided emigration, his refusal to declare for universal suffrage, and his opposition to intervention in European wars of liberation, had been barriers in his way. Those barriers were not yet surmounted, but the common sympathy felt in this work for the cause of freedom contributed toward diminishing their importance. What the effect of the victory of the North would mean for Bright's position was expressed by Charles Francis Adams, who said that if the North won, Bright would be the most powerful man in England.[1]

The democratic enthusiasm inspired by the American struggle was augmented at the same time from another source. In April, 1864, Garibaldi came to England. A Trades Garibaldian Committee had been in existence since 1862 for the purpose of collecting funds for a testimonial and promoting demonstrations in Hyde Park against the French occupation of Rome.[2] It now went heart and soul into the organization of a gigantic workingmen's welcome to him, whom the masses had come to recognize as "the exemplar of the modern democratic revolutionist."[3]

The members of the London Trades Council took the lead, together with George Potter and Robert Hartwell, his colleague on the *Bee Hive*. The most gigantic procession that London had even seen, and wholly of workingmen, escorted Garibaldi from the station to Stafford House. The trades marched with trade banners flying. The *Daily News* estimated that fifty thousand men of various labor organizations took part.[4] Their address to him spoke of

[1] Trevelyan, *Bright*, p. 304.

[2] *Reynolds's Newspaper*, October 5 and November 2, 1862.

[3] The phrase is Hobson's, from his *Cobden, the International Man*, p. 323. See *Times*, April 6, 12, 14, 19.

[4] Quoted in *Newcastle Daily Chronicle*, April 13, 1864. *Times*, April 12, declared only 5000 members of organized bodies marched, but there were masses of the unorganized.

"the unbounded fulness of our love for you and liberty."[1]
The whole demonstration was "the people's own." The
editor of the *Newcastle Daily Chronicle* interpreted its
significance aright:

It is useless and foolish to attempt to conceal the fact that the
sole reason of Garibaldi's popularity is his connection with the
cause of liberty. There is no need for alarm at this political
aspect of Garibaldi's welcome. His cause is our cause and the
cause of mankind.[2]

But the ruling classes, Whig and Tory, saw cause for
alarm. The great provincial towns were planning demonstrations that should outdo that of London. Soon Garibaldi had accepted invitations from thirty such towns, and
the list was growing longer each day.[3] If he should be
permitted to tour the North a democratic force might be
created that would render impossible the maintenance of the
political equilibrium. Hence the government, acting
through Gladstone, made known to Garibaldi that he was
desired to leave England. This he did at once.[4]

The indignation of workingmen was great. The Working Men's Reception Committee announced a mass meeting
of protest to be held on Primrose Hill. Acting with them
were Professor Beesly, William Shaen, P. A. Taylor, and
Edmond Beales, who were members of a Garibaldian committee of middle-class Radicals. Beales was to preside.
No sooner had the crowd gathered than the police ordered
them to disperse and began to administer blows. The meet-

[1] Quoted in *Newcastle Daily Chronicle,* April 12, 1864.

[2] April 18, 1864.

[3] Morley, *Gladstone,* II. 112. The episode presents several points
that were diversely explained at the time, especially with reference
to Gladstone's part in it. Besides Morley, see McCabe, *Life and Letters
of George Jacob Holyoake,* I. 329-31. Also *Newcastle Daily Chronicle,*
April 19, 20, 21, 22; May 12, 1864; and *Reynolds's,* May 1.

[4] *Newcastle Daily Chronicle,* May 9, 1864. An editorial. The *Times*
explains that workingmen believed the government was yielding to
pressure from France (April 21).

ing disbanded. The Working Men's Committee met, adopted resolutions in their capacity as representatives of the trade and friendly societies and other organized bodies of workingmen, and sent a deputation to the Home Secretary to ask if it was the purpose of the government to prevent open-air meetings. The reply[1] appeared to the committee full of menace to public liberty. Until 1862, upon the occasion of a riot instigated by Irish Catholics in the course of a Garibaldi meeting, the right to meet in the parks had not been interfered with. Then orders had been issued forbidding meetings there "for the public discussion of popular and exciting topics."[2] The committee, together with the middle-class Radicals who were meeting with them, in the course of these negotiations over the Garibaldi affair took up for discussion a suggestion to form a national reform association.[3] Never was the idea allowed to lapse. The next year it bore fruit in the formation of the Reform League under the leadership of these same men.[4]

And so the Italian question, like the American, was developing the political consciousness of English workingmen. To quote Trevelyan again, "the success of the Italian revolution, like the victory of the North in America, helped to create over here the atmosphere in which democracy triumphed."[5] In the practical field of political agitation, workingmen were learning to prefer their demands as organized bodies that had acquired such social significance as to give their voices influence. Furthermore, in these affairs, they were working in coöperation with middle-class

[1] *Newcastle Daily Chronicle,* April 29, 1864.

[2] *Ibid.,* May 9, 1864.

[3] See Brand in *American Historical Review,* January, 1925, in article on "The Conversion of the British Trade Unions to Political Action." Also a MS letter by Howell to a foreign correspondent, September 24, 1867.

[4] See below, pp. 250-1.

[5] *Bright,* p. 331.

Radicals of various shades.   A preparation was thus being made for the reform agitation of 1866-7.

A third question of foreign politics called for the support of workingmen even at the same time as America and Italy; namely, the Polish revolution of 1863.   The sympathy that had surged up in behalf of the Poles in the period of the Crimean War again possessed English workingmen.   Out of their proceedings on behalf of Poland came the International Working Men's Association.

Public meetings began to be held early in 1863 in London and the provinces to demand that the English government intervene.[1]   Edmond Beales, the same who was active in the Garibaldi affair, was the chief organizer in London. On April 28 a great meeting of trade-unionists was held in St. James's Hall under the auspices of members of the London Trades Council.[2]   To the meeting came certain French delegates, Friburg and Tolain.[3]   A resolution was adopted to send a deputation to Palmerston to urge coöperation between England and France to restore Polish national rights.   The deputation included Odger, Applegarth, Coulson, Cremer, Facey, Potter, Connolly, and representatives of numerous other trades, as well as James Stansfeld and Professor Beesly.   One member, a shoemaker, took advantage of this occasion to inform Palmerston that they did not approve of his domestic policy, which denied them representation.

After the great trade meeting, Howell relates that a group of "leading spirits" met at a tavern in Long Acre and consulted as to a "grand fraternity of peoples."[4] This group drew up an address to French workingmen

[1] *Reynolds's*, March 21, 29, 1863.

[2] *Ibid.*, May 24, 1863; a full account.

[3] Article by Beesly on the International, in *Fortnightly Review*. November 1, 1870.

[4] Article in *Nineteenth Century*, July, 1878.

which was submitted a short time later to a meeting of trade-unionists and other workingmen at the Bell Inn, Old Bailey. There is no question that this meeting was called by the London Trades Council.[1] The address was adopted, signed, "on behalf of the workingmen of England," by Facey, Odger, Cremer, and others, and forwarded to Paris.[2] The tone of it was a distinct foreshadowing of the International. It praised the French visitors for the step they had taken "towards bringing together in common council those whose labours produce all that is essential to human happiness." First, they must aid Poland. In the second place, they must arrange so that foreign labor could not be brought into England to defeat English trade-unionists in industrial disputes. For this purpose a regular system of communication between workingmen of all nations was needed, "which we hope to see speedily effected."

It was this address,[3] combined with the great meeting on the American war, that brought down the wrath of the Bookbinders' Society upon the Trades Council. Dunning declared it had been made "if not the active means, most certainly the nucleus, of the so-called political movements of the working classes," for which it had not been instituted. The Bookbinders withdrew their delegate. Dunning, nevertheless, went on to remark in his discussion that, as for political action, he wished his society would petition as a body for an extension of the franchise.[4]

Certain other antecedents of the International must be noted. Its first germs are to be found in the builders' strike. This strike, says Howell in his history of the Inter-

[1] It was so advertised in *Reynolds's*, November 8, 1863.

[2] Given in full in *Reynolds's*, December 6, 1863. It was written by Odger.

[3] Dunning said of it: "As a Red Republican document . . . it is a fair sample of its class . . . the silliest of all effusions."

[4] *Bookbinders' Trade Circular*, March 2, 1864.

national in the *Nineteenth Century,*[1] aroused the interest of
Continental workingmen because it was for the reduction of
hours and not merely for wages.   Communications were
opened with them, and money came from Paris unions.   At
about the same time Henri Tolain came to London and,
says Howell, in the interviews that followed, the dreams of
founding an international association began to assume definite shape and form.   In 1861 many English workingmen
went to visit French industries and, as *Reynolds's* puts it, to
strengthen friendly relations between the workingmen of the
two countries.[2]   In 1862 French workingmen visited the
International Exhibition in London.[3]   A committee of English workingmen entertained them with a tea at Freemasons'
Tavern, where an address was read setting forth the desirability of some form of international union.   A French delegate present suggested that a correspondence committee be
formed in London for the exchange of ideas with the men
of France.[4]   A little earlier than this, the London Trades
Council had, upon request, sent an address to the General
Neapolitan Society of Working Men, of which Garibaldi
was president, explaining the nature of English trade-unions.
The address, translated and spread all over Europe, led to
much correspondence and was a step towards the International.[5]

On September 28, 1864, the International Working
Men's Association was inaugurated at a meeting in St.

[1] July, 1878.

[2] June 2, 1861.

[3] R. W. Postgate, *A History of the Workers' International,* London.
1920, p. 17.   He says three hundred and forty French workmen were
sent by the aid of Napoleon III.

[4] *Reynolds's,* August 10, 1862.   Howell says this Exhibition had
nothing to do with the formation of the International, but it probably
did.

[5] Howell in *Nineteenth Century,* July, 1878.   For the address, see
Reynolds's, April 20, 1862.

Martin's Hall over which Professor Beesly presided.[1] Present were three French workmen and a few of other nationalities residing in London and English trade-unionists. A provisional council was formed, with Odger for president and Marx as one of the members. Out of several programs submitted, that of Marx was unanimously adopted and embodied in an address and rules.[2] These declared that to conquer political power had become the great duty of workingmen, because "the lords of the land and the lords of capital will always use their political privileges for the defence and perpetuation of their economical privileges." The emancipation of the working classes could be won only by themselves, and their success would mean not class privilege, but the abolition of all class rule. What they meant by emancipation, explains the preamble to the rules, was the abolition of the monopoly of the means of labor. The rules themselves called for annual congresses and a central council to sit in London. The first council included the following Englishmen, all of whom within a year were working members also of the Reform League: Leno, Hartwell, Lucraft, Shearman, Nieass, Odger, Howell, Osborne, Wheeler, Cremer, Longmaid, Worley, Whitlock, Fox, Blackmore, Pidgeon, Weston, Dell, Shaw, Lake, Buckley, Carter, Gray, Stainsby, Morgan, and Grossmith. Marx was on the council as corresponding secretary for Germany. Odger was president of the council, and Cremer was secretary.

The Englishmen who accepted the address interpreted it, according to Howell, in such practical terms as higher wages, shorter hours, better conditions of employment, abolition of child labor, extended education, and freedom of asso-

[1] Accounts in Beesly's and Howell's articles above referred to, also in Postgate, *The Workers' International,* pp. 19-20, and Beer, *op cit.,* II. 213.

[2] *Address and Provisional Rules of the Workingmen's International Association,* London, 1864 (a pamphlet.)

ciation.[1]   Howell stated later also that some of Marx's theories were not yet known to his colleagues, and again,[2] that the original program was such as "a Gladstone or a Bright might have accepted with a good conscience." But whatever their understanding of the implication of the movement, English workingmen did within the next three years join or affiliate with the International in large numbers. Such other trade-union leaders as Applegarth and Henry Broadhurst became active. Odger was president as late as 1870, when Applegarth was chairman of the general council.[3] The association permitted affiliation by organized bodies like trade-unions upon the payment of a nominal sum,[4] and numerous English unions affiliated.[5] Webb's *History of Trade Unionism*[6] states that few joined in their corporate capacity, but the minutes make it clear that many affiliated and paid annual dues in their corporate capacity. Nor were they only the London unions. John Kane brought in the National Association of Malleable Ironworkers;[7] the Coventry ribbon-weavers joined; the Lancashire, etc. Block-Printers Union did the same and paid dues for one thousand members; the Executive Council of the Amalgamated Carpenters and Joiners paid two pounds for itself, leaving it to the branches to affiliate separately.[8]

In summary, by September, 1866, seventeen unions had affiliated, and thirteen others had promised to; the number

[1] *Labour Legislation, Labour Movements, and Labour Leaders,* p. 150.
[2] Postgate, *op. cit.,* p. 24.
[3] Webb, *op. cit.,* p. 235, note 1. Coulson, another of the Junta, was on the Council in 1867 (MS Minutes of General Council of I. W. M. A. —entry for March 21). (In Bishopsgate Library.)
[4] Minutes of General Council, September 1866 to 1867. This rule was carried October 9, 1866.
[5] Postgate, *op. cit.,* Appendix I, tabulates those that took this step, as he found the data in the MS Minutes. Any study of these minutes reveals the large number that so joined.
[6] Page 235, note 1.
[7] Minutes, July 16, 1867.
[8] Minutes, August 6, 1867

increased each year, so that by 1872 as many as forty-eight such affiliations had been officially recorded, which number included all the chief unions, even the Amalgamated Engineers.[1] The minutes of the general council reveal much concern to obtain the adhesion of the London Trades Council. Deputations were sent to them several times; the final decision of the council merely to "co-operate" was reported at the meeting of January 15, 1867. The fact is, that the association had proposed to the council not merely affiliation, but amalgamation, and the council, after lengthy consideration, resolved to retain its corporate identity.[2] The Birmingham Trades Council appointed a committee to consider the principles of the I. W. M. A. Their report approved its program,[3] but there seems to be no record of the council's affiliation.

The favor in which the International stood with trade societies is indicated also by the action taken by the organizers of the immediate forerunner of the Trade Union Congress; viz., the "United Kingdom Alliance of Organized Trades." The conference of trade delegates that formed this body at Sheffield in 1866 adopted a resolution that they, "fully appreciating the efforts made by the 'International Association' to unite in one common bond of brotherhood the working men of all countries, most earnestly recommend to the various societies here represented the' advisability of becoming affiliated to that body."[4] The Trade Union Congress itself, in 1869, urged the same step.[5] That Marx hoped to use the trade organizations as instruments in his economic transformation of society is evident from

---

[1] Postgate, *op. cit.*, Appendix I, p. 111.

[2] Full account of the discussions in the Trade Council reported in the *Morning Star*, December 21, 1866, and January 15, 1867.

[3] *Birmingham Daily Post*, December 6, 1867.

[4] *Printers' Journal and Typographical Magazine*, August 20, 1866.

[5] Postgate, *op. cit.*, p. 44.

an address he drafted for the General Congress, 1866. He declared the ultimate purpose of trade societies must be the abolition of wages-slavery and of capitalist domination, which mission they had not yet been fully conscious of. They must learn to act as *foci* of the movement for emancipation and must regard themselves as the champions of the whole working class, including the unskilled and badly paid workers.[1] As a comment by English trade-unionism on such a conception of its function, the fact may be cited that the admission of the United Excavators Society, unskilled workers, to the Association led to a coolness on the part of the London Trades Council.[2]

It is beyond the scope of this study to describe the work of the Association as carried on at its annual congresses.[3] English delegates attended all of them up to 1871 and often took an active and moderating part. But as the association grew increasingly political, their sympathy with it waned. From 1868 the disruptive influence of Bakunin was at work; then came the Franco-Prussian War, and the Commune, which wholly discredited the association in the eyes of the moderate English section. By 1871 it had ceased to hold the allegiance of any important group of English workers, though for a while longer a few extremists were faithful to it.[4]

The International Association played a part in developing the whole of the English political situation just prior to the reform act of 1867. Its first declaration of policy stressed the importance of gaining political power as a means to ulterior social aims. The English section at once made this their chief object, entering into the franchise agi-

---

[1] Beer, *op. cit.*, II. 219.

[2] Postgate, *op. cit.*, p. 29.

[3] A contemporary work that is valuable because of its documentation is O. Testut, *L'Internationale,* Paris, 1871.

[4] Howell in *Nineteenth Century,* July, 1878. Postgate, *op. cit.*, p. 71.

tation accordingly.   Already trade-union leaders had parted company completely with a policy of no politics.   To recapitulate : since 1860 there had been political action in connection with the nine-hours movement; the Glasgow Trades Council had proposed trade-union action for franchise reform; an organized effort to secure the repeal of the Master and Servant Law had been undertaken; the Miners' Association had been formed at Leeds in 1863 with a concrete political program and committees to promote it; the London Trades Council had officially or unofficially participated in political meetings with regard to the American Civil War, Garibaldi, and Polish liberation; a trade-unionists' manhood suffrage association had been formed.   And now the International, resting its support in England during its first years very largely upon trade organizations, gave both a theoretical and a practical basis for politico-economic activity.[1]

The reason for most of the incursions made by organized labor into politics from the sixties to 1875 was, of course, its sense of the legal restraints under which it operated. Simultaneously with their developing interest in the franchise, in European and American liberalism, and in labor internationalism, trade-unionists were fighting their opening battles with parliament for the removal of restrictive laws and the enactment of enabling ones.   This story has been adequately recounted elsewhere;[2] it must be referred to here merely in order that its bearing upon politics as a whole may be gauged.

[1] Another international movement in which individual workingmen were interested, as well as the London Trades Council, was the International League of Peace and Liberty, formed at a peace congress held at Geneva in 1867.   Edmond Beales, by that time the idol of workingmen, Cremer, whose life-work henceforth was to be for peace, and Odger helped to form it.   The London Trades Council in December, 1867, Appointed Odger to assist in forming branches.   See *Morning Star,* September 7, December 14, 17, 1867.

[2] Webb, *History of Trade Unionism,* pp. 249-53; Howell, *Labour Legislation,* etc., pp. 151 ff.

The first of this series of parliamentary agitations was concerning an amendment to the Master and Servant Law. By making the breach of contract by a workman a criminal offense, while the same act committed by an employer constituted merely a civil case, the law appeared grossly unjust. Furthermore, the method of its enforcement by the magistrates entailed intolerable oppression, hardly inferior, say the Webbs, to that suffered under the old anti-combination laws.[1]

This law, it will be remembered, had been urged by William Newton as early as in 1852 as an argument for political action.[2] The suggestion to renew efforts to amend it came from the Glasgow Trades Council in 1863.[3] This body opened negotiations with the trade councils of London and other cities and in 1864 convened a conference of delegates to organize for action, which conference "marks an epoch in Trade Union history."[4] It was the first of its kind and the first of a series that culminated in the Trade Union Congress. The conference had a bill prepared, conducted a parliamentary agitation, as well as one throughout the country, and succeeded in securing the adoption of an amendment in 1867 through the assistance especially of Lord Elcho. This was the "first positive success of the Trade Unions in the legislative field."

This agitation connected itself directly with that for suffrage reform. Even conservative, non-political T. J. Dunning of the Bookbinders wrote in 1863:

[1] *Op. cit.*, p. 250, note 1. Prosecutions under the Act reached as many as ten thousand a year (*American Historical Review,* January, 1925, p. 257).

[2] Above, pp. 47-8.

[3] *Report from the Select Committee on Master and Servant,* H. of C., 1866, contains an account of the inauguration of the movement, as given by George Newton, secretary of the Executive Council of the movement, and Alexander Campbell, of Glasgow, one of the members (*Second Report,* pp. 1, 14, 15).

[4] Webb, *op. cit.*, p. 252.

This Act is indubitable evidence that the "workman" class is not represented in the House of Commons, while that of the "masters" indubitably is. We are very far from recommending political action by trades' unions, but there is such a thing as the opposite extreme. There could not be a better course in our opinion than for trades' unions as such to petition for such reform as would ensure a better representation of their own class in the House of Commons.[1]

In 1865 this program won increased favor. The new National Association of Miners under Macdonald was reported as taking up the question of a reform agitation favorably at their conference.[2] At a public meeting of the Boiler Smiths' and Iron Ship Builders' Union of the Tyne and Wear, the chairman advocated going in for general politics.[3] The newly formed Reform League, through its secretary, George Howell, issued a strong appeal to trade-unionists to throw themselves into the manhood-suffrage movement they were launching. The ground of the appeal was the Master and Servant Law and other grievances of unionists.[4]

The years 1864-5 were marked by much industrial unrest.[5] Numerous masters' associations were formed to combat those of the workers. Thus, when the strong builders' unions in the Midlands in this year demanded an increase in wages, the masters' organized an association with three hundred fifty firms in it and again adopted the discharge note as a means of subjecting the men completely.

[1] *Bookbinders' Trade Circular*, June 30, 1863.
[2] *Newcastle Daily Chronicle*, June 3, 1865.
[3] *Ibid.*, June 6.
[4] *Reynolds's Newspaper*, June 18, 1865.
[5] Some figures on trade-union strength may here be given. In 1866 the Amalgamated Engineers had 30,984 members, 229 branches, and a balance on hand of £115,359. The Carpenters and Joiners had 187 branches and 8002 members. Unions with five thousand members or more numbered sixteen, not counting the Miners' Association with thirty-six thousand and the Engine Drivers and Firemen with fifteen thousand (Ludlow and Jones, *Progress of the Working Classes*, pp. 200-205). See also Webb, *op. cit.*, edit. of 1894, Appendix V.

The building trades in eight counties went out on strike and eventually won an unconditional victory.[1]

In the iron district an ugly conflict developed which agitated the whole labor world. In 1862 and 1863 two unions of iron-workers were formed which were said to embrace three fourths of all the workers in those trades.[2] Two strong masters' associations already existed, and in 1864 they determined to break the new unions. They reduced wages, insisted on "the document," and, when the men struck, imported Belgian workers.[3] All the men eventually submitted except a small section in North Staffordshire. In order to subjugate them, the masters stopped the entire iron-trades of England for a fortnight.[4] Their organ, the *Iron Trade Circular,* frankly admitted the issue to be destruction of the new unions.[5] Rumors spread that the masters intended to appeal to the government for aid, and the matter actually was brought up in parliament.[6]

The struggle aroused nation-wide interest among workingmen. The London Trades Council took up the matter, but were opposed in their policy by Potter, who called an important conference of trade-unionists to consider the question and there adopted a more militant attitude. The case created a bitter feud between the two groups of London trade-unionists which persisted for several years.[7] The

[1] *Reynolds's,* February 5, 1865.
[2] Comte de Paris, *Trade Unions of England,* London, 1869, pp. 94-5.
[3] *Reynolds's,* May 1, 1864.
[4] See Comte de Paris, *op. cit.,* pp. 95-100, for description.
[5] Quoted in *Newcastle Daily Chronicle,* March 7, 1865.
[6] *Ibid.,* and *Bookbinders' Trade Circular,* March 28, 1865. The men finally submitted after much suffering.
[7] On the whole question see Webb, *op. cit.,* pp. 254-5. Full discussions in *Reynolds's,* March 19, September 3, 1865; *Newcastle Daily Chronicle,* March 16, 23; August 30; September 11, 16. On the timid policy of the Trade Council and the amalgamated unions, see *Bookbinders' Trade Circular,* January 31, 1866, for a severe attack, and July 23, 1868. See also evidence by John Kane in *Report of the Commission to Inquire into the Organization and Rules of Trade Unions and Other Associations,* London, 1867, I. 14.

schism is significant. The council was displaying that "extreme caution in trade matters" which the Webbs have described and were angrily charged in this heated controversy with "gross neglect" of the economic interests of the workers.

It is a mistake to depreciate the influence of Potter, whatever criticism may be directed against him in certain respects. It is evident that he represented a counter-policy to that of the Junta, and the importance of his following, or allies, including Dunning, Kane of the Iron-workers, Macdonald of the Miners, and Henry Broadhurst, signifies that the temper of large sections of trade-unionism was not the cautious, middle-class temper of Allan and Applegarth. Politically, Potter's importance was conspicuous.[1]

The ironworkers' strike and lockout attracted wide public attention. Denunciations of the masters were numerous.[2] *Reynolds's Newspaper,* violent and extreme, but perhaps reaching the eye of more workingmen than any other paper, declared these masters likely to prove "pioneers of the mightiest and most terrible revolution that ever took place in England"; certainly they were "convincing the toiling millions that, under existing political arrangements, they have no protection against the most cruel wrongs."[3]

In such fashion was the division of society into two hostile sections threatening. The strength of labor was challenging the strength of capital to put it down by the use of industrial and political power. Not only did employers

[1] His economic-political London Working Men's Association was active in the reform agitation, 1866-7, and organized the Labour Representation League, to attempt direct labor representation. (See below, pp. 258, 294.) Potter was several times Liberal-Labor candidate for parliament and was the second workingman elected to the London school board.

[2] *Newcastle Weekly Chronicle,* March 16, 23, December 5, 1865, quotes many from other papers. For an extreme statement of the employers' views, see the *Fortnightly,* I, 1865, pp. 742 ff., "An Iron-Master's View of Strikes," by W. R. Hopper.

[3] April 2, 1865.

sense this, but the general public also, as the Webbs explain;[1] and the fear of trade-unionism was now increased by the resumption of trade outrages at Sheffield. Plainly the industrial question was approaching a crisis. For the purpose of meeting national masters' associations, the "United Kingdom Alliance of Organized Trades" was formed at Sheffield in 1866. The conference that formed it consisted of one hundred fifty delegates claiming to represent two hundred thousand men. It resolved to agitate for an amendment to the law regarding masters and servants as well as to act industrially.[2]

The outstanding events that in 1867 brought to a focus all the energies of organized labor, both industrial and political, were two: the simultaneous appointment by the government of a commission to investigate the whole subject of trade-unions and the discovery by trade-unions, through a judicial decision, that they had no legal status and could not claim protection for their funds from the Friendly Societies Act of 1855, as they had hitherto believed they could. From two sources, then, came an attack on trade-unions that, unless repelled, might prove fatal. The Trade Union Commission, growing out of the tense industrial situation of those years and the Sheffield outrages, was ominous of a purpose to destroy trade combinations by law; the lack of legal protection placed the funds, and hence the life, of trade societies in jeopardy. The result was the marshalling of the forces of organized labor in such strength that parliament and the country dared not ignore it.

The story of the parliamentary effort does not need to be retold here[3]—the taking over of both questions by the in-

[1] *Op. cit.*, pp. 256-7.
[2] Webb, *op. cit.*, pp. 257-9. Also the *Working Man*, July 28, 1866, for resolutions passed.
[3] See Webb, *op. cit.*, pp. 263 ff. Also the MS minutes of the Conference of Amalgamated Trades (in the British Library of Political Science).

formal Junta, comprising the secretaries of the great amalgamated trades; the aid given them by certain middle-class
friends, chiefly the Positivists and Thomas Hughes, M.P.;
the giving of testimony before the commission that cleared
the name of trade-unionism from the worst charges against
it and dispelled the danger of destructive legislation; and the
agitation in parliament for enactments to give trade societies
legal status and freedom, which after some years of arduous
effort were won in 1871-6.[1]

Meanwhile, the hostility of the general public toward
trade combinations had manifested itself from the first of
the year. The *Pall Mall Gazette* declared of unions:

Almost every one in the upper and middle ranks of life has got
more or less into the way of speaking of them in terms of something approaching horror. They are regarded as the antipodes
of respectability. Trades unionism, socialism, atheism, red republicanism, and we know not what other terrible 'isms, are associated
together in the minds of large numbers of the classes which are
conservative and timid by nature. . . . These accusations probably do more to estrange from each other the different classes of
English society than almost any other which are current amongst
us. . . . It will be an object of the highest possible importance
to exorcise, if possible, this spectre.[2]

The *Manchester Examiner and Times,* at that very moment
agitating for working-class enfranchisement, yet wrote of
unions:

We admit their baneful character, we entirely deny the economical
maxims upon which they are based, we believe that their extinction
would be a blessing to the working classes and a real emancipation
of industry; but those admissions do not conduct us a single step
toward recognizing the expediency of legislative interference.[3]

[1] In these agitations also Potter and the Junta were often at war. It
has not been suggested by students of this question that the Junta represented the great, pacific unions, concerned more with their insurance
funds than with industrial activity. Potter's following comprised the
type of union that was not primarily an insurance society, but existed
for trade purposes of wages and hours. The Junta in 1867 was working
for a bill to secure the funds of societies, but Macdonald, at Potter's
conference, declared it would not protect those unions that used their
funds in strikes. (See *Morning Star,* March 6, 8, 9, 1867, for this conference.)
[2] Quoted in *Manchester Examiner and Times,* February 23, 1867.
[3] Editorial, February 9, 1867.

The *Birmingham Post,* ardent advocate of extension of the franchise, spoke its disapproval of trade-union policies.[1] A member of the Manchester Chamber of Commerce published a denunciatory tract, which may be taken as typical; in it he declared that trade-unions existed for the purpose of perpetuating industrial war.[2]   A few voices were raised on the other side. Professor Beesly defended unions in great meetings in Exeter Hall;[3] John Morley explained the fundamental issue to be the disastrous continuance of unlimited competition and praised, by contrast, the "social temper" of trade societies.[4]

The crisis in trade-unionism brought trade organizations into the reform agitation, then itself at a critical stage, upon a large scale and with determination of purpose. They joined the Reform League, or marched in its huge processions with trade banners unfurled. Significantly, Disraeli stated later that not until January of 1867 did he become convinced of the serious nature of the reform agitation. By July the suffrage act had been won from a parliament whose majority was hostile to the very thought of enfranchising members of trade-unions. Working-class political action in conjunction with that of John Bright and his Radicals had effected this result. We may now consider this agitation with a view to discovering its contribution to the development of political relationships that were to persist in the new era introduced by the democratic triumph of 1867.

[1] August 26, 1867.

[2] *Labour and Capital,* by a Member of the Manchester Chamber of Commerce, London, 1867 (in the Goldsmiths' Library).

[3] Webb, *op. cit.,* p. 269, note 1.

[4] In *Pall Mall Gazette,* quoted in the *English Leader,* May 11, 1867. The *Times* in an editorial of May 4, 1865, argued against reform, on the ground that workingmen would demand "reactionary measures on trade and legislation." It declared that members in all parts of the House were alive to these dangers, and that the ministers had done no more than act in accord with the change of feeling in parliament.

CHAPTER IX

THE REFORM LEAGUE, THE NATIONAL REFORM UNION, AND THE REFORM ACT OF 1867

Parliament in 1860 by general consent had dropped the reform question. The conservative forces of both parties united behind Palmerston on this understanding. Old party designations meant nothing. The Radicals no longer held the balance of power, nor could they regain it until the death of Palmerston should loose the bonds of the coalition and set free party strife again.

In the country, the early sixties witnessed a corresponding inertia among all but certain small groups, and for the same reason. The body of the electorate was content. The aggressive spirit shown by organized labor and the intensity and prevalence of industrial contests drove a deep wedge between the working classes and the majority of the upper groups. Workingmen were absorbed to a great extent in these industrial matters. They also realized the unfavorable change in the reform situation with Palmerston's return to power. Gladstone's budget of 1860, abolishing or lowering tariffs on hundreds of articles, had done something to lessen the force of the argument that had prevailed strongly with both the middle and working classes, that the burden of indirect taxation was crushingly heavy and could not be removed without parliamentary reform.

Nevertheless, reform did not at any time cease to be a live issue with workingmen. Certain small groups felt all the more keenly the responsibility to organize and work for it, as the impossibility of its enactment without agitation became apparent. Confidence in the imminence of reform had deluded reformers since 1848. Now that that confidence was dispelled, certain working-class leaders realized distinctly the obligation resting upon their class to take in hand its own enfranchisement.

We have seen above how even trade-unionists in 1862 formed a Trade Union Manhood Suffrage Association designed to enlist the trades in a franchise agitation, as they were entering into other political movements; and how in 1864 the inauguration of their campaign for amendment of the laws bearing on labor had furnished a concrete object to be gained by the acquisition of political power; and how this new motive was increasingly insistent, down to 1867, when it became imperative, in view of the prospect of hostile legislation and the realization of the insecure status of labor organizations. The influence of foreign politics and of the International has been noted also, as creating a politically charged atmosphere, from which even non-political trade-unions were unable to escape. The agitation of 1866-7 was very much the work of trade-unions, but even more the work of trade-unionists organized with their non-union fellows in political associations.

In 1865 the death of Palmerston released the reform question from bondage, and these associations developed vitality and effectiveness. The Radicals of the middle class, again under the leadership of Bright, reawoke to their now historic position as allies of the workingmen for parliamentary reform, and they too organized for that object. In earlier years this alliance had been accompanied by serious misgivings and a consciousness of a difference of objectives that had rendered it difficult. Manhood suffrage and household suffrage had been phrases covering more than appeared; they meant working-class political control, or middle-class control with working-class support. Intelligent workingmen in the fifties would have accepted household suffrage or even less, as an installment, but they could not arouse an agitation upon anything less than manhood suffrage, which still sounded as the trumpet-call of a class. The revival of reform in 1865-7 was again to reveal the identical division among reformers. To the middle-class demand for a limited reform, the working class answered with a cry for manhood suffrage. The enthusiasm created by the latter made possible the fulfillment of the former.

After 1865 the parliamentary situation delivered the question into the hands of the Radicals, if they should be supported strongly in the country. The old parties came to life. Liberals began again to talk a liberalism in which many did not believe and to pit it against a conservatism in which they did. And Conservatives, alive to the fateful import for future party power of attitudes now assumed toward the dominant question of increasing the electorate, found themselves involved in the difficult maneuver of harmonizing their principles with their prospects. Division in parliament along the line of principle gave way to division along the line of partisan advantage, made decent by party shibboleths. But if they were shibboleths to the parties in parliament, they had in reality been informed with the living spirit of the great social forces that were greater than parties—that were even then reshaping parties in the moment of their reappearance. The new authoritative voice that was to interpret these forces to an insincere Liberalism and make of it something earnest was that of Gladstone. And the skill that was to adjust Conservative principles to these same forces was that of Disraeli. The time had come when Bright's long labors were to fructify in the new Liberalism for another than he to lead; and the Tory-democracy of *Sybil* was to appear in the concrete form of Conservative workingmen's associations maneuvered from the Carlton Club.

In 1860 a manhood-suffrage association was started at
Leeds. Several similar associations had been formed elsewhere in 1859-60, as has been already explained. Those in
London were little streams that lost themselves in 1865 in
the larger manhood-suffrage Reform League. This association at Leeds became the point of origin for the rival
association to the League, the Reform Union, organized at
Manchester by Bright's party and working-class allies in
1864. The Leeds Working Men's Parliamentary Reform
proposed at the outset a program of winning the coöperation
of the middle and upper classes for reform.[1] It stood for
manhood suffrage, but would take less as a step toward its
goal. The members of the Association were all workingmen,
but there is little doubt that Bright was the inspiration of it.
The phrasing of the plan of action has a tone that indicates
it; furthermore, Bright was present at the inaugural meeting,
and the burden of his address was the need of workingmen
to prefer their claims to the vote more insistently.[2] Edward
Baines, a local member of parliament and parliamentary
leader of the nonconformists, was present. Thus once again,
as so often before, the three groups were united whose interests required an alteration in the constitution.

In the autumn of the next year this Leeds Working
Men's Association called a reform conference to which came
delegates from middle- and working-class reform bodies.
George Wilson, the veteran free trader and delegate of the
Lancashire Reformers' Union, presided.[3] The only significance the conference possesses is that several working-class
delegates stood out for their democratic measure, while the
Lancashire Reformers' Union (in reality the remnants of
the Anti-Corn Law League) upheld a household suffrage, as

[1] *Leeds Mercury*, December 1, 1860.
[2] *Ibid.*, December 13.
[3] The *National Reformer*, November 30; December 7, 1861.

it had done steadily since Hume devised his "Little Charter" in 1848. In the second place, this conference provided for the calling of another the next year and thus instituted a series, at the third of which the Reform Union was organized.

In this year, 1861, several other manhood-suffrage Political Unions, upon the order of those in London, were formed—one at Norwich, with C. J. Bunting, the well-known workingman writer of political pamphlets,[1] for president;[2] and one at Bradford.[3] A new one was launched in the metropolis (or it may have been a consolidation of the four earlier Unions), at whose inaugural meeting were gathered together such diverse democrats as unreconciled Chartists like James Finlen, Washington Wilks, the journalist, Lucraft, McHeath, who had organized the unemployed in 1857, William Newton of the Engineers, and Lord Teynham, a peer of the realm.[4] These organizations, all of them taking form in March, were doubtless in answer to Russell's announcement in February of the abandonment of reform by the government. The influence of the radical Lord Teynham is also evident. He was present at the inauguration of all these organizations and advocated a network of manhood-suffragist "political unions" over the land.

A second reform conference was held in London in 1862, of larger proportion than the one at Leeds.[5] The proceedings are of importance because of the clearer definition there achieved of the divergence of the two classes from each other in regard to the extent of reform to be advocated. Baines and the other middle-class delegates insisted upon the neces-

[1] He wrote under the name of "A Norwich Operative." He had advocated a union of classes for reform since 1848.
[2] Reynolds's, March 17, 1861.
[3] Reynolds's, March 24, 1861.
[4] National Reformer, March 18.
[5] Account in Reynolds's, May 25, 1862, and the National Reformer, May 24, 31.

sity of adopting a moderate program as a means of securing
that union of classes which was their prime object.   Certain
workingmen agreed to the wisdom of this course.   Among
them was George Newton of the Glasgow Trades Council,
promoter of the agitation against the Master and Servant
law.   Others, on the contrary, were vehement in their assertion that no agitation was possible except for manhood
suffrage.   Of such were Lucraft, of London, and Alderman
Livesey, of Rochdale, who declared that the men of the
North could never again be drawn into a sham agitation.   A
Manchester delegate, who claimed a wide acquaintance with
workingmen, maintained that nine tenths of them were manhood-suffragists, and unless the conference wrote that on its
banner, it would better not unfurl one at all.   The committee
on resolutions was urged at least to declare for the principle
of manhood suffrage.   The end of the discussion was the
complete defeat of the extremists.   What was practically the
"Little Charter" of 1848, the program of the Parliamentary
and Financial Reform Association in the early fifties and of
John Bright's agitation in 1858-9, was adopted.   In other
words, it was the regulation program of the Manchester
Radicals.

The year 1863 was full of political excitement for workingmen, as we have seen.   This excitement, however, centered mainly around events in foreign countries or the inauguration of a parliamentary campaign against the Master
and Servant law.   In this year alone, in the interval between
1861 and 1867, there was no reform conference.

By the next year a sort of nervous consciousness of the
approaching revival of the reform question began to manifest
itself among the governing classes.   The mere title of a
pamphlet published at Liverpool suggests apprehension:
*The Danger of a Democratic Reaction and Suggestions for
Placing the Franchise in a Sound and Defensible State*

While Still Possible. The author of the pamphlet feared a period of excitement, "an accident," which would precipitate sweeping changes. The rehabilitation of the cause of democracy by the turning of the tide of war in America and the response of the government to working-class pressure upon that issue were signs that were not misinterpreted. Nor was the democratic fervor evoked by the visit of Garibaldi overlooked. The increasing political activity of trade-unions was coincident with keen industrial strife. So ominously were the anti-reform forces in the country consolidating, in view of these facts, that Cobden, in a speech to his constituents, described the reform question as having assumed of late a dangerous aspect by becoming a question of the total exclusion of a class. Never had it presented itself so before.[1]

The one single event that, more than any other, crystallized this apprehensive sentiment, and at the same time vitalized the reform question, was Gladstone's epoch-making speech on that subject in the House of Commons in May, 1864, in the course of a discussion of Baines' annual motion for a six-pound franchise. The argument of the speech was that there ought to be "not a wholesale, but a sensible and considerable" addition to the number of working-class voters, such as the bill of 1860 might have provided. But its theoretical justification of reform implied vastly more than this: "I venture to say that every man who is not presumably incapacitated by some consideration of personal unfitness or of political danger, is morally entitled to come within the pale of the constitution." Such fitness for the franchise had already been shown by a select portion of the working classes, Gladstone declared, and therefore the desired union of all classes should be promoted "by a reasonable extension,

[1] *Newcastle Daily Chronicle,* November 25, 1864.

at fitting times and among selected portions of the people, of every benefit and every privilege that can be justly conferred upon them."[1]

These utterances electrified the country. The Whiggish limitations imposed in this same speech and in the preface to a pamphlet edition of it were swept aside by public opinion, radical and conservative alike; it was accepted as a pronouncement for democracy.[2] The *Newcastle Daily Chronicle* saw already the outlines of a "Great Party of the People," with Gladstone as its chief.[3] Throughout the rest of the year, the fact was assumed as established that Gladstone was now the leader of a revivified Liberalism.[4] The democracy had adopted Gladstone, whether Gladstone had adopted democracy or not. "One of the fated words had been spoken that gather up wandering forces of time and occasion and precipitate new eras."[5]

Gladstone's progress toward the point where he could assume the leadership of a liberalized Liberal party is one of the most interesting studies in nineteenth-century English politics. His Conservatism and Church-of-Englandism were gradually transformed into political and religious liberalism. On the question of religious liberty he had drawn so close to the Dissenters as to be able to say in 1865 that he believed the interests of the Church of England would be best served by complete equality.[6] On fiscal and colonial policy he agreed with Manchester.[7] In regard to European liberal movements, he was in sympathy with the working-class posi-

---

[1] *Hansard,* CLXXV. 312 ff., especially p. 324.

[2] The *Newcastle Daily Chronicle,* May 13, 1864, summarized the press comment which shows this. Many assumed it to advocate manhood suffrage. See also *Times,* May 12, 31.

[3] *Newcastle Daily Chronicle,* May 13, 1864.

[4] *Ibid.,* September 16, 1864. Speech of Henry Fawcett.

[5] Morley, *Gladstone,* II. 127.

[6] In a speech in the campaign of 1865 (*Newcastle Daily Chronicle,* July 20, 1865). On this question see Morley, *Gladstone,* I. 385.

[7] Morley, *Gladstone,* I. 361-2; also Greville, *Memoirs,* VIII. 297.

tion. And, finally, his judgment of workingmen had been rendered much more favorable by their heroism in the cotton famine. All these influences had prepared Gladstone for the step he took in 1864.

Nor can the influence of political expediency be overlooked as playing its part in his conversion. Many English politicians saw the direction in which the current was flowing. Gladstone threw himself into the current, which he knew to be irresistible, and was borne by it into power. By 1862 he was beginning to pay visits to industrial centers.[1] In 1863 he was laying a cornerstone in the Potteries and receiving an address from the workingmen.[2] In 1864 his contact with trade-unionists was frequent, especially in regard to his Annuities Bill. Potter led a delegation to him to protest against the bill, while the London Trades Council sent one to disavow Potter and express approval of the measure.[3] Upon this latter occasion, the deputation secured from Gladstone a statement that "the franchise ought to be extended to the working classes." This was a month before his speech in parliament. In the autumn of this year he toured the manufacturing districts and spoke cautiously, yet reassuringly, of reform, and received addresses asking for the franchise.[4]

In 1864, the year of Gladstone's speech, was organized the association which became the instrument of the Manchester party in the agitation about to commence; namely, the National Reform Union. Like all similar bodies that had been formed since 1848, it sought the united action of both industrial classes, but, also like its predecessors, the work-

[1] Holyoake, *Bygones Worth Remembering*, I. 289-90, gives an account of a visit to Tyneside.
[2] *Reynolds's*, November 1, 1863.
[3] Humphrey, *Life of Robert Applegarth*, pp. 52-55.
[4] Morley, *Gladstone*, II. 153. *Reynolds's Newspaper*, October 23, 1864 (speech at Manchester); October 16 (Bolton); *Newcastle Daily Chronicle*, November 9 (Lambeth).

ingmen who came into it had to come in upon middle-class terms, not upon their own.

The third of the series of conferences initiated by the Leeds Working Men's Association in 1861 was held at Manchester, 1864,[1] and here the Union was formed. In the discussions attending its formation, the gulf separating manhood-suffragist workingmen and the household-suffragist middle classes, which had appeared at every such conference in the previous fifteen years, showed itself to be as deep and as wide as ever.[2] For this reason the Union was never able to create the united popular movement which it had in view. The partnership between Radicalism and labor it proposed appeared to labor to be unequal.

Accordingly, to the middle-class Reform Union, typifying as it did one form of a Liberal-Labor alliance, was soon opposed the Reform League, typifying that form of alliance which workingmen sought to achieve. Its program gave expression to the deep and abiding sentiment of the working masses for the full enfranchisement of the manhood of England in the name of right and justice. Behind both programs —of Union and of League—were to be seen the outlines of the ulterior objectives each had in view. It was the consciousness of this that made compromise impossible for the middle classes. Their program, therefore, prevailed, and workingmen in 1867 came into the Liberal-Labor alliance not in their full numbers nor upon their own terms.

A study of the activities of these two associations prior to the triumph of the principles of the Union in 1867 possesses interest in that it reveals this divergence. The approaches made, the hesitancies, the antagonisms, the mutual dependence necessitating coöperation in spite of distrust—

[1] None was held in 1863, because of the cotton famine.
[2] Account of conference is in *Reynolds's,* April 3 and 24. Bradlaugh deplored the bitterness displayed by extremists. *(National Reformer,* May 21, 1864. See also *Times,* April 21.)

these were the psychological material of the Liberal-Labor alliance. Looked at thus, the reform agitation becomes something more than a series of processions and harangues. The forces that were to shape English history were at work in it.

That the program of either League or Union was too wide for parliament or electors is certain. In 1865 the first general election since 1859 forced the question of reform into the forefront of general discussion. Men knew that the Palmerstonian lethargy on the subject was approaching its end. The moderation of the utterances of Bright and Gladstone is significant. They expressed their desire for a practical and possible measure.[1] Charles Buxton, Liberal M.P. for Maidstone, told his constituents there was no disguising the fact that the existing electorate was becoming alarmed at the prospect of being swamped by workingmen, and justly so.[2] The *Times* boasted of the apostasy of Lord Grosvenor, M.P. for Chester. In 1864 he had voted for Baines's bill, in 1865 against it. His explanation was that, whereas he had viewed the measure as merely a testimony to the principle of reform, he now saw it as a specific proposition fraught with revolutionary peril.[3] The *Times* declared such fears were the consequence of the constant iteration by Radical orators that any measure would be accepted "as an installment."

That the industrial question had much bearing upon political opinion is plain. Certain proposed schemes of reform favored a frank recognition of the principle of labor representation. Earl Grey proposed that workingmen should be treated as a distinct class and allowed representation as such, the registered trades being allowed to elect members to

[1] *Reynolds's Newspaper,* January 22, 1865, for Bright's speech at Birmingham; *Newcastle Weekly Chronicle,* June 2, 1865, for Gladstone's at Chester.

[2] *Reynolds's,* January 8.

[3] Quoted in *Reynolds's,* May 28.

voice their interests.[1]   John Stuart Mill made a similar suggestion in a letter to T. B. Potter of Rochdale. "The most
important questions in practical politics," he declared, "are
coming to be those in which the working classes as a body
are arrayed on one side and the employers as a body on the
other, as in all questions of wages, hours of labour, and so
on."   Hence he argued that workingmen should command
half the votes in the House of Commons.[2]   Cobden read
this letter and wrote to Potter: "I do not like to recognize
the necessity of dealing with the workingmen as a class in
the extension of the franchise."[3]

The *Newcastle Weekly Chronicle* declared that strikes
and lockouts were being used as an argument against reform.[4]   Sir George Grey, home secretary, in a hustings
speech,[5] said that, from public and private discussions on
the subject, he knew there was an honest apprehension in
many minds against a wide extension of the franchise because of the prevalence of strikes and the readiness with
which workingmen listened to agitators in disputes with
employers, thus being led to take a course which fostered
the alienation of classes.   If workingmen would base their
trade-unions upon justice and let them and strikes be voluntary, he considered that one strong argument against giving
them the vote would be removed. Presenting views that justified such fears, *Reynolds's Newspaper* was then writing to its
many working-class readers: "Let the working classes fully
understand that their political degradation is at the bottom
of all their social and industrial grievances";[6] and again,

----

[1] A pamphlet quoted from and replied to by Bright in a speech at
Birmingham (*Newcastle Weekly Chronicle,* January 19, 1865).
[2] Letter written March 16, 1865. Quoted in *Reynolds's,* April 23,
1865.
[3] *Ibid.* This was the last letter Cobden ever wrote.
[4] May 16, 1865.
[5] *Newcastle Daily Chronicle,* July 12, 1865.
[6] April 16, 1865.

that all schemes of reform being devised were a tacit confession of a conflict of interest between classes:

The great problem now attempted to be solved by aristocratic statesmanship is how to confer on the unenfranchised millions the form without the reality of political power. The wealth producers of England . . . are quick enough to discern all this . . . therefore they refuse to agitate or to work themselves into a bellowing enthusiasm in favour of reform schemes which are transparent shams.[1]

In this election workingmen exerted a certain amount of solid influence.[2] Their most notable victory was in the choice of Thomas Hughes for Lambeth. His success was distinctly a triumph for labor. His candidacy had been suggested in the first place by Holyoake.[3] Leading trade-unionists formed themselves into an electoral committee; on it were all the members of the Junta, together with other prominent workingmen, such as Cremer, Dunning, and T. J. Mottershead.[4] Hughes said afterward that two hundred workingmen gave their spare time without pay to his canvass.[5] The minutes of the newly formed Reform League show it collecting funds for his election expenses.[6] Hughes had been a friend of labor since the days of Christian Socialism, was a promoter of coöperation, and a democrat. As M.P. for Lambeth, he became peculiarly the representative of labor, acting with the Junta to secure trade-union legislation.

Another metropolitan election of special concern to workingmen was that of John Stuart Mill for Westminster.

[1] January 1, 1865.
[2] On their participation see *English Leader*, March 17 and April 7, 1866.
[3] Holyoake, *Bygones Worth Remembering*, II. 106 ff.
[4] From a pamphlet, *Mr. Hughes and the Election of Lambeth: The Call to Duty to Working Men*, London, 1868—a handbill issued in the campaign of 1868 calling together the committee of 1865.
[5] *Newcastle Weekly Chronicle*, July 11, 1865.
[6] Minute Book of the General Council and Executive Council of the Reform League, for 1865-6.

There is not much evidence available as to their direct participation in his election beyond the fact that one large working-class meeting was addressed by Ogder in his behalf.[1] But it is a safe assumption that they were much interested. By this time Mill was on close and friendly terms with them.[2] Early in 1865 he had published a cheap edition of certain of his works at the express wish of workingmen.[3] There can be no doubt that by that year his connection with labor leaders was intimate. The three names that provoked most enthusiasm in working-class audiences during the reform agitation were those of Bright, Gladstone, and Mill. After his election, he was regarded by workingmen as a representative upon whom they could count.

At Manchester the manhood-suffragists met with the same treatment at the hands of the Radicals that their successors in the labor world were to receive so often at the hands of their Liberal allies. They tried to secure the choice of Abel Heywood as running mate for Bazley, but the Radicals refused. The workingmen persisted; the Radicals cried that they were splitting the party. The result was that a nondescript Liberal was elected by the aid of the Conservative vote—evidence of the coalescing of the propertied classes regardless of party. Heywood again, as in 1859, received over four thousand votes, almost the total number of workingmen upon the register.[4]

[1] Mill's *Autobiography*, p. 163. That the new Reform League took part in the electoral meetings appears from an account in the *Times* (March 29) of a meeting for Mills's opponent, which was practically captured by the Mill group led by Leno (ex-Chartist) and S. Morley, both among the organizers of the League.

[2] His economic principles had come to accord to a large extent with theirs. For these principles see Beer, *History of British Socialism*, II. 187-8, 231; Barker, *op. cit.*, p. 205; also J. S. Mill, *Socialism*, ed. by W. D. P. Bliss, New York, 1891 (a rough draft by Mill written in 1869).

[3] *Autobiography*, p. 154.

[4] Account in the *Lankishire Loominary un Wickly Lookin' Glass.* July 1, 8, 15, 22; August 12, 1865; *Newcastle Weekly Chronicle*, June 30, 1865.

At Newcastle the patient efforts of democrats of both classes were rewarded in the election of Joseph Cowen, Sr. Workingmen played a conspicuous part in his election. John Kane, secretary of the National Association of Ironworkers, was active in his behalf.[1] At Sunderland, the greatest ship-building center of Great Britain, the Radicals and working-men, who had been struggling to emancipate the borough from the control of the ship-owners, brought forward an employer who stood for "all points of the Charter" except annual parliaments.[2] In the most bitter contest in the history of the borough, he was defeated by a Whig-Tory alliance.[3] At Tynemouth an equally exciting election resulted more happily for the advanced party with the success of G. O. Trevelyan. He was supported by a Non-Electors Association, and at one great non-electors' meeting for him upon the platform were joiners, painters, tailors, and other workingmen. A joiner occupied the chair.[4]

The net result of the election was a considerable strengthening of the advanced Liberals. The election was generally interpreted as meaning a reform bill, though only a moderate one. Disraeli was alarmed over the added strength of Bright's party[5] and over the growing strength of Liberalism generally, and he began to suggest to Derby that Conservative hopes might depend upon extending the basis of representation.[6] In the campaign those Conservatives who had pronounced for reform at all had advocated only a lateral extension.[7] Many Liberal candidates had been vague

[1] *Newcastle Daily Chronicle*, February 15; July 6, 7, 12, 1865.

[2] *Ibid.*, July 4; August 28, 1865.

[3] *Ibid.*, July 13. He was elected a short time afterward at a bye-election.

[4] *Newcastle Daily Chronicle*, November 11, 1865; July 11, 1865.

[5] Speech to his constituents (*Reynolds's*, July 30, 1865).

[6] Monypenny and Buckle, *op. cit.*, IV. 416.

[7] Lord Stanley did this (*Reynolds's*, July 16) and Beresford Hope at Stoke (*ibid.*, July 2).

on the subject and had led the people to consider them more sincere reformers than they were.[1]

It was not the election of 1865 that brought the reform question sharply to a crisis, but the death of Palmerston in October of that year. Disraeli wrote to Derby that there was now danger of changes occurring in both Church and State "which neither the necessities of the country require, nor its feelings really sanction."[2] Shaftesbury wrote:

We must now be prepared for vast and irrevocable changes. . . . We seem as though we were going to do everything that we most disliked. No one wishes for Reform, and yet every one will give it. The Parliament is called moderate, and even "liberally Conservative"; but it will prove decidedly revolutionary. The period is fast approaching, when the real effects of the Reform Bill [of 1832] will begin to be felt.[3]

It has already been noted that in 1864 the National Reform Union was formed. In 1865 its rival, the Reform League, was constituted upon a basis of registered, residential, manhood suffrage and the ballot. The activities of this league present the most complete picture of general working-class politics between the date of its formation and its dissolution in 1869 that can be found. It was distinctly a working-class organization, though it had the support of certain middle-class individuals. It possessed a temper and a purpose that differentiated it sharply from its Radical contemporary. Since it was organized as an agitating body, it was usually favored by the Radicals, but at times a sharp antagonism arose because of the abiding differences between a middle- and a working-class political movement.

The League owed its origin to Garibaldi's visit in 1864.[4] When the public meeting on Primrose Hill, called by the

[1] H. Cox, *The Reform Bills of 1866 and 1867*, London, 1867, p. 28.
[2] Monypenny and Buckle, *op. cit.*, IV. 426.
[3] Hodder, *Shaftesbury*, III. 201.
[4] The account in Howell's MS letter to a foreign correspondent, dated September 24, 1867, is the best there is of these events (in the League Letter-Book).

Working Men's Garibaldi Committee to protest against the curtailment of his visit, was broken up by the police, the committee, with certain middle-class sympathizers, among them Edmond Beales, barrister, met later in the day, and it was here that George Howell proposed the formation of a political association.[1] Beales presided at a number of preliminary meetings to that end. The franchise and the right of public meetings were the two questions discussed. At one of those meetings a letter from Bright was read that gives the key to his relations with the manhood suffragists. He wrote:

I think you are quite right to move for manhood suffrage, for that is what you must approve. . . . I think the people everywhere should ask for what they want, but, at the same time, I would recommend that they who ask for much should not regard as enemies and opponents those who ask for less. By a combined and friendly movement we shall get something, and that once gained is never again lost, but becomes an additional power to obtain more.[2]

It is certain that the Radicals had been negotiating with Beales and the workingmen. The above letter from Bright is evidence. At that same meeting letters were read from other members of parliament, who had been invited, but who did not attend. The *Observer* mentioned in this connection Bright, Forster, Samuel Morley, and others.[3] It declared that if the workingmen showed they were in earnest the Radicals were willing to put down five thousand pounds with which to carry on the agitation. Those negotiations must not have been satisfactory, for never did the Radicals contribute a quarter of that sum in the whole course of the agitation. The League was constantly in want of funds. Those middle-class Radicals who were actively and openly con-

[1] This was shortly after the formation of the National Reform Union at Manchester. See above, p. 219.

[2] *Times*, June 23, 1864.

[3] Quoted in Park, *The Reform Bill of 1867*, p. 89, as quoted in the *Times* of February 21, 1865.

nected with it were tried democrats, and not Manchesterites
—such men as P. A. Taylor, Beales, and Samuel Morley.
Morley was a leading nonconformist politician and a democrat of the type of Joseph Sturge and Edward Miall. But
that Bright was in touch with the League fairly constantly is
also certain. Since he was in reality guiding the whole agitation, he could not afford to act otherwise, and he and the
Radicals found the zeal and enthusiasm aroused by the
League a most potent whip with which to scourge Whigs
and Tories into a reforming frame of mind.

In February, 1865, the League was formally constituted
by resolution at a public meeting in St. Martin's Hall.[1] In
March Beales was chosen as president of the League, Howell
as secretary; a permanent executive committee was formed
and offices opened in Adelphi Terrace. It is interesting to
note that the rules adopted provided for the formation of
autonomous branches and also for the affiliation of bodies
which could not become branches.[2] This latter scheme,
identical with that adopted a year later by the International,
was no doubt designed for trade-unions. In May an Address to the workingmen of Great Britain and Ireland was
issued, some phrases of which indicate the Chartist tone of
the document: "The Working Classes in our Country, the
producers of its wealth, are in a degraded and humiliating
position . . . the men who have fought her battles,
manned her ships, tilled the soil, built up her manufactures,
trade and commerce . . . are denied the most essential
privileges of citizens," without which "we are powerless for

---

[1] Short account in the *Times* of February 24. Hartwell (ex-Chartist
and Potter's henchman) presided. Potter took a prominent part. Beales
and Mason Jones represented the middle-class group. Jones soon fell
into disfavor with the League. The minutes record many complaints,
and he soon ceased to be active—evidence again of the failure of middle-
class coöperation.

[2] A printed copy of the *Rules and Address* is inserted in the MS
Minute Book for April 15, 1865, to November 7, 1866.

the present and hopeless for the future." Let workingmen, therefore, organize and agitate, but peacefully and legally. "Take courage from the triumph of our brethren in America." Finally, on May 13, 1865, the inaugural public meeting of the League took place, and it was formally launched into politics.[1]

The minutes of the League for the first few months reveal among those active in it the trade-unionists, Odger, Applegarth, Coulson, Cremer, Stainsby, and Nieass; several who were active in the International, as George Eccarius, the Marxian tailor; several ex-Chartists, as Robert Hartwell and J. B. Leno; and several middle-class democrats, as J. A. Nicholay, J. Baxter Langley, and Charles Bradlaugh. In June Ernest Jones, now residing at Manchester, was made a vice-president. By this time also branches had been formed in Birmingham, Manchester, Huddersfield, and other provincial towns, and soon lecturers were being sent out to speak on various political questions. The land is mentioned as one. Applegarth was among the lecturers.

Thus before the death of Palmerston two national organizations were at work for reform. The problem had at once arisen as to the relation between these two bodies. Two months after the formation of the League, the Union called a national conference to meet on the eve of the election in the Free Trade Hall, Manchester, for the purpose of unifying the agitation.[2] Two hundred delegates represented many associations or geographical districts. Among the associations represented, those that were evidently made up of workingmen were the Manhood Suffrage Association of

[1] A pamphlet is in the British Library of Political Science entitled *Speech of Edmond Beales, Esq. M.A., President of the Reform League. at a meeting in St. Martin's Hall in support of the League, May 13, 1865, with notes.*

[2] *Report of Proceedings at the National Reform Conference, held in Free Trade Hall, Manchester, May 15 and 16, 1865. George Wilson, chairman* (printed for the National Reform Union).

Bury, one of the same name at Manchester, as well as the Manchester Working Men's Parliamentary Reform Association, the International Working Men's Association, and the Reform League. The rest probably were Radical organizations with some working-class members. From the moment that the question of the extent of reform to be demanded was raised by Jacob Bright, the debate waxed hot between the proponents of the two principles represented. The Reform League delegates took up the challenge at once, saying that London workingmen could not accept less than manhood suffrage, because anything else would not enfranchise them. Cremer, speaking for the International, said that its twelve thousand members had sent him to speak for manhood suffrage. The Manchester men retorted that London blocked every movement for reform by such uncompromising tactics and accused the League of having organized expressly to thwart the Union.

Not only was there disagreement as to principle, but also as to method of procedure. The moderate, middle-class group advised proceeding with such moderation as to win support in parliament, but the extremists thought of coercing parliament. In the words of E. O. Greening, delegate of the Manchester manhood-suffragists: "What was really wanted was the arousing of such a feeling throughout the country in favour of the full principle that they [parliament] would be obliged, from the very fear of that moral pressure, to give way."[1] Ernest Jones pronounced all the resolutions proposed by the resolutions committee nonentities. A Huddersfield delegate of the Reform League stated that the men of that town would not agitate except for the widest franchise. Finally, Beales urged the conference to accept at least the *principle* of manhood suffrage, but P. A. Taylor per-

[1] *Report of Conference,* p. 53.

suaded him reluctantly to withdraw his motion. In the end
the League lost on every round, but George Howell wrote
soon afterward that neither did the Union carry their program, but merely a few colorless resolutions. He asserted
that when Beales was speaking to his last motion, the Union
packed the hall to defeat it.[1] George Newton, organizer of
the agitation against the law on Masters and Servants then
in progress, was one of the working-class delegates who sym-
pathized with the middle-class position. He declared it hopeless to expect parliament to accept manhood suffrage; "if
they went to the House of Commons and asked for it they
might as well stay at home and whistle jigs."[2] The League
delegates hoped for either of two things: to frighten parliament by Chartist methods into granting a Chartist reform,
or, as Howell wrote to Lucraft later in the year, "if we work
we may be landed somewhere *nearer* manhood suffrage."[3]

The Reform League adopted the policy at the outset of
trying to enlist the trades. In June, 1865, it addressed to
them the appeal which has already been quoted above,[4]
pointing to their grievances as unionists that resulted from
their powerlessness to voice their interests in the House of
Commons. The minutes record discussions as to how to
bring the trades in. Practically all the prominent trade
unionists were active in the League from the start; even
George Potter was, though he was then waging war upon
the London Trades Council over the matter of the Staffordshire ironworkers and, for that reason, soon carried his
quarrel into the League, upon whose council most of the
Trades Council sat. The minutes contain denunciations of
his machinations.[5] Within a few months he set up his

[1] Reform League Letters, November 17, 1865 (to W. L. Evans).
[2] *Reynolds's,* May 21. This issue gives an account of the Conference.
[3] Reform League Letters, November 9, 1865.
[4] P. 229.
[5] *E.g.,* for August 11, 1865.

London Working Men's Association, designed to be his organ in distinction from the Trades Council in matters industrial and from the League in politics.

The first trade-union recorded as paying a contribution to the League and voting to form a branch among its members was the Finsbury Branch of the Amalgamated Cordwainers.[1] Soon Odger reported the ironworkers of Grantham warm in support.[2] Letters were sent to over a hundred officials of the various lodges of the Operative Bricklayers, and hundreds of others to the Cordwainers, Carpenters and Joiners, Amalgamated Engineers, the Potters of Staffordshire, etc.[3]

In December, 1865, the League initiated a policy designed to draw closer its relations with all organized bodies of workingmen, which became a permanent and effective part of its machinery. This was to hold periodical conferences with delegates from trade, friendly, temperance, and other working-class societies. The first conference was apparently a success. The public meeting upon the occasion filled St. Martin's Hall and necessitated two overflow meetings. This interest was not created by the presence of any popular orator, for all the speakers were workingmen.[4] Upon the eve of the introduction of Gladstone's bill in 1866, another conference was held, and the council's minutes record that delegates were sent by the Operative Bricklayers, the Amalgamated Carpenters, the Shoemakers' Amalgamated Society, "etc., etc."[5] Howell's letters inviting the

[1] Minutes, August 18, 1865.

[2] *Ibid.*, September 22.

[3] Reform League Secretary's Petty Cash Book. Entries for June, 1865.

[4] *Reynolds's*, December 17, 1865.

[5] February 23, 1866. See an account also in the *Morning Star* for March 1 and 2, 1866.

unions to participate on this occasion all used as an argument
the need of trade-union legislation.[1]

Relations between the League and the Union were verging on hostility by the end of the year.[2]   Howell wrote
to Greening of Manchester that if a break came he desired
it to be from the other side.[3]   Not even Bright was approved of.   Beales called his recent acts "unworthy"; and
another member of the council said the less they depended
on Bright the better, for he was fast verging on Conservatism and had begun to preach reaction.[4]   When Bright
stated that a measure similar to that of 1860 would give
satisfaction, the council was indignant.

Nevertheless, by the opening of 1866 it is noticeable that
a few middle-class Radicals were beginning to contribute to
the funds of the League, though in small amounts.[5]   The
council was in correspondence with Gladstone, Fawcett,
Hughes, T. B. Potter, Frederick Harrison, and other Liberals in and out of parliament.

The League was meanwhile expanding and improving its
organization.   The council was regular in attendance, and
the minutes reveal its admirable spirit and method, moderate, earnest, and circumspect.   This was due in large part
to the wise and high-minded guidance of the President,
Edmond Beales.   His lofty character impressed its own
quality upon the organization over which he presided for
four years.   Repeatedly, the minutes, as well as Howell's

[1] Reform League Letters, January and February.
[2] Minutes, November 10, 22; December 8, 1865; *Reynolds's*, November 26.
[3] Reform League Letters, November 6, 1865.
[4] Minutes, September 22, 1865.
[5] Secretary's Petty Cash Book. Amounts varied from a few pounds
up to fifty. Among the donors were P. A. Taylor, S. Morley, S. Pope
(a permissive bill advocate), Wm. Hargreaves, of the Ballot Society,
and Sir Wilfrid Lawson, M.P.

letters, give evidence of the respect and affection in which he was held and of his wise and moderating leadership.[1]

Another working-class organization that was to figure prominently in politics, 1866-7, was Potter's London Working Men's Association. About this body there has been a good deal of misconception.[2] It was formed in March, 1866.[3] Its political program was registered, manhood suffrage, the ballot, and more equal representation, but it, unlike the League, announced its readiness to accept less, Potter declaring that manhood suffrage was impossible in their lifetime.[4] From the first, it made the insertion of a lodger clause in any reform bill its special cause. This was a matter of vital interest to London. The membership of the Association included T. J. Dunning of the Bookbinders; T. Connolly, president of the Operative Stonemasons; Joseph Leicester, secretary of the Glass-makers' Society; Henry Broadhurst, and other less conspicuous trade-unionists.

[1] He was an idealist fighting against all forms of oppression. He belonged to Polish Committees, a Circassian Committee, the Emancipation Society, the Garibaldi Committee, the Jamaica Committee, etc. (From a MS article on Beales written by Howell in 1874.)

[2] West, *History of the Chartist Movement*, p. 277, note 1, says wrongly that it grew out of the Reform League. Beer, *History of British Socialism*, II. 223, considers Hartwell and not Potter the leading figure, identifies it with Chartism, and says it did no more than adopt a program. All are incorrect. (Beer calls it "Union.") Webb, *op. cit.*, p. 255, calls it unimportant and of nondescript persons. It was important politically, and even its trade-union following for a time was as large as that of the Junta. Its members were hardly nondescript. G. Güttler, *Die Englische Arbeiterpartei*, Jena, 1914, p. 42, confuses it with the League.

[3] So Hartwell stated. See *Morning Star*, October 1, 1867. Humphrey, *History of Labour Representation*, says it was formed February 16 (p. 10). Potter, in his evidence before the Trade Union Commission in March, 1867, stated that the association had been in existence about fifteen months. Its prospectus declared its object to be "to procure the political enfranchisement and promote the social and general interests of the industrial classes." Potter likened it to a trades council and stated that its industrial objects were its major concern. (*First Report of the Commissioners Appointed to inquire into the Organization and Rules of Trade Unions*, etc., H. of C., 1867, p. 16.

[4] *Morning Star*, August 2, 15, 1866.

John Kane, president of the Ironworkers, was in close touch with it.[1] The purpose of the organization was two-fold: to act as a political organ of trade-unions and to perform trade-union functions as well.[2] It was able to draw the trade-unions of London into its political agitation upon a large scale and thus exerted much influence upon the progress of the reform question. It revealed its industrial influence when it convened an important conference of trade delegates from all over the country upon the appointment of the Royal Commission on Trade Unions early in 1867. In this it was opposed unremittingly by the Junta, who succeeded in largely nullifying the conference.

With the opening of 1866, the prospect of a reform bill was near. A deputation from the Reform League waited on Russell in January and secured from him the first official statement that reform would be a cabinet question.[3] In March Gladstone introduced his measure, which was to enfranchise seven-pound householders and ten-pound lodgers in boroughs, and fourteen-pound occupiers in counties—a more restricted measure than had been presented by any Liberal government since 1848. The abundant testimony to the anti-reforming sentiment of parliament and the electorate that can be gained from pamphlets, the press, and public speeches, is sufficient explanation of that fact.[4] Gladstone

---

[1] *Ibid.*, September 5, 12, 1866.

[2] *E.g.*, two months after it was formed it was considering the lockout in the file trade of Sheffield (*Morning Star*, May 2, 1866).

[3] *Morning Star*, January 13, 17, 1866; *Reynolds's*, January 21.

[4] Some pamphlets of this nature are: Richard Varden, *Hints on the Principles of Self-Government and their Application to Parliamentary Reform*, London, 1866 (in British Library of Political Science); E. J. Gibbs, *Parliamentary Reform Considered as a Question of Principle and not of Party*, London, 1866 (in the same library); *The Final Reform Bill of Earl Russell, K. G.*, London, 1866 (in British Museum); H. W. Cole, *The Middle Classes and the Borough Franchise*, London, 1866 (in the British Museum); E. Wilson, *Principles of Representation, in order to secure due balance of classes*, London, 1866. Plurality of voting and proportional representation were much discussed; *e.g.*, a pamphlet giv-

estimated that four hundred thousand new voters would be added, of whom about half would be artisans; but this would leave the middle classes still in the majority in boroughs, which he considered a six-pound franchise would not have done.[1]

Radicals and workingmen were disappointed, but generally bowed to the inevitable and accepted it. Joseph Cowen, M.P. for Newcastle, wrote his constituents that household suffrage would not secure fifty votes in the House.[2] The Reform League Council debated long on its policy, but decided to accept the bill and assist to pass it.[3] Its advice was followed by all its branches, of which there were now seventy;[4] but Ernest Jones withdrew from the League because of their decision.[5]

The League had by this time won for itself a position of some importance. Its first annual report showed that it had held six hundred meetings, sent out over one hundred thousand tracts, and spent £1603. It now called for an agitating fund of ten thousand pounds. It was sweeping into its organization all the small and struggling political associations that existed among workingmen. A glance at the membership of its general council reveals the factions and movements, or fragments of movements, which it had absorbed.

Its support of the government bill was therefore important. Howell's letter book shows Bright urging it to strengthen the hands of the government,[6] and it acted ener-

ing a speech by R. D. Macsie, *Speech delivered at the meeting of the Liverpool Reform League . . . on plurality of votes as a needful element in any final scheme of Parliamentary Reform,* London, 1867.

[1] C. Seymour, *Electoral Reform in England and Wales,* pp. 250-1 and note 1, p. 251. Also H. Cox, *The Reform Bills of 1866 and 1867,* pp. 35-6.

[2] *English Leader,* April 7, 1866.

[3] Minutes, March 10 and 20.

[4] First Annual Report, to April 13, 1866.

[5] Reform League Letters, May 7 and 14, 1866.

[6] March 19, 1866.

getically toward that end. Howell wrote that only lack of
funds prevented its holding an enthusiastic meeting every
night,[1] yet contributions from the middle-classes came in
slowly and in small amounts.[2] Evidently the Radicals did
not yet need the League sorely. The most important of its
demonstrations in these two months was a large meeting,
chiefly of trade-unionists, addressed by Professor Beesly,
Thomas Hughes, Cremer, and Bradlaugh.[3] Meetings to
support the bill seem to have been general over the country.
The National Reform Union was especially active. On
March 27 it held a conference of one thousand delegates,
who were addressed by Bright.[4] By the time of the Easter
recess, it was apparent that the bill was in grave danger
from the Conservatives and obstructive Liberals, consequently the agitation out of doors increased in vigor.[5]

As the League had accepted Gladstone's bill, so had Potter's L. W. M. A.[6] It arranged a trade-union demonstration when danger to the bill was threatening.[7] Representatives of sixteen unions, some of them national, were on the
platform, and all of the speeches were made by trade-unionists. A notable one was that of Dunning, who now came
out for the policy of political activity by trade societies in
view of the repeated treachery of the government on reform.
That this was regarded as a trade-union demonstration is
shown by the comment of the *English Leader,* that it proved

[1] Letter to Greening, March 30, 1866.
[2] Petty Cash Book records only about two hundred pounds contributed thus in the two months the bill was pending.
[3] *Morning Star,* April 12, 1866.
[4] H. Cox, *op. cit.,* p. 42.
[5] Park, *The Reform Bill of 1867,* p. 95, gives a list of ten large
meetings noted in the *Times* between April 2 and April 5. He under-
estimates the expression of approval of the bill *before* the recess, because
he follows the *Times,* which did not report such meetings regularly.
The best source for such information is the *Morning Star.*
[6] *Morning Star,* March 21, 1866.
[7] *Ibid.,* March 24, and April 4 and 6. (The last number describes the
demonstration.)

the trades could look beyond questions merely of work and wages.[1]

Another cause of the mounting public interest, besides the evident danger that the bill would fail, was the vituperative language used of the working classes in the debate. Bradlaugh's paper said it was this which had raised interest to the pitch of a real agitation in the Easter recess.[2] That these popular demonstrations came from the lower orders of society, and not from the more respectable middle class, during the whole time that Gladstone's bill was pending, is indicated in a series of detailed confidential reports made by a certain Conservative agent during those months. Time after time the statement is made that no important persons, no men of weight or respectability, took part, while frequently the meetings are reported as composed of Chartists, extremists, artisans, Dissenters, or rabble.[3] That the middle-class electorate on the whole were not behind even this moderate measure seems certain.[4]

In parliament the bill was under discussion nearly four months. It split the Liberal party along a line that marked off democratic progress from a political system based upon classes and property. Those who upheld the latter joined with the Conservatives to defeat the pending measure. The Liberal schism was not permanent, so far as actual personnel was concerned, but it foretold the coming adhesion of conservative Liberals to the Conservative party, which gradually took place after 1867.

[1] April 21, 1866.

[2] *National Reformer*, May 13, 1866. How important a factor this was can be judged by the denunciation of Lord Elcho by the London Trades Council, though he was even then conducting their cause in parliament for an amendment of the Master and Servant Law (see *Morning Star*, April 12, December 14, 1867, and May 21, 1868).

[3] *Reform Meetings, the Real Facts*, London, 1866. Reports to J. Spofforth. A pamphlet in the British Museum.

[4] The *Fortnightly* wrote in May that reform was "the most unpopular subject of the day with existing constituencies."

It was felt that Gladstone's measure was the "thin edge of a wedge." It was believed that there would be constant pressure for a lowering of the qualification until universal suffrage should be reached.[1] Bright, during the Easter recess, urged that the bill be used as a "lever" for the obtaining of a great deal more, an argument that drew from a member of the government the remark: "Confound Mr. Bright; his lever has done for our bill." This consciousness of the lack of finality in the proposed settlement was further strengthened by expressions of public meetings, which almost universally pronounced it to be only a step in the right direction. The effective speeches of Robert Lowe, leader in the "Cave of Adullam" that joined the Conservative opposition, "arrested all careless legislation on reform." So stated the *Fortnightly*.[2]

The Conservative attitude toward the bill was determined partly by principle and partly by party expediency. There can be no doubt that the party as a whole was opposed to any measure that would increase the proportionate power of the middle and working classes. To maintain the present balance of classes, so favorable to the land, was their general desire. Even Lord Stanley, one of the most liberal of his party, in the recent electoral campaign had favored no more extension of the suffrage than Disraeli's bill of 1859 had proposed—a lateral extension only. Conservatives would, however, be so implacably opposed to a measure such as this, which would increase middle-class influence in counties while preserving a middle-class majority in boroughs and adding the upper artisans who were Liberal almost to a man, that they would be willing to go much lower, if that should be

---

[1] Monypenny and Buckle, *op. cit.*, IV. 431-3. Cox, *op. cit.*, p. 38.

[2] For these arguments see Seymour, *op. cit.*, pp. 252-3, and G. C. Broderick, *The Utilitarian Argument against Reform, as stated by Mr. Lowe* (in *Essays on Reform*, London, 1867). For an analysis of the whole debate, see Trevelyan, *Bright*, pp. 352-3.

the only possible escape from such a middle-class measure. Tory democracy might be an available counter-policy to such a measure as this; but it is difficult to believe that Tory democracy was a policy sought for its own sake. To a suggestion made to Disraeli that he permit Russell to pass a moderate measure and so settle the question, he had replied that "such a course would seat the Whigs for a lifetime."[1]

Finally, on June 19, the government was beaten upon an amendment that would have nullified the bill;[2] and within two weeks it had resigned, in spite of numerous indignant public meetings calling upon it to dissolve parliament. The Reform League held huge meetings of twenty thousand or more on Clerkenwell Green and in Trafalgar Square.[3] Banners with the League tricolor were borne. Beales said he was leaving these meetings to be organized spontaneously by the workingmen.[4] In the provinces similar meetings were general.

The crisis brought the National Reform Union and the Reform League temporarily into harmony. The Union held a great delegate meeting, with representatives from three hundred towns, at which Cremer, for the League, said they were willing to coöperate for household suffrage and would not block the movement by insisting upon their own program.[5] And Beales, in a public letter, declared the willingness of the League to accept household suffrage as the basis of a renewed agitation, since it would be "a link between Manchester, Birmingham, and London."[6]

[1] Monypenny and Buckle, *op. cit.*, IV. 430. For the middle-class nature of the bill, see this volume, pp. 430-3, and R. D. Baxter, *Distribution of Seats and the Counties,* London, 1866.

[2] To substitute rating for rental. A house rated at seven pounds would rent for eight or nine pounds.

[3] *Morning Star,* June 23 to 29.

[4] *Ibid.,* July 3.

[5] *Ibid.,* June 23, 26.

[6] *Ibid.,* June 21.

With the accession of a Conservative government, the reform question entered upon a new phase. It now developed dynamic possibilities which came near to achieving a dangerous crisis for the country. It was complicated by economic distress; it became entangled with Fenianism; it gave prospect at times of developing the ever ominous qualities of a class war through the operation of Tory opposition and the rapidly developing sense of antagonism of interests which the crisis in trade-unionism produced. It resulted in the enactment of democratic reform by a parliament which had a year before dedicated itself to the warding off of precisely that eventuality.

Mention has been made of economic distress as a factor in the political agitation after the middle of 1866. Late in the spring of that year a sudden, sharp panic occurred, whose influence spread rapidly over industrial England and whose evil effects were increased by simultaneous bad harvests. These conditions gave a threatening and menacing aspect to the reform agitation in the mind of the upper classes that it would perhaps not have otherwise possessed.[1] It developed a psychological situation that far outweighed in significance the real importance of the economic crisis as a political factor. The lesson of Chartism had not been forgotten; unemployment and a drop in wages, coupled with an agitation for democracy, presented a specter of frightful mien to a generation that remembered the hungry forties. Bright had for nearly ten years been prophesying just such a combination of circumstances which would finally wreak vengeance upon an obstinate parliament, that would not heed the people's demands while there was yet time.

The details of the crisis and its economic effects have been worked out in detail elsewhere.[2] From May to Aug-

[1] Some evidence on this may be found in Park, *op. cit.*, pp. 80-86.
[2] In Park, *The Reform Bill of 1867*, chapter II. Also R. Baxter, *The Panic of 1866, with its Lessons on the Currency Act*, London, 1866.

ust the discount rate stood at ten per cent.; investment was curtailed, production lowered, wages decreased, and unemployment was general. At the same time, the prices of food rose rapidly on account of bad crops. Pauperism increased steadily from the middle of 1866 to 1871, showing the lingering effects of the depression.[1] Especially in the poorer quarters of large cities, most of all in London, where the population was perpetually near the starvation level, was the distress acute.[2] The *Spectator* in January, 1867, described the misery of Greenwich, Deptford, and Poplar, where thirty thousand more dock laborers were out of work than usual, and the poor-rates were rising ominously.[3] The distress all over the country continued through 1869. The organized trades were greatly affected; as to the great mass of unskilled labor, Howell wrote in that year, "no one can . . . sound the depths of its absolute, deplorable misery."[4]

It was at the very beginning of the period of distress that Russell's ministry resigned. From that moment the Reform League grew in influence and numbers, so that it became a powerful organization. It organized the major part of the agitation which converted the Conservative cabinet to reform and enabled—or forced—Bright and Gladstone to give final shape to the measure. Two things made the League formidable to the conservative classes—its numbers and extent, particularly its close alliance with trade-unions, and, secondly, its coöperation with Bright. All the forces of democracy seemed to be allied together for the undoing of the constitution and the destruction of the vested interests of property that flourished under its wing.

[1] Mackay, *History of the Poor Law,* III. Appendix III.
[2] Pauperism in London rose twenty-nine per cent. between 1866 and 1868 (the *Coöperator,* October 10, 1868). For a description of the wretchedness of East London, see Baxter, *The National Income,* London, 1868, pp. 45-6.
[3] Quoted by Park, *op. cit.,* pp. 81-2.
[4] MS article in his Letter-book for 1869-72.

There is not space to relate the full story of the agitation. Its more significant features alone must suffice. Beginning with a huge meeting of artisans in Trafalgar Square, where Beales and Bradlaugh spoke on the disaster which had befallen their cause,[1] the League promoted an agitation nation-wide in extent. The League believed, with Ernest Jones, that temporizing with Whiggery had brought the reformers to the present pass, and that only by a vigorous manhood-suffrage movement could any reform be forced from an unwilling parliament. In truth, the agitation from this point bore a decidedly Chartist aspect, and there is no question that while Bright and his party saw the value of it to coerce opposition, they were also nervous over the latent possibilities that resided in it. Before Derby had been in office a month, the League and the Hyde Park riots had put this new face upon the movement.

The League planned a demonstration in Hyde Park for the double purpose of "intimating the national will" on reform and testing the right of the police commissioner to forbid such meetings in parks. It will be remembered the League grew out of just such a prohibition, and the right of public meetings had been from the first one object it championed. The police commissioner forbade this meeting. Beales led one section of the huge procession to the gates to assert their right to enter, then returned quietly to Trafalgar Square. Another and larger section approached the park from another direction. The crowd swelled with the addition of workmen just out from work. It became a huge, swaying mass of human beings and at the entrance to the park its pressure forced the railings to give way. Contem-

[1] *Morning Star*, July 2, 3, 4, quotes *Pall Mall Gazette*, that the crowd was made up of earnest artisans, and that there was no question that they wanted votes. The *Star* reckoned the number present at thirty to fifty thousand.

porary accounts of the affair vary, but it seems to be probable that this result was not contemplated or the result of an
angry demonstration.[1] Police to the number of about
eighteen hundred were drawn up in the park; they now
charged the crowd, but were powerless before it. Two
troops of Horse Guards and two companies of Foot Guards
were called in, but no further violence took place.

An ugly temper had been aroused in the people, however, and for three days they surged through the park in
defiance of the police and the military. Walpole, the home
secretary, was reduced to despair. The League council considered whether to hold another meeting in the park. John
Stuart Mill, fearing the people would go armed, went to the
council meeting to use his influence to prevent a trial of
strength with the government. He said afterwards that
Beales and his chief colleague, Colonel Dickson, did not need
persuading, but the workingmen did, and he could move them
only by showing it meant revolution. He says in his *Autobiography* he believes he was the only man, except Bright or
Gladstone, who had influence enough with the workingmen
to restrain them.[2] Finally Beales prevailed upon Walpole
to remove the soldiers and police, promising that the League
would restore order. This it had no difficulty in doing. The
whole episode was a humiliation for the government and an
exhibition both of the influence of the League and the good
sense of its officers.[3]

[1] One of the best descriptions is in Henry Broadhurst's *Autobiography*, pp. 33-40. He was present. See also *Morning Star*, July 20,
23, for preliminary plans, and July 24, 27, for very full account of the
affair. Also, the *English Leader*, July 28. An account hostile to the
League, and patently unfair, is in a pamphlet, *The Government and the
People! The Great Reform League Demonstration in Hyde Park*.

[2] Pp. 165-7.

[3] For further important details see the *English Leader*, August 11,
1866, and the *National Reformer*, July 29.

The League followed up the Hyde Park affair with a great meeting in Agricultural Hall, where it was said between twenty-five thousand and forty thousand people gathered, the organized bodies of workingmen coming with banners flying.   Mill was there to speak in behalf of the right of public meeting; P. A. Taylor also spoke, and Bradlaugh.   The *English Leader* rightly declared, "Such an assembly in London reduces the Reform question to one simply of date and extent."[1]   The impetus given to the agitation by this clash with the government was marked. The *National Reformer* wrote at once that if the Tories kept up such tactics they would find "that they, and not the Radicals, are tending in a very summary manner to Americanize British institutions."[2]

But the effectiveness of the whole reform agitation of 1866-7 lay above all in the participation in it of organized labor.   This fact gave weight to the Reform League and also to the London Working Men's Association.   Goldwin Smith said to the Oxford Reform League, soon after the Hyde Park episode, that he feared that—

The struggle may in the end cease to be one between parties in Parliament and become one between classes, the class represented by the House of Commons on the one side, and the class represented by the trade unions on the other. . . . The true statesman would almost rather drag the working men within the pale of the constitution by force than suffer them thus to organize themselves into a separate community outside it.[3]

It should be noted that the United Kingdom Alliance of Organized Trades was just being formed at Sheffield.   In the background of the developing agitation constantly ap-

[1] August 4.   Also *National Reformer,* August 5.   See Broadhurst's *Life,* p. 33.   The agitation of the Queen and ministry on this occasion was so great as to cause the use of troops.   A message was sent to the Queen every half-hour upon the state of London (The *Working Man,* August 4, 1866).
[2] August 12.
[3] *Morning Star,* July 24, 1866.

pears the embittered industrial struggle, which reached a crisis in 1866-7.

The conjunction of League and trade-unions was portentous enough; their coöperation with Bright completed a sum of threats to the stability of English institutions that could not be withstood by those in authority. The last months of 1866 saw a series of joint demonstrations by the three. In August, at Brookfield, in Birmingham, a crowd of, it was said, two hundred thousand gathered from the Midlands country to hear John Bright. Many of the trades in Birmingham had already joined the League in their corporate capacity,[1] and all joined in this demonstration, by advice of the Trades Council.[2] One whole division of the monster procession, ten thousand strong, was made up of the trades marching with their banners. Other divisions were of friendly societies, temperance societies, and of non-society men from the local works. Thousands of artisans wore the badge of the Reform League. Resolutions were adopted for manhood suffrage, Bright declaring he had no fear of it.[3] The significance of the demonstration was at once recognized. The *Economist* said the Conservatives could not shelve reform now, even for one session.[4] The press united in admitting that it was an event of importance.

Other League meetings were held—at Manchester with Ernest Jones for chief speaker;[5] at Halifax, where the Trade Council joined with the League to convene it;[6] at the Guild Hall in London, where the League and the L. W. M. A. acted in concert and where the speakers were all work-

[1] Webb, *op. cit.*, p. 248, note 1.
[2] *Morning Star*, August 16, 1866.
[3] *Ibid.*, August 28, September 3.
[4] Quoted in the *Morning Star*, September 3.
[5] *Ibid.*, August 11, 13.
[6] *Ibid.*, September 6.

ingmen.[1] All the time the League was growing in membership. By September it was so strong, in Lancashire,
Cheshire, and Derbyshire that those counties were erected
into a Northern Department, with offices and a full staff of
officers at Manchester.[2] On September 17 the Scottish
National Reform League was formed, identical with the
Reform League in program and closely affiliated with it,
practically its Scottish section.[3] Constant improvement in
the central machinery of the League was made. It was trying also to raise ten thousand pounds for agitation purposes,
and Howell wrote to many Liberals for contributions, explaining that the League hoped to follow the procedure of
the Anti-Corn Law League. It asked for aid even if its
principles were not accepted, for it would accept any good
measure that had a chance of passing.[4]

Yet the Liberals, even the most advanced, except Bright,
held back from the League. By October three men had
given two hundred fifty pounds[5] each and one one hundred
pounds. Howell sadly wrote that the fund was not growing,
adding a sentence that reveals to the historian, if it did not to
Howell, the reason for the ill-success : "If we had the money
our movement would become one of the greatest triumphs of
modern days."[6] It was precisely such a triumph that middle-class Liberals and even Radicals would have done much
to prevent.

[1] *Ibid.*, August 9.

[2] *Ibid.*, September 10, 1866. Ernest Jones was very prominent here.

[3] Facts given in a pamphlet, *The Great Reform Demonstration at
Glasgow, 16 Oct. 1866*, Glasgow, 1866. (In Manchester Free Reference Library.) Howell's correspondence shows that Glasgow had hesitated to go as far as the League did. (Letters December 19, 1865, and
February 24, 1866.)

[4] See letter to J. W. Woodley, September 29, and others dated
September 15, 19, 1866 (to R. C. Hanbury, M.P., and Isaac Holden,
M.P.).

[5] These were S. Morley. Sir W. Lawson, and T. Thommison.

[6] To R. Kell, of Bradford, October 17, 1866.

But Bright was willing to use the League as an instrument against the government, and its meetings multiplied.[1] A second great meeting of Bright, the League, and the trades, and, this time, the National Reform Union, was held in Manchester, where Bright found himself in company with orators of the stamp of Ernest Jones, E. O. Greening, Odger, Lucraft, and W. P. Roberts, the "pitmen's attorney."[2] On every such occasion Bright denounced the Tories unsparingly, hoping thereby to create greater popular pressure, and also, perhaps, to draw the prospective working-class electorate more closely toward the Liberal camp.

Next Bright appeared at a West Riding demonstration at Leeds, where Beales and Ernest Jones also spoke. Many trades and friendly societies marched in the procession. Chartist emblems of white and green were conspicuous. In concluding its description of this demonstration, declared to be the most magnificent of all, the *English Leader* wrote: "The blood of the Chartists of 'forty-eight is the seed of the Reform movement of 1866." All the members of parliament for the West Riding declined to be present, Baines frankly because of his opposition to manhood suffrage.[3] A week later occurred at Glasgow another exhibition of the Bright-League-trades alliance.[4] It was the greatest political demonstration that had ever been held in Scotland. A procession of thirty thousand, formed of the organized trades and men from workshops, mines, and foundries, covered five

---

[1] Bright was writing the Council to push their agitation (Minutes, September 7, 1866). Bradlaugh's paper declared that in September hardly a night passed without a meeting somewhere, and in one week it noted thirty (*National Reformer,* September 9, 16, 1866).

[2] *Morning Star,* September 26; *English Leader,* September 29, 1866.

[3] Account in *Morning Star,* October 9, and *English Leader,* October 20, 27. The president of the League here was Alderman Carter, who was elected to Parliament in 1868 by the votes of workingmen.

[4] Pamphlet, *The Great Reform Demonstration at Glasgow, 16 Oct. 1866,* Glasgow, 1866 (Official account by League). Also *Morning Star,* October 17, and Trevelyan, *Bright,* p. 362, note 1.

miles of the Glasgow streets; then came the open air meeting, which adopted resolutions for manhood suffrage and the ballot, and at night Bright spoke in the City Hall. Thus was the regular procedure at all these events complete. Among the speakers here were George Potter, Alexander Macdonald of the Miners' Association, George Newton of the Glasgow Trades Council and also secretary of the committee on the Master and Servant Law, the president and secretary of the Amalgamated Tailors, and other trade representatives. It is worth noting that the operative masons carried a banner inscribed: "Nine hours—a new era in the history of Labour." Bright's speech discussed the reasons why the poor should have the vote; then only would legislation be just to them, the land monopoly disappear, and with it unemployment.[1]

The League was not altogether contented with its relations with Bright. The council, just before the Leeds demonstration, seriously discussed the matter and dwelt upon the fact that they could not do without Bright's leadership, yet could not give up their principles. Beales stated that at Manchester he had offered to turn over the whole League organization, then numbering two hundred branches, to Bright, if he would come out for manhood suffrage.[2] The League earnestly sought the coöperation of the middle classes and was disappointed not to achieve it any more extensively. Thus Howell consoled a League correspondent:

Don't be disheartened at not having big names on your committee; it's our work and we must plod on in good faith and hope. Let the middle classes see that we fight our own battles and they will come to us.[3]

[1] *Speeches on Questions of Public Policy, by John Bright*, ed. Rogers, London, 1868, II. 199-212. Also Trevelyan, *Bright*, pp. 365-7.

[2] Reform League Letters, October, 1866, discuss this; also *Morning Star*, October 6, 1866, reports council's discussions.

[3] Written October 15, 1866. A comment on the official Liberal attitude toward the League is afforded by the fact that Beales was dismissed

The trades were taking constantly a larger part in the agitation. In October the Hatters' Society of London, by vote of the members, became a branch of the League.[1] In December the London Working Men's Association succeeded in bringing the unions out on a large scale in a strictly trades' demonstration. It was estimated that from twenty to thirty thousand artisans marched in the procession,[2] though it was said several large trades refused to take part because of those who were managing it[3]—again perhaps the feud between Potter and the council. The next day the same trades held a meeting in St. James' Hall, which was addressed by Bright. Only two metropolitan members were present, though all had been invited. Bright again expressed his approval of political action by the trades, which he had advised eight years before.[4]

A few weeks after this the Reform League began to plan a similar demonstration to take place the next February, upon the day Disraeli was to introduce his reform proposals. The London Trades Council unanimously adopted a resolution declaring its adhesion to the principles of the Reform League and advising all trade-unionists, either as corporate bodies or individually, to participate in the forthcoming demonstration.[5]

The increasing interest of the trades was evinced in many ways. The West End Cabinet Makers formed into a League branch in January,[6] and their example was soon followed

from his office of Revising Barrister for Middlesex because of his connection with it. (*Morning Star*, November 3, 1866.)

[1] *Morning Star*, October 24, 1866.

[2] *Ibid.*, December 4, 10, 11. The *Working Man*, December 8.

[3] The *Examiner*, quoted in the *Manchester Examiner*, January 14, 1867.

[4] *Morning Star*, December 5. G. B. Smith, *Bright*, pp. 265-6. Jephson, *The Platform, Its Rise and Progress*, II. 456.

[5] *Morning Star*, December 20, 1866.

[6] *Morning Star*, January 15, 1867.

by the West End Shoemakers and the Tailors.[1]   Another
London branch was of the goldsmiths and jewellers.   As to
the provinces, in Birmingham nearly all the trades joined the
League in their corporate capacity, while in Wolverhampton
the carpenters and upholsterers became branches.[2]   Howell's
correspondence contains a letter to a man in Camberwell,
which refers to his trade's taking up the League principles
unanimously, and another to a man in Merthyr thanking him
for bringing his trade into the League.[3]   The League minutes contain a report by Odger of the formation of a branch
in Leamington by the trades.[4]   Early in 1867 the Edinburgh Trade Council became a branch of the Scottish National Reform League.[5]

The rapid increase of interest in the reform question on
the part of the trades early in 1867 was due mainly to the
judicial decision handed down in January in the case of
Hornby v. Close, which rendered the legal status of trade-
unions extremely precarious by taking from them the protection of the Friendly Societies Act of 1855 and thus placing their funds at the mercy of defaulters.   At the same
moment, it had become certain that the government intended
to issue a Royal Commission to investigate the whole subject
of trade combinations, having been provoked thereto by the
Sheffield outrages, among other causes.

[1] An announcement of the opening of a branch by the West End
Society of Boot Closers on March 24, 1867, appears in the League letter
book. A letter of Howell's dated January 18, 1867, mentions the Shoemakers, Cabinet Makers, Hatters, "etc.," as having formed branches.
The *Star* of April 10, 1867, notes the Tailors' branch of the Reform
League. This is also mentioned in an official list of branches published
some time in 1867 in the form of a circular. (In the Howell collection.)

[2] Official list of branches mentioned above. This list may have been
published early in the year and cannot be taken as complete evidence as
to the number of trades that joined the League. The Webbs perhaps
underestimate the number (*Trade Unionism*, p. 248, note 1).

[3] Letters dated April 16 and January 18, 1867.

[4] Minutes for October 12, 1866.

[5] *Manchester Examiner and Times,* February 9, 1867.

Delegate meetings of the League and trade-unions together with representatives of friendly and temperance societies met to plan the above-mentioned reform demonstration. These meetings were largely attended. The individual trades held aggregate meetings and for the most part adopted the advice of their delegates to take part.[1] At the delegate meetings the Royal Commission and the new status of unions were frequently discussed.[2] The *Manchester Examiner* considered the commission to be the government's answer to the political activity of trade societies.[3] Beesly wrote that the decision in Hornby *v.* Close brought the Amalgamated Carpenters almost to a man into this League demonstration, whereas in December they had refused to participate.[4]

The public was much disturbed over the prospect of the demonstration. Derby admitted in the House of Lords that it was dangerous. The *Morning Star* wrote that trade-unions had been transformed into "a grand and irresistible machinery for the promotion of the reform cause."[5] Especially significant is the fact that even the Radical press opposed the coming event with what one of them described as a note of terror in its discussions. "They appeal, conjure, and threaten as if peril were imminent. They talk of the projected demonstration as if it were to be the first act in the drama of civil war."[6]

The demonstration itself was of the usual character. Many trades marched with banners and bands; League branches were there and delegations from the allied Scottish, Oxford, and Irish Reform Leagues, the last of which had recently been formed. The National Reform Union and

---

[1] *Morning Star,* January 23, 26.
[2] Minutes, February 6, 1867.
[3] Editorial of February 9, 1867.
[4] In the *Fortnightly Review,* March 1, 1867.
[5] January 17, 1867.
[6] *Manchester Examiner* remarked this of the *Daily News,* the *Examiner* and the *Nonconformist* (January 15, 1867).

the London Working Men's Association were also represented. At a huge meeting in Agricultural Hall speeches were made by Beales, Beesly, Ernest Jones, Professor Thorold Rogers, and The O'Donoghue. The last two were presidents respectively of the Oxford and Irish Leagues.[1]

Disraeli finally brought in his measure in March. Derby, convinced of the genuineness of the agitation by the close of 1866, had had much to do to convince Disraeli, who hoped, if he delayed, the Liberals would become disorganized over the question.[2] Disraeli's correspondence with Derby in December shows how averse he was to a reduction of the borough qualification and to a lodger franchise.[3] By January, however, he considered the question of reform "paramount"—a change "clearly based on a revised estimate of the state of public opinion."[4] And so the cabinet seized upon the "great phrase," household suffrage, as the basis of their measure, meaning to hedge it about with such safeguards as dual voting and personal payment of rates in order to render it safe and maintain the balance of classes with little change. The cabinet was torn asunder over the question. The bill proposed to enfranchise householders in boroughs who had a residential qualification of two years and paid their rates in person. It would also have given two votes to those who paid a certain amount in direct taxes.

Buckle remarks that "strangely enough" great popular meetings treated the bill as a virtual denial of workingmen's rights.[5] This is not in the least strange, in view of the fact that it disfranchised compound householders, to

[1] Accounts in *Morning Star*, February 12 and a circular: *Only Authorized and Official Programme. National Reform League Demonstration, Monday, February 11, 1867* (in British Museum).

[2] Monypenny and Buckle, *op. cit.*, IV. 453, 459 ff.

[3] *Ibid.*, p. 461.

[4] *Ibid.*, pp. 486-7.

[5] *Ibid.*, p. 536.

which class the vast majority of the occupiers of cheaper houses belonged; that it provided no lodger franchise, which was an especial grievance in London; that it required two years' residence and gave a dual vote to property. The bill was condemned on one or more of these grounds by all reform organizations.

The Reform League realized that its agitation would have to continue to keep the Liberals screwed up to the point of rejecting the bill or improving it. Howell's letters declared that they had not only the government to fight but the House of Commons.[1] Once he wrote: "Gladstone seems trimming. We must keep him up to the mark."[2] The council of the Northern Department of the League voted to recommend to the London executive a "people's parliament" to prepare their own bill.[3] A week later a delegate meeting of the League and the trades in London adopted a resolution for a national convention of delegates from all the League branches, other reform bodies, and trade, friendly, and other societies of workingmen. A circular was printed calling for the election of these delegates. One argument it used was the danger in which trade-unions stood.[4]

These delegate meetings in London had now become fortnightly occurrences at the Sussex Hotel in Bouverie Street.[5] Often as many as two or three hundred delegates were present. Public meetings were now held weekly in Trafalgar Square, both by the League and the L. W. M. A.

---

[1] Letter of March 3.

[2] Letter of March 22. This was doubtless in view of Gladstone's attempt to have a five-pound rating franchise substituted for the government measure. It must be remembered that five-pound rating meant six-pound to eight-pound rental. This move of Gladstone's was bitterly denounced by the League. See League Letters, April 10, 15, 18.

[3] *Manchester Examiner*, March 12.

[4] A copy of the circular is inserted in Howell's letter book.

[5] Resolutions to make them such passed February 13. (Minutes of General Council of League.)

Both organizations sent large deputations to Gladstone to protest against the bill.[1]

The Reform League was by this time strong enough to be a power and to create the fear in those who hesitated on reform that it was capable of becoming a nation-wide, revolutionary, class movement. It was not that; perhaps it never could have been; but to the governing classes, with memories of the not wholly dissimilar Chartist movement present in mind, the risk that might be involved in stubborn opposition was too great to be taken lightly.

The formation of the closely affiliated Scottish League in 1866 has been noted. It seems to have been strongly supported by the Scottish trades.[2] In December, 1866, the former Northern Political Union of Tyneside was revived as the Northeastern Department of the Reform League under Joseph Cowen, Jr.; and, by the opening of 1867, an Irish Reform League, identical in program with the English and Scottish Leagues and in close alliance with them, was in operation. There was also an Oxford Reform League that held the same relation to the original League. Its president was Professor Thorold Rogers, who soon lost his chair in the University on that account.[3]

As to the principal League, by the first of December, 1866, it had sixty-three metropolitan and one hundred and seventy provincial branches.[4] At the time of its second annual report, April 20, 1867, its branches numbered one hundred and seven in London and three hundred and

[1] *Morning Star,* March 25, 26; April 1. See Broadhurst's *Biography,* p. 33, for an account of the busy life then led by a workingman reformer.

[2] *National Reformer,* January 13, 1867, for demonstration at Dumfries; *Manchester Examiner,* February 9, 1867, for one at Edinburgh. Both were largely trade affairs.

[3] *Birmingham Post,* February 8, 1868.

[4] These and the following data are taken from the MS of the second annual report, and from a printed circular describing the organization of the League in 1867.

thirty-seven in the provinces. It had now four departments, each with a full staff of officers—the Midlands Department, with headquarters at Birmingham; the Northern, centered at Manchester; the Northeastern; and the West Riding Department, whose center was Leeds. These were in addition to the area directly organized under the London executive. The League claimed its organization to be "more complete in its details than any other political association this country has seen."

The League, by April, 1867, was taking to itself the credit for the fact that the Tories were then outbidding the Liberals. The prospective victory would, it considered, have to be followed up by further reforms and by sending workingmen to parliament.[1] The League council had already advised its branches to form into electoral committees.[2] The dissolution of parliament on the reform question was, of course, a possibility at any moment.

To add a few more data with regard to the League: the Midlands Department in its second annual report stated that in the year following August, 1866, it had held six hundred public meetings, had enrolled twenty thousand members, its executive had met one hundred fifty times, and its income had amounted to seven hundred seventy-six pounds, of which amount only one hundred seventy pounds had been donated.[3] The Northern Department during 1867 had a total income of £1002, to which no single contribution was larger than seventy pounds.[4] The ledger of the central executive at London shows total receipts of £1429 between September, 1866, and April 20, 1867. These figures indi-

[1] Second annual report.
[2] Resolutions adopted at Council meeting, from Howell's letter-book. No more definite date than March, 1867.
[3] Printed in the *Birmingham Daily Post*. August 6, 1867.
[4] Reform League. Northern Department. Report of First Annual Meeting, Manchester, November 9, 1867. (In Manchester Free Reference Library.)

cate the slight financial support the League received from the middle classes and make it clear that it was not a middle-class movement. The council was constantly lamenting the lack of adequate funds. Beales stated at the second annual meeting that so little help had come from the middle classes that had it not been for the unpaid services of workingmen the League could not have accomplished its great work.[1]

The fact is, that the middle-class Radicals were operating through their own National Reform Union. Some working-men belonged to both League and Union, but the former remained primarily a working-class body and the latter mid-dle-class. A list of the leading members of the Union, fill-ing two columns of the *Morning Star* for September 25, 1866, is practically the roster of the Radical party leaders, Manchesterite, nonconformist, and independent.

By that date the Union claimed a hundred and eighty-six branches. At a conference in November, to which six hundred delegates came from a hundred and fifty towns, plans were made to raise fifty thousand pounds. Several thousand-pound subscriptions were made on the spot.[2] Here the question of relations with the League came up, and the discussion revealed general opposition to any concession to the League's platform, but also a lively apprehension of "dividing the Liberal party" now and in the future after reform should have been won. The annual report of the Union in February, 1867, placed the number of branches at one hundred and ninety-two. The Union had held six hun-dred and thirty meetings in the previous year and had pre-sented petitions with over half a million signatures; it had issued over half a million tracts and thirty thousand mem-ership cards.[3] It was under the management of a regular

[1] *Morning Star*, May 23, 1867.
[2] *Morning Star*, November 20, 1866.
[3] *Manchester Examiner*, February 20, 1867. Compare the size of the League, which in April of this year had 440 branches, exclusive of

paid agent and kept prominent advertisements in the newspapers.

It has been explained in this study that such a union of classes as Radicals and working-class leaders had striven for since the time of the Complete Suffrage Movement had until now proved impossible to effect, chiefly because of antagonistic ultimate aims. The agitation of 1866-7 presented the same elements, though under cover of a certain amount of coöperation between the two classes. An examination yet a little further into expressions of opinion during the agitation tends to substantiate this statement. This evidence goes far to justify Dicey's judgment that the reform of 1867 was sought by labor to secure legislation in favor of collectivism, its object being social rather than political.[1] It also confirms the belief that this essential feature of the agitation was much clearer to the minds of all classes than is sometimes supposed. If that be true, then the amount of coöperation that took place between labor and the middle classes can be accounted for only on the following grounds: (1) the strength of labor that compelled a political readjustment; (2) Victorian optimism, which was confident that the dangerous tenets of workingmen would yield to good bourgeois sense, when workingmen were no longer excluded from the common life of the state; and (3) the fact that Radicalism without labor was a stunted growth.

Edmond Beales frankly avowed his objects to be social rather than political. His aim was "that of promoting as much as possible the political power, and by that power, the physical welfare of the people. Reform of the representation is only the means to our end, the end being the material welfare of the great masses of the community."[2] In a

the Scottish, Irish and Oxford Leagues. It had thus increased from 230 branches in December.

[1] A. V. Dicey, *Law and Public Opinion*, p. 253.

[2] *Morning Star*, August 3, 1868.

speech before the Reform League early in its career he had declared that reform would mean the securing to labor of a fair and just recompense and the banishment of much poverty and misery.[1] Howell's correspondence during the period contains such arguments as that political power would prove the best cure for periodical distress,[2] and that the League's program would be a remedy for landlordism.[3] The abolition of pauperism and unemployment was a constant objective with workingmen reformers. Thus Holyoake placed that as a motive second only to the one that was ever first with him, the honor and dignity of full citizenship.[4] Thomas Hughes, one of the few members of parliament workingmen could claim as their own, declared compulsory education and extension of the factory acts as objectives of reform; while Henry Fawcett, another, to his constituents of Brighton, answered the argument that parliament already listened to the working classes by pointing to the fever dens of great cities, the poor law system which imposed the burden of the poor upon the poor, and the lack of universal, free education.[5] George Odger declared in a League meeting in 1865 that among the objects in view were a reduction of hours for women and children and an increase in wages for agricultural labor.[6]

Evidence enough has already been adduced to show the prominence of the trade-union question in the agitation. The alliance between the League and the trades seemed to the propertied classes to threaten the country with Chartism under a new form. In fact, Chartist tactics were really threatened by the League. Plans for a national convention

[1] *Ibid.*, March 5, 1866.
[2] Letter of January 24, 1867.
[3] Letter of March 21, 1867.
[4] From a petition he presented to parliament through Mill. See *English Leader*, April 6, 1867.
[5] *Morning Star*, January 16, 1867.
[6] *Quarterly Review*, January, 1866, pp. 262 ff.

were actually made, as has been pointed out above. At one
League-trades conference of two hundred and fifty delegates,
it was resolved enthusiastically that unless some prospect of
the enfranchisement of the working classes were held out, it
would "be necessary to consider the propriety of those
classes adopting a universal cessation from labour until their
political rights are conceded."[1] Potter made a similar suggestion at Trafalgar Square a week later.[2] Bradlaugh's
paper suggested a refusal to pay taxes and a people's parliament.[3] A deputation of three hundred from the League
and trades, including all the largest unions, waited on Disraeli and expressed disapproval of his measure in belligerent
words.[4] A comment of the Radical *Manchester Examiner*
after the agitation was over is worth quoting:

The questions at issue between Capital and Labour have thrust
themselves into the very front rank of practical problems. . . .
The Geneva conference [of the International] illustrates the connection between the trades' unions in England and the democratic
movements on the continent; an international fact analogous to
that suggested by the co-operation between Mr. Beales and Mr.
Potter, between the Reform League and the London Trades.[5]

That certain of the social implications of reform were
apparent to the upper and middle classes is unquestionable.
The *Spectator* believed that a House of Commons that represented labor as well as capital would provide compulsory
education, compulsory hygiene, and perhaps compulsory insurance against thriftlessness, sickness, and old age; would
settle the difficulties between labor and capital so as to render
strikes obsolete, would revolutionize housing conditions, and
would ultimately extinguish pauperism.[6] The *Times* de-

[1] Minutes, February 27, 1867. Also *Morning Star,* February 28.
[2] Park, *Reform Bill of 1867,* p. 125.
[3] *National Reformer,* April 21, 1867.
[4] *Morning Star,* April 3, 1867.
[5] December 31, 1867.
[6] Quoted in *Morning Star,* January 14, 1867. See also the *Quarterly Review* for April, 1866, pp. 543 ff.

clared workingmen only wanted reform to strengthen their
hands against their employers and that the middle classes
feared nothing so much as democracy. Mill wrote soon after
1867 that he believed the active leaders of English workingmen were socialists of one sort or another, though believing
in gradual change.[1]   Shaftesbury's speech in the Lords on
the reform bill emphasized the danger of socialism.   After
asserting his intimate knowledge of workingmen and their
ideas, he declared, "I am sure that a large proportion of the
working classes have a deep and solemn conviction   .   .   .
that property is not distributed as property ought to be;
.   .   .   that to take away, by a legislative enactment, that
which is in excess, with a view to bestow it on those who
have insufficient means, is not a breach of any law, human
or Divine."[2]   Dicey, in one of a volume of essays on
reform published in 1867, enumerated as arguments valid
with the opponents of reform that taxes collected from the
rich would be spent on the enjoyments of the poor, and that
workingmen would "establish laws for the protection of
labour as oppressive as the laws which English gentlemen
established for the protection of corn."[3]   One pamphleteer
besought Derby to prevent if possible the "political extinction
of intelligence and property,"[4] while another baldly stated
the whole issue to be one of the rich against the poor, of
which fact he believed most people to be conscious.[5]

The difficulty the middle classes felt in coöperating
with workingmen became acute in April.   Then it was that
the National Reform Union began to try to establish itself

[1] Mill, *Socialism*, ed. Bliss, p. 65.

[2] Hodder, *Shaftesbury*, III. 221.

[3] A. V. Dicey, "The Balance of Classes," in *Essays on Reform*,
London, 1867, p. 74.

[4] E. W. Cox, *A Proposal for a Constitutional Reform Bill; a Letter
to the Rt. Hon. the Earl of Derby*, 3d. edit., London, 1867.

[5] *A Letter to the Rt. Hon, the Earl of Derby. By One of the People*,
London, 1867.

in London.   This dismayed the League.   It believed that
the Union was preparing to try to win the trades away
from it.[1]   In May Howell wrote that such a move would
"throw back our cause immeasurably."[2]   When the Manchester men actually came to London to launch their movement, Beales, at a conference called for the purpose, besought them to do nothing that would seem hostile to the
League, which possessed, he asserted, the hearts of ninety-
nine out of every hundred workingmen in the country.[3]
The tone of the negotiations between the two bodies reveals
much unfriendliness and suspicion, especially on the part of
the League, which saw in this another attempt to sacrifice a
working-class to a middle-class movement.   The Union,
on the other hand, insisted that the strength of the manhood
suffrage movement in London had prevented the middle
classes there from speaking out effectively for reform.
Bright, Mill, Forster, and Baines were behind the new policy.
Within less than a fortnight after it was initiated, the reform bill was enacted into law, and it embodied the essential
principles of the program of the Union.

If advanced reformers were divided between Union
and League, the whole Liberal party was in no better state.
Gladstone refused to stand for household suffrage.[4]   This
alienated a body of influential Radicals.   In fact, when the
Liberals a few weeks later came to contend for straight
household suffrage, they had no thought of getting it.[5]
At the same time, Gladstone's proposed five-pound line was
too democratic for the Whig element in the party.

---

[1] *Morning Star*, May 11, 1867. Also Howell's correspondence for
April.
[2] Letter to the Manchester secretary, May 15.
[3] *Morning Star* and *Manchester Examiner*, May 11.
[4] At a party meeting. See *Morning Star*, March 22, 1867.
[5] Morley, *Gladstone*, II. 224-6. Gladstone stated this later.

Thus the Liberal members had no agreed policy toward the pending measure. It went into committee, therefore, to be shaped by Radical hands. Neither Liberals nor Conservatives were courageous enough to withstand the democratic proposals there made, with the agitation out of doors in full swing. One by one Disraeli abandoned the checks that were to have made household suffrage safe, and Gladstone found himself abetting an amendment that would abolish compounding for rates and thus admit all householders, even the poorest, who paid their rates at all.

One author says that the final act was "the half accidental result of the balance of forces in the House, and of the evolution of attack and defence performed on a swamp of party expediency."[1] This is perhaps a fair judgment so far as the major parties in parliament were concerned, but outside of parliament men were demanding reform with a voice that spoke even in parliament through John Bright and John Stuart Mill. The country was wrought to a high pitch of excitement. A settlement of the question, and a fairly democratic settlement, had become a necessity. When the repeal of the local and other compound householder acts had been carried, which democratized the measure, Disraeli wrote:

Two months ago such a repeal was impossible; but a very great change has occurred in the public mind on this matter. Two months ago Gladstone would have placed himself at the head of the Vestries and "civilization"; now, we were secretly informed, he intended to reorganize on the principle of the repeal of the Local Acts.[2]

Disraeli, practically upon his own responsibility, accepted the amendment for his party, which step he said "would destroy the present agitation and extinguish Gladstone and Co."[3]

[1] G. L. Dickinson, *Development of Parliament in the Nineteenth Century*, p. 63.
[2] Monypenny and Buckle, *op. cit.*, IV. 540.
[3] *Ibid.*, p. 540.

The actions of both party leaders were dictated primarily by the fact that, as Morley expresses it, "the tide of public opinion had suddenly swelled to flood."[1] Neither could face the prospect of an antagonized new electorate. Disraeli's expression during the progress of the bill of his hope of "realizing the dream of my life and re-establishing Toryism on a national foundation," is to be reconciled with his constant opposition to even a moderately democratic reform to the very last only by attributing such opposition to the party rather than to Disraeli himself. Or perhaps it may be legitimate to surmise that Disraeli's active imagination in those months of 1867 was already sketching plans for the winning and organizing of the new voters for Conservatism, as an offset to middle-class Liberalism.[2] That such a possibility had occurred to him even earlier is certain.

The net result of all these party struggles was the enactment of the essential principle for which the Radical party had been contending since 1848, though on a more sweeping scale than even Bright had ever stood for. Bright had succeeded at last because, after repeated failures, he had been able to call in the people to redress the balance in the House of Commons. The *Manchester Examiner* attributed the result to the determined expression of the people's own demand: "The nation decreed its own political organization. Mr. Gladstone and Mr. Bright were the organs of its will."[3]

[1] Morley, *Gladstone*, II. 222.
[2] Suggested by Seymour, *Electoral Reform in England and Wales*, p. 276.
[3] Editorial of December 31, 1867.

CHAPTER X

CONCLUSION

Thus were the majority of English urban workers "brought within the pale of the Constitution." The Act of 1867 was the culmination of a development that had been continuous since the agitation for the first reform bill. It was the inevitable result of policies forced upon all classes in the state by the facts of the social and industrial world.

As the Act was a point of culmination, so was it a point of departure. It was to prove the initial force in another cycle of political evolution. The full effects of the enfranchisement of workingmen were slow to manifest themselves, but from the first a profound modification of the political system and its legislative fruits is evident to those who can look back from the vantage point of a later period. The policy of most of the upper and middle classes since the opening of the century had been to prevent workingmen from achieving a position where they could exert direct political influence through the suffrage. Their policy after 1867 was to minimize the effects of the success of workingmen in having won such a position. The method adopted was to strive to attach the labor vote to one or the other of the old parties. The era of Liberal-Laborism and of Tory-democracy was at hand.

The first of these alliances is the more important in English labor history. Tory-democracy possessed no possibilities of development from the point of view of labor. It meant simply the securing of labor support for Conservatism by means of organization, patronage, and occasional social legislation. It was not based upon any idea of equal partnership.   Liberal-Laborism, on the contrary, in theory at least, recognized labor as an integral section of the party, free to exert as much influence therein as it might show strength enough for.   If labor exerted a minimum of influence, it was due partly to the fact that it lacked any well-defined program, either as to policy or electoral activity, and partly to its political inexperience.   Liberal-Laborism offered to workingmen a needed training school in politics. Because it was not a static régime like Tory-democracy, but recognized the life principle of freedom of action, it permitted to labor a gradual political growth.   When labor had outgrown the framework of the Liberal alliance and when changed economic conditions made it no longer serviceable, labor was sufficiently experienced and disciplined in political methods to become an independent party.

Not only did Liberal-Laborism serve as a means for the political development of the working classes.   It has to its credit great acts of legislation, which it would have been impossible to secure if Liberalism had not rested upon a broad national support.   Not only that, but much of the legislation it fostered after 1867 took its character from labor. Especially was the new political status of workingmen largely responsible for divorcing the party from the individualistic principles it had inherited from the Manchester School. That this divorce was not effected sooner was due in part to the fact that labor itself during two decades after its enfranchisement inclined toward individualism.

The foundations of the Liberal-Labor alliance were laid in the period treated in this study.   The Radical wing of the Liberal party had striven persistently to bring a portion at least of the working classes within the body of the electorate, well knowing that only by such support could Whig and Tory domination of the national policies be broken.   Working-class leaders were convinced, in their turn, of the need of such an alliance in order to secure the suffrage for their class. The coalition between the two groups contained elements that were at the same time compatible and incompatible. The latter consisted in the opposition of the views held as to industrial and social interests. The fluctuation in the influence of this fundamental consideration during the period between 1850 and 1867 is described in these pages.

The Act of 1867 gave the Radical faction the ascendency within the Liberal party, and its allies in the agitation now became its allies in the party. The identical divergence of views and policy that had characterized the earlier attempts at coöperation was carried over into their new relationship. In the program of the party, as in those of Reform Union and Reform League, a lack of harmony became apparent whenever labor preferred special claims in the social and economic field. Only on the ground of political radicalism could there be thorough coöperation, unless these antagonisms should be softened. A gradual assuagement of them had been going on ever since 1850. That fact accounts in part for the degree of coöperation that was evident in the agitation for reform. The Liberal party of Gladstone came to achieve a conspicuous amount of harmony, because on both sides this assuagement continued. Labor became less and less insistent upon its special claims; on the other hand, the party as a whole, through the almost unconscious pressure of labor, became partially reconciled to collectivist principles.

Herein lies one reason for a careful study of the two decades before 1867. It serves to make clear the continuity of political developments. From the special point of view of the political history of the working classes, this study reveals the fact that the divisions between its various phases in the nineteenth century were not so sharp as is sometimes believed. Its development was uneven, it is true, but its transitions were made without any great degree of abruptness. Finally, this study makes it clear that both the direct and the indirect influence exerted by the working classes upon English politics in the third quarter of the century reached notable proportions in spite of the exclusion of the majority of those classes from the suffrage.

A word needs to be added concerning the future of the various organizations that had participated in the successful movement for reform. During the last months of the agitation both the Conservatives and the Liberals were bidding for the support of the prospective voters.[1] The Conservatives claimed gratitude for their reform bill and began at once to organize workingmen's associations. During 1867 the press reported several deputations of workingmen to Disraeli to convey the gratitude of their class.[2] Even before the bill was passed, steps were taken by the Conservatives to organize the labor vote, and before the end of the year a National Union of Conservative and Constitutional Associations had been formed with many working-class constituent bodies.[3] This work was entrusted to a firm of solicitors. There can be no doubt that the Liberals were much concerned over these activities.[4]

Meanwhile, the Liberals neglected to pursue a similar policy, trusting too much, no doubt, to the native liberalism

[1] An excellent analysis of the electoral results of the Act of 1867 and of the way in which the labor vote was cast in the next three elections is to be found in Seymour, *Electoral Reform in England and Wales,* ch. x., pp. 280-316.

[2] *Manchester Examiner,* February 4; April 23; May 1; *Morning Star,* April 8, 9, 20, 30; May 1, 6; June 10.

[3] *Morning Star,* November 12, 13, 1867. Also a pamphlet, *Principles and Objects of the National Association of Conservative and Constitutional Associations,* London, 1872; and another, *The Metropolitan Conservative Working Men's Association,* London, 1868.

[4] *Manchester Examiner,* June 29; *Morning Star,* March 1, October 16, 1867.

of workingmen. They even began to antagonize the Reform League as soon as the agitation was over. The League exulted greatly in the reform victory which it believed to have been won by its efforts. The executive council was so filled with a consciousness of the strength and effectiveness of the League that it planned to continue as a permanent working-class political organization—a labor wing of the Liberal party. Through it, they hoped to organize the new electors. In April, 1867, the Second Annual Report set forth the aim of perfecting the organization until no member of parliament could be elected without its support. It advised its branches to form themselves into electoral committees, one aim of which should be to send workingmen, or others who truly represented the interests of the wage-earners, to parliament.[1]

Soon, however, the League found itself in financial straits. The Radicals now paid it only scant respect; their press belittled it. Its efforts to have amendments in the registration system made in the interests of the new voters were ignored by them.[2] Its enemies were furnished an excellent weapon against it in the fact that it undoubtedly temporized with Fenianism.[3] Finally, it became torn with internal dissensions.[4]

In 1868, however, came the first election under the new law. Leaders of the Liberal party bethought themselves of the possibility of using the nation-wide organization of the

[1] MS of the Second Annual Report. Also resolutions adopted at a Council meeting in March, copied in the League Letter-Book. Also *Morning Star*, May 28, and *Manchester Examiner*, June 1, 1867.

[2] *Birmingham Post*, February 10, 1868, quoting *London Review* to the effect that Bright had removed from the League the light of his countenance. Howell's letters show the chagrin the League felt in the matter of the registration amendments.

[3] The League minutes record stormy sessions on the subject. They were reported in the press, often in detail.

[4] League Letter-Book, July 26 and September 27, 1867; also the League minutes.

League to marshall the new voters. They gave it their favor once again, therefore, contributed nineteen hundred pounds to it for electoral purposes, and found it an effective aid in carrying a number of seats. The League, in turn, sought to secure from the Liberal organization support for a list of League candidates, definitely put forward as candidates of the working classes, and also recognition of the new voters by the party in making party nominations. If they expected fraternal treatment from the party, they were disillusioned. A detailed study of this election makes it clear that the new voters, through the League, took a larger part than is usually supposed, though in the main an unsuccessful part. The trades coöperated with the League in several constituencies.[1]

The Reform League, broken and dispirited after the election, dissolved early in 1869. Its attempt to become an organized labor wing of the Liberal party had failed. The effort to carry on some form of labor electoral organization was left to its rival, the London Working Men's Association, which organized the Labor Representation League in 1869. It played some part in the next two elections.

As for the middle class counterpart of the League—the National Reform Union—it disbanded in 1869, was revived in 1876, and took part in the movement for a reform of the county franchise.[2]

[1] These statements are based upon a careful survey of the Radical press during the election, the minutes of the League and its Letter-Book, and upon a series of MS confidential reports on the campaign made to the League Council by its agents (in Bishopsgate Institute).

[2] It would appear that it was not the League that was revived in 1876, as stated in Park, *Reform Bill of 1867*, p. 266, but the Union. See *Reform Gazette and Manchester Critic*, October 11, 1878, as to the latter.

BIBLIOGRAPHY

Unpublished Material

In the Library of Bishopsgate Institute (the Howell Collection):

Minute Books of the General and Executive Councils of the Reform League, 1865-1869.

Cash Book of the Reform League, 1865-1869.

Letter Books of the Secretary of the Reform League, 1865-1867.

Letters and Articles by George Howell, 1867-1875.

Reform League Election Reports, 1868.

Minutes of the General Council of the International Working Men's Association, 1865-1869.

In the British Library of Political Science:

Minutes of the Conference of Amalgamated Trades, 1867-1871.

Official Documents

Hansard, *Parliamentary Debates,* Third Series (cited as *Hansard*).

Report of the Select Committee on Bleaching and Dyeing Works. House of Commons, 1867.

Report of the Select Committee on Masters and Operatives. House of Commons, 1860.

Reports of the Select Committee on Master and Servant. House of Commons, 1865-6.

Report of the Commissioners appointed to Inquire into the Organization and Rules of the Trades Unions and Other Associations. First Report, House of Commons, 1867.

Report of a Select Committee of the House of Lords on the Elective Franchise in Counties and Boroughs. House of Lords Reports and Bills, 87, Parliament of 1860.

Secondary Works

Note—Only a few general works or even special studies that are listed here proved to be of extended usefulness. Certain biographies and works dealing with special aspects of social developments, such as trade-unionism or socialism, were most valuable. From others, however, suggestions or discussions of special incidents could be drawn that aided in interpretation or added something to the sum of available information.

ADAMS, E. D., *Great Britain and the American Civil War.* 2 vols. New York, 1925.

BAERNREITHER, J. M., *English Associations of Working Men.* Tr. A. Taylor. London, 1893.

BARKER, E., *Political Thought in England from Herbert Spencer to the Present Day.* New York, 1915.

BEER, M., *History of British Socialism.* 2 vols. London, 1919, 1920.

BONNER, H. B., *Life of Charles Bradlaugh.* 2 vols. London, 1895.

BOWLEY, A. L., *Wages in the United Kingdom in the Nineteenth Century.* London, 1900.

BRIGHT, JOHN, *Speeches on Questions of Public Policy.* Ed. J. E. T. Rogers. London, 1868.

————, *Public Letters.* Ed. H. J. Leech. London, 1895.

BROADHURST, HENRY, *The Story of His Life from a Stonemason's Bench to the Treasury Bench.* Told by himself. London, 1901.

CHAPMAN, S. J., *The Lancashire Cotton Industry.* Manchester, 1904.

COBDEN, R., *Speeches on Questions of Public Policy.* Ed. Bright and Rogers. London, 1870.

COLLETT, C. D., *History of the Taxes on Knowledge.* 2 vols. London, 1899.

COOPER, T., *Life of,* written by himself. London, 1882.

COX, H., *The Reform Bills of 1866 and 1867.* London, 1867.

DAVIDSON, J. M., *Eminent Radicals in Parliament.* London, 1879.

DEWSNUP, E. R., *The Housing Problem.* Manchester, 1907.

DICEY, E. V., *Lectures on Law and Public Opinion.* London, 1914.

DICKINSON, G. L., *Development of Parliament in the Nineteenth Century.* London, 1895.

DIERLAMM, G., *Die Flugschriftenliteratur der Chartistenbewegung und ihr Widerhall in der öffentlichen Meinung.* Leipsig, 1909.

DOLLÉANS, E., *Le Chartisme.* 2 vols. Paris, 1912.

DUNCAN, W., *Life of Joseph Cowen.* London, 1904.

DUNCOMBE, T. H., *Life and Correspondence of Thomas Slingsby Duncombe.* 2 vols. London, 1868.

Essays on Reform. London, 1867.

FAULKNER, H. U., *Chartism and the Churches.* New York, 1916.

FROST, T., *Forty Years' Recollections, Literary and Political.* London, 1880.

GAMMAGE, R. G., *History of the Chartist Movement.* Edit. of 1894, Newcastle-on-Tyne.

GARNETT, R., *Life of W. J. Fox, Public Teacher and Social Reformer, 1786-1864,* London, 1910.

GIBBINS, H. DE B., *English Social Reformers.* London, 1892.

GIFFEN, SIR ROBERT, *Progress of the Working Classes in the Last Half of the Nineteenth Century.* London, 1884.

GREVILLE, G. C. F., *Memoirs.* 8 vols. London, 1896-9.

GUTTLER, G., *Die englische Arbeiterpartei; ein Beitrag zur Geschichte und Theorie der politische Arbeiterbewegung in England.* Jena, 1914.

HARRISON, F., *Autobiographic Memoirs.* 2 vols. London, 1911.

————, *National and Social Problems.* New York, 1908.

HINTON, R. J., *English Radical Leaders.* New York, 1875.

HOBHOUSE, S., *Joseph Sturge.* London, 1919.

HOBSON, J. A., *Richard Cobden, the International Man.* New York, 1919.

HODDER, E., *Life of Samuel Morley.* New York, 1888.

————, *Life and Work of the Seventh Earl of Shaftesbury.* 3 vols. London, 1888.

HOLYOAKE, G. J., *Bygones Worth Remembering.* 2 vols. London, 1905.

————, *Sixty Years of an Agitator's Life.* 2 vols. London, 1906.

HOWELL, G., *Conflicts of Labour and Capital Historically and Economically Considered.* London, 1878.

————, *Labour Legislation, Labour Movements and Labour Leaders.* London, 1902.

HOVELL, M., *The Chartist Movement.* Edited and Completed by T. F. Tout. Manchester, 1918.

HUMPHREY, A. W., *History of Labour Representation*. London, 1912.

————, *Robert Applegarth*. London, 1913.

HUTCHINS, B. L., and HARRISON, A., *History of Factory Legislation*. 2nd Edit. London, 1911.

JEPHSON, H., *The Platform, its Rise and Progress*. 2 vols. London, 1892.

LEARY, F., *Life of Ernest Jones*. London, 1887.

LEVI, L., (Ed.), *Annals of British Legislation*. 14 vols. London, 1856-65.

LOVETT, W., *Life and Struggles of, in his Pursuit of Bread, Knowledge and Freedom*. London, 1876.

LUDLOW, J. M., and JONES, L., *Progress of the Working Classes, 1832-1867*. London, 1867.

McCABE, J., *Life and Letters of George Jacob Holyoake*. 2 vols. London, 1908.

MACKAY, T., *History of the English Poor Law from 1834 to the Present Time*, Vol. III (supplementary to Sir George Nicholls, *A History of the English Poor Law*). London, 1898-9.

MAURICE, F., *Life of Frederick Denison Maurice*. 2 vols. New York, 1884.

MENGER, A., *The Right to the Whole Produce of Labour*. Introduction by H. S. Foxwell. London, 1899.

MILL, J. S., *Autobiography*. London, 1873.

MILL, J. S., *Socialism*. Ed. W. D. P. Bliss. New York, 1891.

MOLESWORTH, W. N., *History of England from 1830 to 1874*. 3 vols. London, 1886.

MONYPENNY, W. F., and BUCKLE, G. E., *Life of Benjamin Disraeli, Earl of Beaconsfield*. 6 vols. London, 1910-1920.

MORLEY, J., *Life of Richard Cobden*. Boston, 1881.

PARIS, COMTE DE, *Trade Unions of England*. London, 1869.

PARK, J. H., *The English Reform Bill of 1867*. New York 1920.

PORTER, G. R., *Progress of the Nation from the Beginning of the Nineteenth Century, in its social and economic aspects*. Revised by F. W. Hirst. London, 1912.

POSTGATE, R. W., *The Workers' International*. London, 1921.

RAVEN, C. E., *Christian Socialism*. London, 1920.

RICHARDS, C., *A History of Trades Councils from 1860 to 1875*. Introduction by G. D. H. Cole. London, 1920.

ROBINSON, M., *The Spirit of Association; Gilds, Friendly Societies, Coöperative Movements and Trade Unions of Great Britain.* London, 1913.

ROSE, J. H., *The Rise of Democracy.* London, 1912.

ROSENBLATT, F. F., *The Social and Economic Aspects of the Chartist Movement.* New York, 1916.

SCHULZE-GAEVERNITZ, G. VON, *Social Peace: A Study of the Trades Union Movement in England.* Tr. Wicksteed and Ed. Wallas. London, 1893.

SEYMOUR, C., *Electoral Reform in England and Wales; the Development and Operation of the Parliamentary Franchise 1832-1885.* New Haven, 1915.

SLATER, G., *The Making of Modern England.* Boston, 1915.

SLOSSON, P. W., *The Decline of the Chartist Movement.* New York, 1916.

SMITH, G. B., *Life and Speeches of John Bright.* New York, 1881.

SOLLY, H., *These Eighty Years, or the Story of an Unfinished Life.* 2 vols. London, 1893.

STANMORE, LORD A. H. G., *Sidney Herbert, Lord Herbert of Lea, a Memoir.* 2 vols. London, 1906.

STUBBS, C. W., *Charles Kingsley and the Christian Socialist Movement.* New York, 1899.

TESTUT, O., *L'Internationale.* Paris, 1871.

TREVELYAN, G. M., *Life of John Bright.* London, 1913.

————, *British History in the Nineteenth Century.* London, 1922.

WALLAS, G., *Life of Francis Place.* London, 1898.

WALPOLE, SIR S., *History of Twenty-Five Years, 1856-1880.* London, 1904-5.

WEBB, S. and B., *History of Trade-Unionism.* Edits. of 1894 and 1920, London.

WEST, J., *History of the Chartist Movement.* London, 1920.

WOODS, R. A., *English Social Movements.* 3rd Edition. New York, 1921.

WOOD, G. H., *Some Statistics of Working Class Progress since 1860.* London, 1900.

NEWSPAPERS

Age. Founded 1852.

Albion. Protectionist journal in the fifties.

Atlas. 1850-1867.

Ballot. Founded 1859. In 1860 became the *Elector.*

Bell's News: A London Weekly Newspaper advocating the Progress of the People. File in British Museum begins with 1856.

Birmingham Daily Post.

Borough of Greenwich Free Press, and Kent and Surrey Commercial Advertiser. Founded 1855.

Britannia: A Weekly Journal of News, Politics and Literature. Founded 1841.

British Banner. Founded 1848. Dissenting.

British Standard. Dissenting.

Builders' Salesman and Mechanics' Advertiser.

Christian Cabinet. Founded 1865. Dissenting.

Christian Times. Founded 1848. Became *Beacon and Christian Times* in 1858. Dissenting.

Christian World. Founded 1858. Dissenting.

Christian Weekly News. Dissenting.

Clerkenwell News. File in British Museum begins with 1857.

Elector.

English Leader. 1864-6. Democratic.

East London Observer and Weekly Local Journal. 1857.

Freeholders' Circular, 1852-1884. Organ of the National Freehold Land Society.

Gazette of the Association for Promoting the Repeal of the Taxes on Knowledge. 1857-61. Issued gratis.

Labour League, or Journal of the National Association of United Trades. Isle of Man, 1848-9.

Leeds Mercury.

Manchester Examiner and Times. Organ of the Manchester Radicals.

Morning Star. 1855-1869. Radical.

National Reformer. 1860-1893. Edited by Charles Bradlaugh and others. Democratic.

Newcastle Daily Chronicle. Founded 1858. Purchased in 1859 by Joseph Cowen; then became radical.

Newcastle Weekly Chronicle. Long-established Whig paper until it became the property of Cowen in 1859.

Northern Star. Chartist organ.

Political Examiner, a Weekly Democratic Journal. 1853.

Red Republican. 1850. Ed. G. J. Harney.

Reform Gazette and Manchester Critic. 1878-9.

Reynolds's Newspaper. 1850 to date. Ultra-radical.

St. Pancras Chronicle. 1857.

Shoreditch Herald and East London Rambler. 1852.

South London Local Journal. 1855.

South London News. Founded 1853.

Times.

Tower Hamlets Mail. 1857.

Vanguard: A Weekly Journal of Politics, History, Biography and General Literature. 1853. Ed. G. J. Harney.

Watchman and Wesleyan Advertiser. Founded 1848.

Weekly Advertiser and Parochial Reformer. 1853.

Weekly Christian News. Founded 1854. Dissenting.

West Middlesex Advertiser and Family Journal. 1857.

Whitehaven Herald.

PERIODICAL PUBLICATIONS

Advocate of National Instruction: for promoting the establishment of a general system of secular instruction, supported by local rates and under local management. 1853-4.

American Historical Review.

Barker's Review of Politics, etc. 1861-3.

Bentley's Quarterly Review.

Bookbinders' Trade Circular. 1850-77.

Champion of What is True and Right and for the Good of All. 1849-50. Ed. Rev. J. R. Stephens.

Christian Socialist: A Journal of Association. 1850-1.

Constitutional Press, a review of politics, etc. 1859-60.

Contemporary Review.

Coöperator. A record of coöperative progress conducted exclusively by working men. 1860-71.

Cooper's Journal, or Unfettered Thinker and Plain Speaker, for Truth, Freedom, and Progress. 1850.

Democratic and Social Almanac for 1850. London, 1849.

Democratic Review of British and Foreign Politics, History, and Literature. 1849-50. Ed. G. J. Harney.

Edinburgh Review.

English Republic. 1851-5. Ed. W. J. Linton.

English Leader. 1866-7.

Fortnightly Review.

Fraser's Magazine.

Freethinkers' Magazine, and Review of Theology, Politics, and Literature. 1850-1.

Herald of Peace: A monthly journal published under the auspices of the Peace Society.

Illustrated Builders' Journal. 1865-6.

Industrial Partnerships Record. 1867-8.

Investigator.

Journal of Association. 1852.

Journal of Progress. 1854.

Journal of the Typographic Arts. 1860-2.

Lankishire Loominary un Wickly Lookin Glass. 1864-5.

Leicestershire Movement: or Voices from the Frame and the Factory, the Field and the Rail. Leicester, 1850.

Liberator. A monthly journal of the Society for the Liberation of Religion from State Patronage and Control. 1855.

London Review and Weekly Journal of Politics, Literature, Art and Society.

Midland Progressionist; a periodical for the people, devoted to popular enfranchisement and progress. 1848.

Monday Review. 1862.

National Union: A Political and Social Record and Organ of the "National Political Union for the Obtainment of the People's Charter." May to December, 1858.

Nineteenth Century.

Northern Tribune. A Periodical for the People. 1854-5.

Notes to the People. By Ernest Jones. 1851-2.

Operative. 1851-2.

Operative Bricklayers' Society's Trade Circular and General Reporter. 1861-2.

Parochial Reformer and Tower Hamlets Chronicle. 1850.

Peace Advocate and Correspondent. 1851.

People, The: Their Rights and Liberties, their Duties and their Interests. 1848-9.

People's Review of Literature and Politics. 1850.

Political Annual and Reformers' Handbook. 1854-6.

Political Science Quarterly.

Politics for the People. 1848.

Printers' Journal and Typographical Magazine.

Provident Times. 1854.

Quarterly Review.

Reformer's Almanac and Political Year Book. 1849-50.

Republican. 1848.

Saturday Review.

Staff of Life, a Bakers' Journal. 1866-7.

Truth Promoter. 1850.

Universal Review in Politics, Literature and Social Science. 1859-60.

Voice of the People and Rights of Industry. 1848.

Yorkshire Tribune; a monthly journal of Democracy and Secularism for the People. 1855-6.

Westminster Review.

Woollen, Worsted and Cotton Journal; or Monthly Magazine of Industry. 1853-4.

Working Man. 1866-7.

Working Men's College Magazine. 1860.

PAMPHLETS

ADAMS, W. P., *An argument for complete suffrage.* London, Manchester, Hulme, and Newcastle, 1860.

Address of the Metropolitan Trades' Delegates to their Fellow Countrymen, etc. London, 1850.

Address and Provisional Rules of the Working Men's International Association. London, 1864.

Address of the Executive Council of the Amalgamated Engineers to the Fellow Workmen, etc. London, 1855.

Address of the National Reform Conference to the Friends of Parliamentary and Financial Reform. London, 1850.

Association for Promoting Equalization of the Poor Rates and Uniformity of Assessment Throughout the Metropolitan Districts. London, 1857.

BAXTER, R. D., *The New Reform Bill.* London, 1866.

———, *Distribution of Seats and the Counties.* London, 1866.

———, *The National Income.* London, 1868.

Bright's Speeches at Birmingham, etc. London, 1859.

CALLENDER, W. R., *The Commercial Crisis of 1857; its Causes and Results.* London, 1858.

CHADWICK, D., *On the Rate of Wages in Two Hundred Trades and Branches of Labour in Manchester and Salford and the Manufacturing Districts of Lancashire. . . . 1839 to 1859, with statistical tables,* etc. 2nd Edit. London, 1860.

COLE, H. W., *The Middle Classes and the Borough Franchise,* London, 1866.

Contrast, The; or John Bright's Support of the Present Government Justified. By a Liberal M.P. London, 1859.

Council of the Manchester Chartist Association to the Democratic Reformers of Great Britain. 1851.

Council of the Northern Reform Union to the Radical Reformers of the United Kingdom, October 11, 1859. Newcastle-on-Tyne.

COX, E. W., *A Proposal for a Constitutional Reform Bill: a Letter to the Rt. Hon. the Earl of Derby.* 3d. Edit. London, 1867.

Danger of a Democratic Reaction and Suggestions for Placing the Franchise in a Sound and Defendible State While Still Possible. Liverpool, 1864.

DRUMMOND, H., *A letter to Mr. Bright on his Plan for Turning the English Monarchy into a Democracy.* London, 1858.

DUNNING, T., *Trade Unions and Strikes: their Philosophy and Intention.* London, 1860.

Emancipation Society (no date).

Ernest Jones. Who is he? What has he Done? Manchester, 1867.

Extension of the Franchise: a Letter Addressed to the Rt. Hon. Earl Russell, by a Non-elector. London, 1866.

A Few Facts and Fallacies about Parliamentary Reform. London, 1859.

FIELDEN, S., *The Turn-out by the Master Mechanics. A Letter Addressed to the Editor of the Times.* Bolton, 1852.

Final Reform Bill of Earl Russell, K.G. London, 1866.

First Report of the Society for the Promotion of Working Men's Associations. London, 1852.

The Franchise Considered, in a Letter to the Rt. Hon. W. E. Gladstone, M.P. London, 1866.

FREARSON, J., *The Relative Rights and Interests of the Employer and the Employed Discussed; and a System Proposed by which the Conflicting Interests of all Classes of Society May be Reconciled. By Justitia.* London, 1855.

GIBBS, E. J., *Parliamentary Reform.* London, 1867.

The Government and the People! The great Reform League Demonstration in Hyde Park. London, 1867.

Great Reform Demonstration at Glasgow, 16 October, 1866. Glasgow, 1866.

GREENING, E. O., *Complete Enfranchisement of the Manhood of England. Speech Delivered at the Inaugural Soirée of the Newark Reform Association.* Newark, 1867.

HILL, F., *Parliamentary Reform. How the Representation may be Amended.* London, 1865.

HOLE, J., *Lecture on Social Science and the Organization of Labour.* London, 1857.

HOLYOAKE, G. J., *The Liberal Situation: the Necessity for a Qualified Franchise.* London, 1865.

————, *G. J. Holyoake to W. H. Brown.* (No date).

————, *Deliberate Liberalism.*

————, *The Workman and the Suffrage.* London, 1858.

————, *Working Class Representation; its Conditions and Consequences.* London, 1868.

JONES, ERNEST, *Evenings with the People. No. 1. The Workman and his Work. An address delivered . . . at St. Martin's Hall, London, October 7, 1856.* London, 1856.

————, *Evenings with the People. No. 7. The Unemployed. An address at the great Smithfield meeting . . . Feb. 17, 1857. To which is added a Reply to the "Times," etc.* London, 1857.

Labour and Capital. By a Member of the Manchester Chamber of Commerce. London, 1867.

Labour and Wages. Six prize essays. . . . By Six Working Men. Leicester, 1849.

The Land of England Belongs to the People of England. London, 1850 (?).

Letter to Mr. George Jacob Holyoake, Containing a Brief Review of that Gentleman's Conduct and Policy as a Reformer. London, 1854. By C. Murray.

Letter to the Right Honourable the Earl of Derby on Political Reform. By One of the People. London, 1867.

Life and Death of Ernest Jones, the Chartist Reformer. A Memoir. Manchester, 1869.

M'LAREN, D., *Information respecting the Cities and Boroughs of the United Kingdom.* London, 1859.

MACSIE, R. D., *Speech delivered at the meeting of the Liverpool Reform League on December 19, 1866, on Plurality of Votes as a Needful Element in any Final Scheme of Parliamentary Reform.* London, 1867.

Manchester Tract on Politics and Trade, a Test for a Shuttle-cock Cabinet. Manchester, 1858.

Meeting of the Journeymen Bakers of the Metropolis. London, 1850.

MIALL, E., *The Franchise; Considered as a Means of a Peoples' Training.* London, 1851.

Mr. Bright: his Thoughts and my Thoughts. By a member of the Carlton. London, 1859.

Mr. John Bright and Labour Representation. (No date).

Mr. Hughes and the election of Lambeth. The Call of Duty to Workingmen. London, 1868.

National Association of Coal, Lime, and Iron-stone Miners. Transactions and Results of the National Association held at Leeds, November, 1863. London, 1864.

National Association of Factory Occupiers. Special Report of the Executive Committee. Manchester, 1855.

National Freehold Land Society, as it Is, and as it Must Be. London, 1853.

National Parliamentary and Financial Reform Association. Address of the Executive Council. London, 1850 and 1851.

National Parliamentary and Financial Reform Association. Tracts. London, 1851.

National Reform League. *Propositions for the Peaceful Regeneration of Society.* London, 1850.

National Reform League. *Only Authorized and Official Program. National Reform League Demonstration, February 11, 1867.* London, 1867.

National Reform Union. *Report of the Proceedings at the National Reform Conference, Manchester, 1865.* (Contains also the first annual report of the Union).

Newspaper Press Census for 1861. London, 1861.

NICHOLLS, J. A., *The Strike. A Letter to the Working Classes on their Present Position and Movement. By a Lancashire Man.* London, 1853.

Our Constitution and the Elective Franchise. London, 1866.

PARE, W., *Claims of Capital and Labour: with a Sketch of Practical Measures for their Conciliation.* London, 1854.

Petitions for Manhood Suffrage and Vote by Ballot. 1859.

POTTER, G., *The Labour Question. An Address to the Capitalists and Employers in the Building Trades, being a Few Reasons in Behalf of the Reduction of the Hours of Labour,* etc. London, 1861.

Prospects of Reform. Letter to Sir Joshua Walmsley. London, 1849.

PRYCE, E. S., *Electoral Action, with Suggestions for its Continuance. A paper read at the Fourth Conference of the Society for the Liberation of Religion from State Patronage and Control, May 7, 1856.*

Questions for a Reformed Parliament. London, 1867.

Reform Bill: An Attempt at an Equitable and Safe Mode of Representation in the Commons. . . . By One Who Loves Old England. Huddersfield, 1859.

Reform. Fingerposts and Beacons. London, 1859.

Reform in Parliament, or the Balance of Political Power. . . . By One Who Loves Old England. Huddersfield, 1867.

Reform League, Northern Department. *Report of the First Annual Meeting—Manchester, November 9, 1867.* Manchester, 1867.

Reform League. *Official List of Branches.* 1867.

Reform Meetings. The Real Facts. Reports to J. Spofforth, Esq. London, 1866.

Reform or not Reform? "That is the question." By an Independent Liberal. London, 1861.

Reply to the Speech of the Rt. Hon. Robert Lowe, Delivered in the House of Commons, May 3, 1865. By a Member of the Committee of the Carlisle Non-electors Association. Carlisle, 1866.

Report of the Central Committee of the United Trades on the Proceedings Connected with the "Combination of Workmen Bill" in the Parliamentary Session, 1853.

Report of the Committee appointed for the Receipt and Apportionment of the Master Spinners and Manufacturers' Defence Fund. Manchester, 1854.

Representation of the Case of the Executive Committee of the Central Association of Employers of Operative Engineers. London, 1852.

RICKARDS, F. P., *Manchester and John Bright.* London, 1859.

RITCHIE, J. E., *Freehold Land Societies—History, Present Position, and Claims.* London, 1853.

Rough Sketch of a New Reform Bill. By a Devonshire Man. Exeter, 1866.

SARGENT, W. L., *A Letter to John Bright, Esq., M.P.* Birmingham, 1861.

Speech of Edmond Beales, Esq., M.A., President of the Reform League—May 13, 1865.

Speech of C. N. Newdegate, M.P., at the Annual Meeting of the Rugby and Dunchurch Agricultural Association, November 26, 1858. London, 1859.

STOKES, W., *Manchester Reform and Manchester Reformers, with Remarks on the Reform Associations Recently Commenced in this City, and Suggestions Tending to the Creation of a Thoroughly Liberal and Independent Constituency.* In a letter to Alderman Heywood. 2nd edition. Manchester, 1859.

STURGEON, C., Esq., *Letter to John Bright, M.P. on Dirt, and on his Speech at Birmingham, 1867, with Notes on the First List of Friends of the Working Classes, Published after the Coup d'etat they Made on the Manchester Radicals.* London, 1868.

Suffrage for the Million: A Suggestion with a View to Reconcile the Full Enfranchisement with a Fair Representation of the People. London, 1860.

Terrigenous. Land, Common Property. London, 1852.

Transactions of the Coöperative League. London, 1852.

United Kingdom Alliance of Organized Trades. Rules for the Government of, as Adopted at a Conference Held in Manchester, January, 1867. Sheffield, 1867.

VARDEN, R., *Hints on the Principles of Self Government and their Application to Parliamentary Reform.* London, 1866.

View of Parliamentary Reform, by a Reformer. Wallingford, 1867.

Who is the "Reformer," John Stuart Mill or John Bright? London, 1859.

Why the Liberals are Leaving the League. A letter Addressed to Sir Benj. Heywood, Bart., and Samuel Fletcher, Esq. By a Manchester Liberal. Manchester, 1857.

WILSON, E., *Principles of Representation, in Order to Secure Due Balance of Classes.* London, 1866.

Working Man's Dream of Reform. London, 1859.

INDEX

Aberdeen, Earl of, premier, 49, 56, 104.

Act of 1867, *see* Reform.

Allan, William, 51, 162, 210 f., 231.

Amalgamated Society of Carpenters and Joiners, 210, 224, 276.

Amalgamated Society of Engineers, 35, 37, 43, 46, 100 ff., 204; and strike of 1851, 52 ff., 97, 100, 138.

American Civil War, significance in England, 213, 217, 227, 241, 253.

Applegarth, Robert, 210 ff., 220, 224, 231, 253.

Anti-State-Church Association, 129.

Ashley, Lord, *see* Cooper, Anthony Ashley.

Ashworth, Henry, 193, 197.

Association for the Repeal of the Taxes on Knowledge, 69.

Aveling, Thomas, 162.

Ayrton, A. S., 127, 135.

Baines, Edward, 14, 193, 238 f., 272, 286.

Bakers, London, protection of, 41 note 1, 64.

Bakers' Gazette and General Trades Advocate, 64.

Ballot, 96, 124, 126 f., 153, 159, 161, 166, 250.

Ballot, the, 165.

Baxter, R. D., 192.

Bazley, Thomas, 183.

Beacon, the, 57, 107.

Beales, Edmond, 215, 218, 220, 227 note 1; and the Reform League, 251 f., 254, 257, 264, 267 f., 272 f., 277, 282, 286.

Bee Hive, the, 209 f., 217.

Beer, M., quoted, 26, 33.

Beer's History of British Socialism, 8.

Beesly, Professor E. S., 140, 215, 218, 220, 223, 234, 261, 277.

Bentham, Jeremy, 78.

Berkeley, F. H. F., 31.

Birmingham, Liberalism of, 146 f.; *Post,* 234; Trades Council, 225.

Black, Adam, 139, 190.

Blanc, Louis, 55, 65.

Boiler Smiths' Union, 229.

Bookbinders' Society, 51; breach with Trades Council, 221.

Bookbinders' Trade Circular, 45, 50 f., 98.

Boot and Shoe Makers Reform Association, 204.

Bootmakers City Reform Association, 204.

Bouverie, E. P., 194.

Boycott, William, 120.

Bowley, A. L., quoted, 199.

Bradlaugh, Charles, 162, 180, 208; and Secularist Movement, 93; in Reform League, 253, 261, 267 f.

Bright, Jacob, 215, 254.

Bright, John, 6, 14, 25; and American Civil War, 214 ff.; and Liberal Party, 96, 99, 104, 177, 181, 186 f., 260; and parliamentary reform, 30, 56 ff., 80 f., 83, 85, 92 ff., 105. 146, 148 ff., 163, 168,—bill of 1859, 174, 177 f., 181, 186, 217, —agitation of 1865-1867, 234, 236, 238, 251, 253, 257, 260, 263, 266, 274, 286; and peace movement, 75, 106, 115, 217; and Reform League, 251 f., 257, 260, 266, 270, 272 f.; and social legislation, 59 ff., 64,